V
ER
TI
GO

Curated by *Matthieu* Poirier
Fondation Carmignac, Porquerolles
Éditions Dilecta
Paris, 2025

V
ER
TI
GO

John Armleder
Oliver Beer
Anna-Eva Bergman
Jean-Baptiste Bernadet
Frank Bowling
Alexander Calder
Lynn Chadwick
Chu *Teh-Chun*
Caroline Corbasson
Isabelle Cornaro
Carlos Cruz-Diez

Philippe Decrauzat
Olafur Eliasson
Helen Frankenthaler
Bernard Frize
Hans Hartung
Raphael Hefti
Jeppe Hein
Leiko Ikemura
Ann Veronica Janssens

Véronique Joumard
Yves Klein
Emily Kraus
Artur Lescher
Heinz Mack
Flora Moscovici
Otto Piene
Gerhard Richter
Bridget Riley
Rotraut
Thomas Ruff
Hugo Schüwer Boss
Conrad Shawcross
Francisco Sobrino
Jesús Rafael Soto
Pier Stockholm
Thu-Van Tran
James Turrell
Günther Uecker
Fabienne Verdier
Jef Verheyen

COSMIC VERTIGO

Charles Carmignac

Porquerolles island © Camille Moirenc, 2025

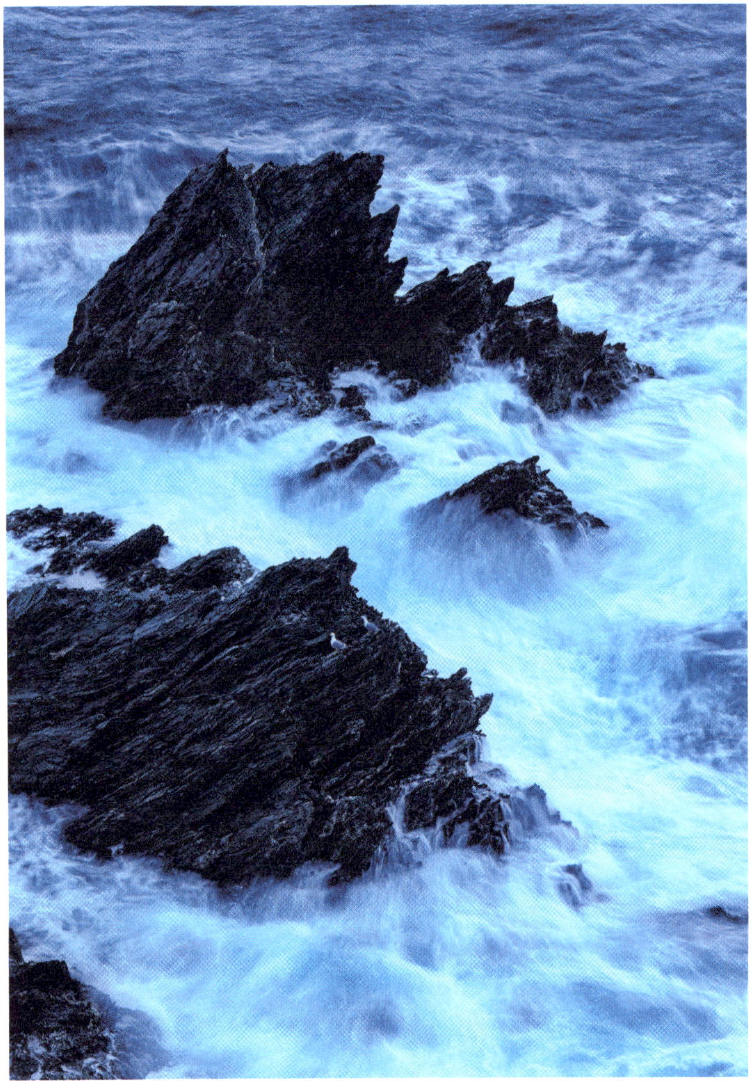

Legend has it that painter William Turner told anyone who cared to listen that he was once attached to the mast of a boat in the middle of a storm, like Ulysses with the mermaids, to feel the power of the elements and better transcribe them.

During the same period, painter Horace Vernet purportedly did the same, off the coast of Toulon, closer to here. Both suggest that art is an experience before it becomes a representation.

Each artist in their own way tested the energy of natural phenomena and rendered it palpable, and Porquerolles certainly provides some fine occasions for this. Here, cosmic elements are powerfully expressed.

The *Vertigo* exhibition was designed to echo the sensorial and emotional vertigo that the experience of intense natural phenomena can generate, such as the ones present on the island.

Continuing to explore, through art, the states of awareness and possibilities of the mind stimulated or modified by the experience of nature, and notably of the island, this year, the Villa Carmignac devotes its exhibition to vertigo. This extreme state can emerge out of fear of the void, visual excitation, a strong exaltation or a confusion between our body and its environment, when the latter oscillates, springs to life or stretches endlessly onwards.

If the experience of a potent and overwhelming nature can generate these various kinds of vertigo, what happens in contact with works of art? When the dynamic forces of nature encounter those that animate artists' inner worlds, what happens? Might the effects be similar, or are they new?

These questions pervade the exhibition, devised by art historian and exhibition curator Matthieu Poirier, a specialist in abstract art, who, in response to our invitation, proposed and designed this exhibition.

For our institution, the choice is radical: share only abstraction with the public. But we are persuaded that the artworks selected here will affect the public through their aesthetic qualities and vertiginous effects.

Our ambition is to lead the visitors towards unknown visual territories, to the limits of their perception, to encounter artists who perceive nature as a world of vibrations in perpetual motion.

I would like to warmly thank Matthieu Poirier for bringing these extraordinary artworks together, which palpitate, oscillate, vibrate and invite us into a truly sensorial immersion. All of our gratitude also goes to the lenders, both public and private, as well as to the artists for their generous contributions; particularly those who created artworks especially for the occasion, to our great delight: Isabelle Cornaro, Philippe Decrauzat, Flora Moscovici, Raphael Hefti, Pier Stockholm and Thu-Van Tran.

We also acknowledge our scenographer and all of the loyal partners and providers we know we can count on. Our heartfelt thanks also go to the authors of the catalogue: naturally, Matthieu Poirier, Nina Leger, Ann Veronica Janssens and Riccardo Venturi, for the exciting texts to discover in this book, as well as the team from Éditions Dilecta for the high calibre of their work for many years now. Finally, thanks to all of the teams from the Fondation and Villa Carmignac for their involvement in the production and presentation of this ambitious project.

VERTIGO

NATURAL AND VISUAL PHENOMENA IN ABSTRACTION SINCE 1950

Matthieu Poirier

Beyond, began the great sea, shimmering and grey, whose farthest reaches were lost in the mist. It was important to watch attentively to understand where the sea ended, where the sky began, given how dubious the limit was, how one and the other had the same uncertain paleness to them, the same stormy palpitation and the same boundless infinity.

Words cannot describe what shared emotion gripped us and how extraordinary this spectacle of immensity became, twice repeated, and consequently a double expanse in both height and depth, seen from the lighthouse platform.

Without a doubt, each of us were struck by it in different ways; but I remember that its effect was to immediately suspend all discussion, and that the same physical vertigo suddenly made us grow pale and serious.

Some kind of anguished cry escaped Madeleine's lips, and, without saying a word, all leaning on the light railing that was the only thing separating us from the abyss, very acutely aware of the enormous tower oscillating beneath our feet with each gust, drawn by the tremendous danger, as though called from below by the clamours of the rising tide, we remained for a long time in the greatest stupor, like people who, with one foothold on fragile life, by some miracle, would one day have the unprecedented adventure of looking and seeing beyond.

EUGÈNE FROMENTIN, *DOMINIQUE*, 1863

Sailing towards Porquerolles Island, then wandering around the Villa Carmignac while paying attention to natural forces plunges us into an incredible landscape of events: we are buffeted by sea breezes or the Mistral, dazzled by the Mediterranean sun, or bathed in myriad luminous phenomena, which are themselves modulated by the shifting atmosphere or the puff of pine trees and clouds. It is a vertiginous, dazzling impression, that of floating or a suspended state between palpitating infinity and aerial swarms, above us, and marine depths, below us, where the Mediterranean Sea attains a depth of three thousand metres. These natural and atmospheric phenomena are associated with our increased awareness of a space that is both limitless and full of life. They resonate within us, modify our state of consciousness during the experience, without resorting to psychotropics. They make us realise that our perception is an artistic medium in its own right.

The *Vertigo* exhibition is an invitation to pursue this "unprecedented adventure of looking and seeing beyond" formulated by Eugène Fromentin. It identifies the many resonances, in abstract art since 1950, of an environment or natural milieu – understood as a set of elements and physical phenomena, ideally exempt from human history and activity. By assembling the artworks of around forty artists from diverse geographic backgrounds and aesthetic affiliations, the exhibition explores the unstable sensations pertaining to loss of bearings or perceptual disorders such as dizziness or dazzlement. Vertigo comes from the Latin *vertere*, meaning both "turn" and "upturn" or "transform". It refers to that modified state of consciousness through the perception of a tormented visual field, when our sensorial compass goes wild.

Phenomenology, whether it concerns nature or human perception, is the common root of diverse individual practices and currents of abstraction.

Naturally, the title *Vertigo* recalls Alfred Hitchcock's eponymous film (1958) and its whirling credits, created by Saul Bass. Although the term refers here to acrophobia, the fear of heights afflicting the film's main protagonist, in the context of the exhibition, it above all invites us on an overview of some of the vertiginous and destabilising effects offered by contemplation and the experience of nature. This term refers to the quest, for many artists, for a more sensitive and embodied emotion, for the expression of a natural phenomenon freed from representation, from the image and its illusionism. Each artwork invites, expresses or channels in an abstract manner (that is, without recourse to mimesis or figurative representation) these natural and optical phenomena usually confined to external space – as per the model of the glass and water conservatory situated in the heart of the Villa Carmignac, which transforms, animates and redistributes the light that enters there.

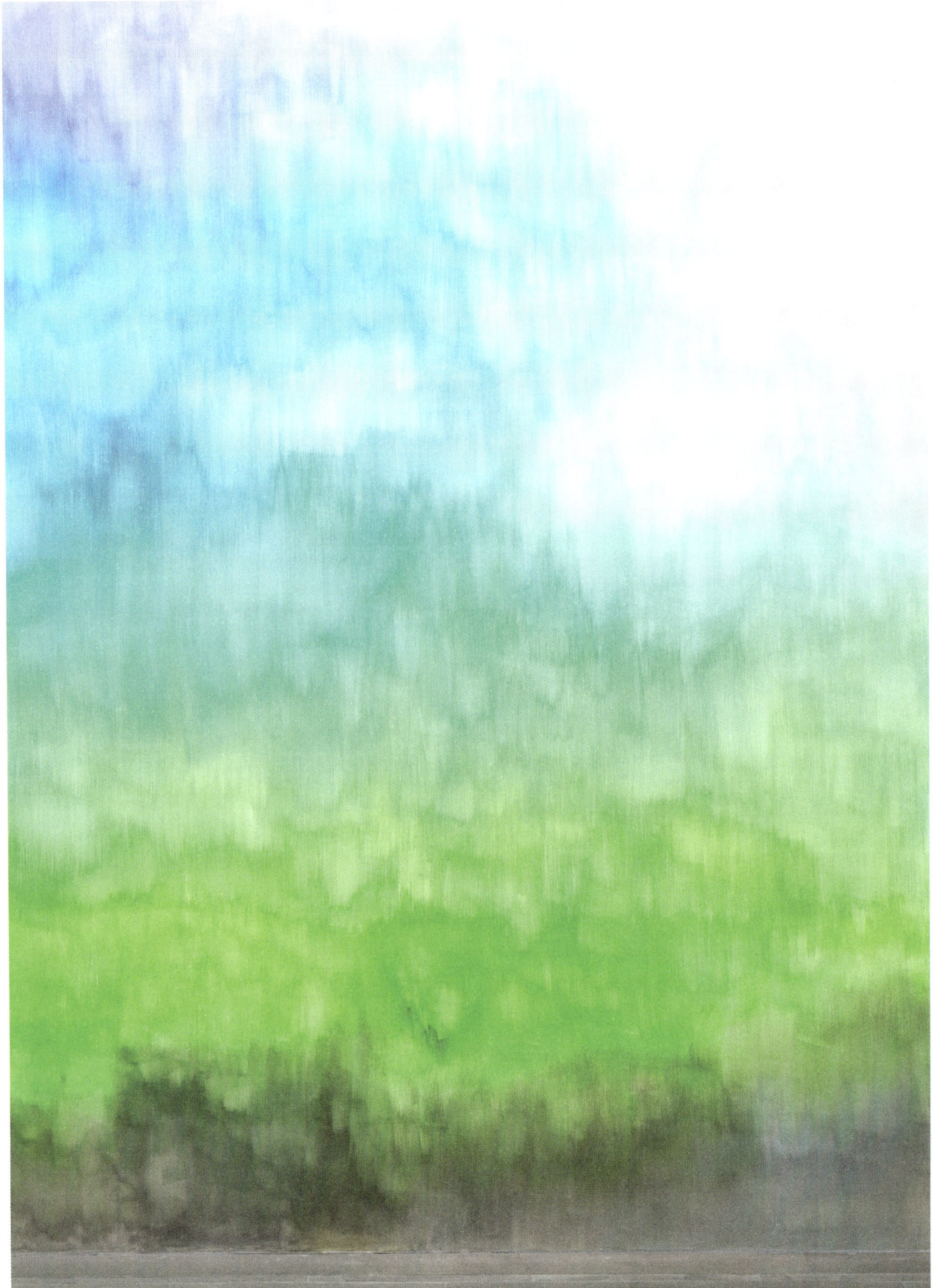

These disruptive effects emerge from various methods and techniques: from the action of the brushstroke, subtle or violent accentuations of light, liquefaction or atomisation of surfaces, mechanical movement or transformations sparked by our own movement. They raise many questions: regarding how to anchor our gaze and our body when we roam through uncertain spaces, when we contemplate vibrant and elusive forms? This dizziness is the product of a discrepancy between our mind and reality, when instability and the disappearance of visual markers make themselves felt in our flesh. What does it reveal to us about the perceptible exertion of the forces of the universe, energies from which we are often cut off, through the omnipresence of screens that saturate us with images, words and information?

From one section of the exhibition visit to the other, traditional, static and reassuring composition has been set aside. For these artists, abstraction is a process more than an end result. It does not target geometric construction as much as a spatiotemporal translation of a natural phenomenon, palpable in the artwork. The identifiable figure, which most often sustains art, here makes way for a shifting field of appearances, ectoplasms or indistinct phantoms, paradoxically filled with a vital tremor – which is really the echo of our own vitality. Each artwork presented is apprehended in a dynamic and no longer passive way; now it is a womb that is at once boundless and enveloping, now a vortex or a maelstrom, haunted by the torments of being and the world, which attracts or, conversely, repels us beyond its field of action.

The exhibition confers a highly dynamic turn to the "sublime", a notion that is traditionally combined with beauty and fear, in classical painting. The artworks brought together, nearly fifty of them, are generally in large format in order to encompass the gaze and the body and thus prevent any cold or distant observation. They represent all sorts of aesthetic scenarios, from dazzlement to cecity, to what happens when we lose control or deliberately let go, when eye and mind, confronted with their optical and semantic limits, fail in their ordinary function that consists of mentally grasping reality. In short, this exhibition considers the experiential dimension of the limits of our visual and spatial connection with natural reality, that is, what escapes our control, when we relinquish ourselves to these forces, during the aesthetic experience.

This vast palette of vertiginous sensations is deployed over a visit divided into seven sections or strata, which represent as many perceptive states associated with landscape in classical painting: the liquid element ("Clouded Turbidity"), cosmogony ("Event Horizon"), the air ("Atmospheric Turbulence"), the infinite ("Threshold, Mirage and Abyss"), terrestrial ("Telluric Visions"), the abyssal ("Maelstroms") and blinking ("Fields of Vision"). They are articulated and attached to the great yellow sphere by Jesús Rafael Soto, floating mid-air in the centre of the Villa, under the glass conservatory, and serving as its magnetic core, around which artworks and viewers gravitate.

Opposite and following pages: Flora Moscovici, *À la poursuite du rayon vert / Romancing the Light* (detail), 2025, pigments and gouache binder, variable dimensions

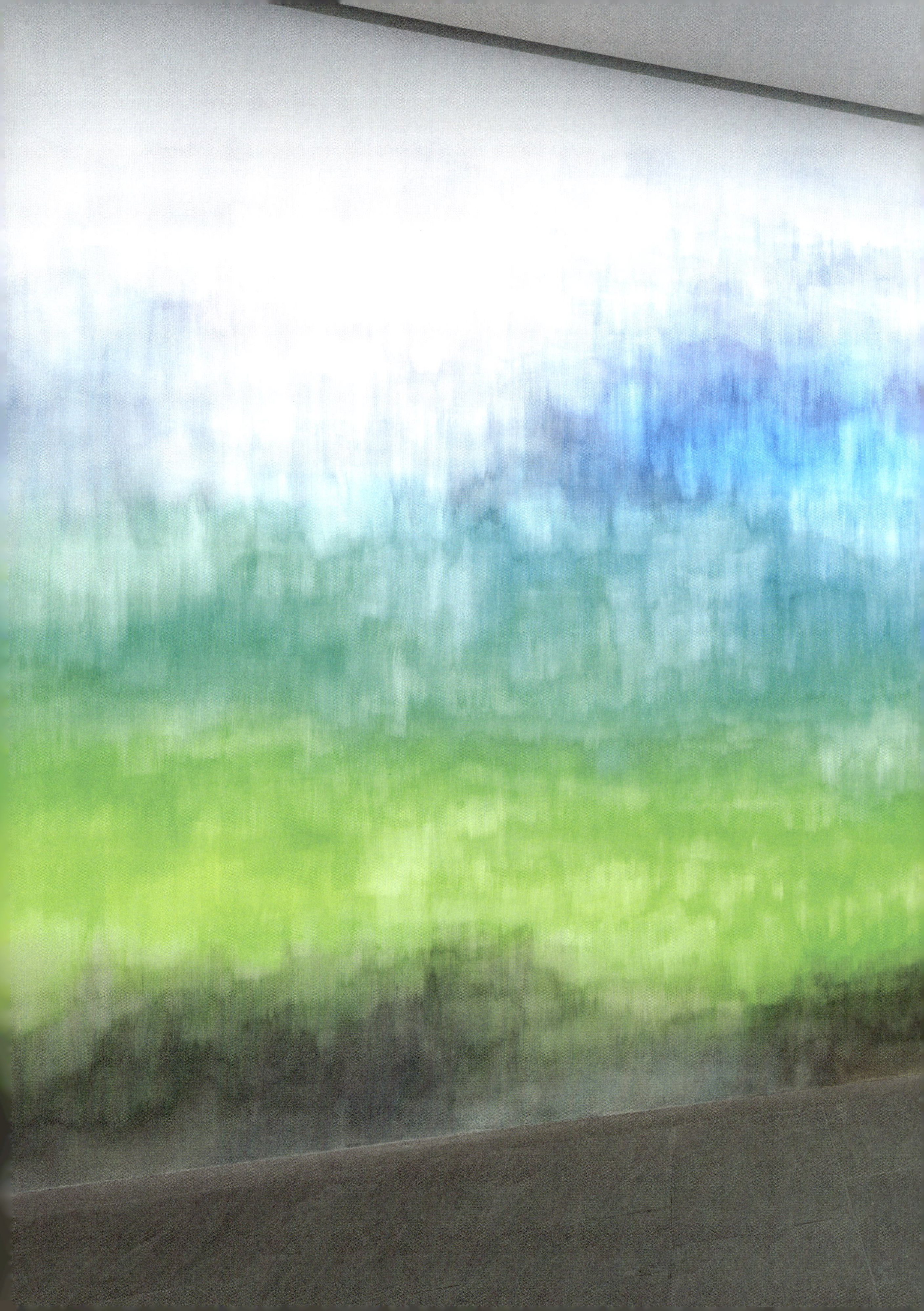

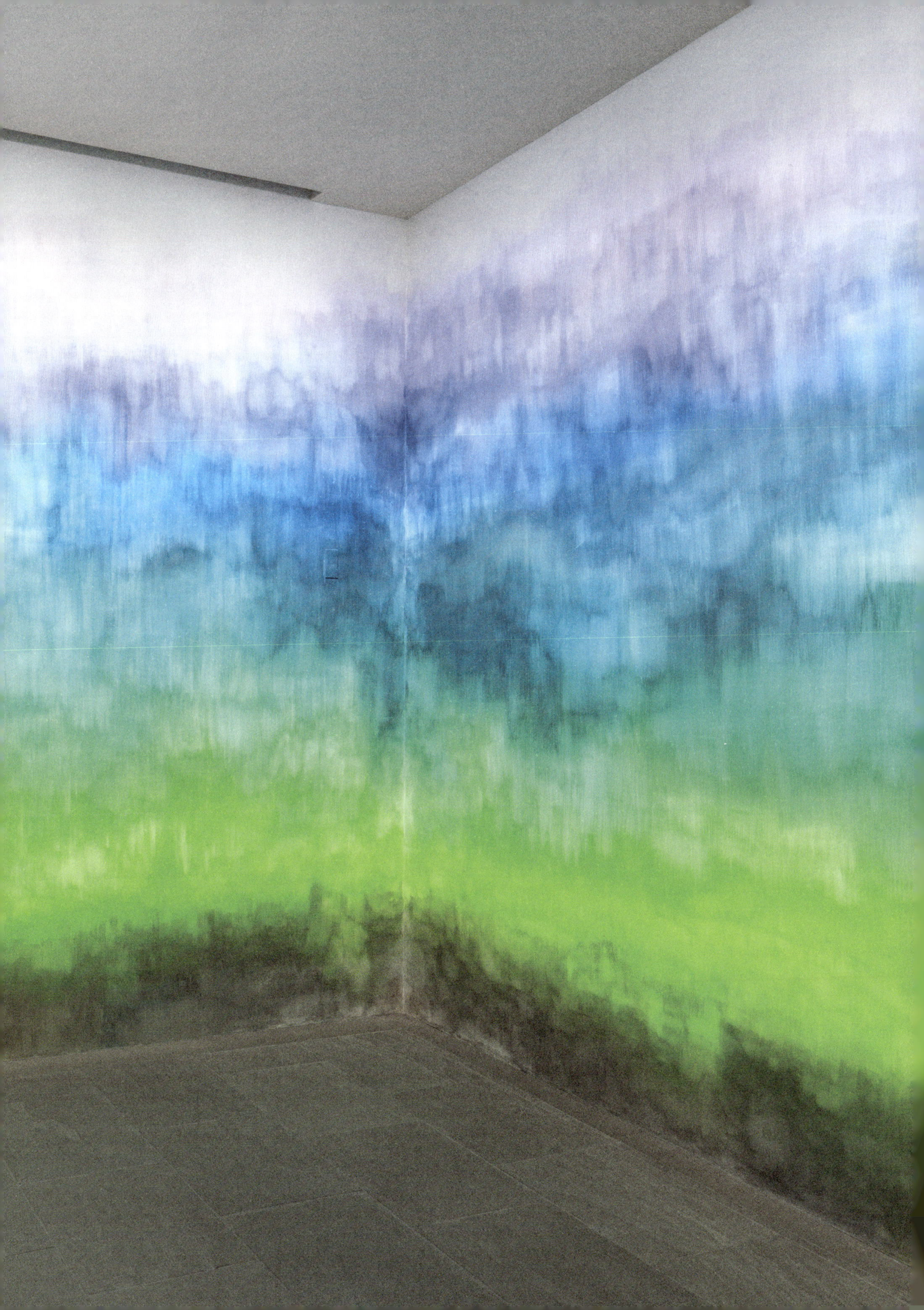

Therefore, depending on our chosen path and visual exploration, we move or float within a colourful milieu with aquatic properties, losing ourselves in the infinity of sparkling constellations, mentally traversing optical abysses, wandering through a diffuse colour, aimlessly, amid instable and turbulent visual content; we explore a field sometimes similar to that of air, whose atmosphere palpitates with plays of light deploying interference and filters; then, finally, we plunge into a telluric material, in which various chemical, eruptive or tectonic transformations operate. From a maelstrom of colour to an optical storm, these works disrupt our habits and semantic, spatial or temporal bearings. They procure a singular intoxication, resonating with the thrilling experience of the vitality of the natural world.

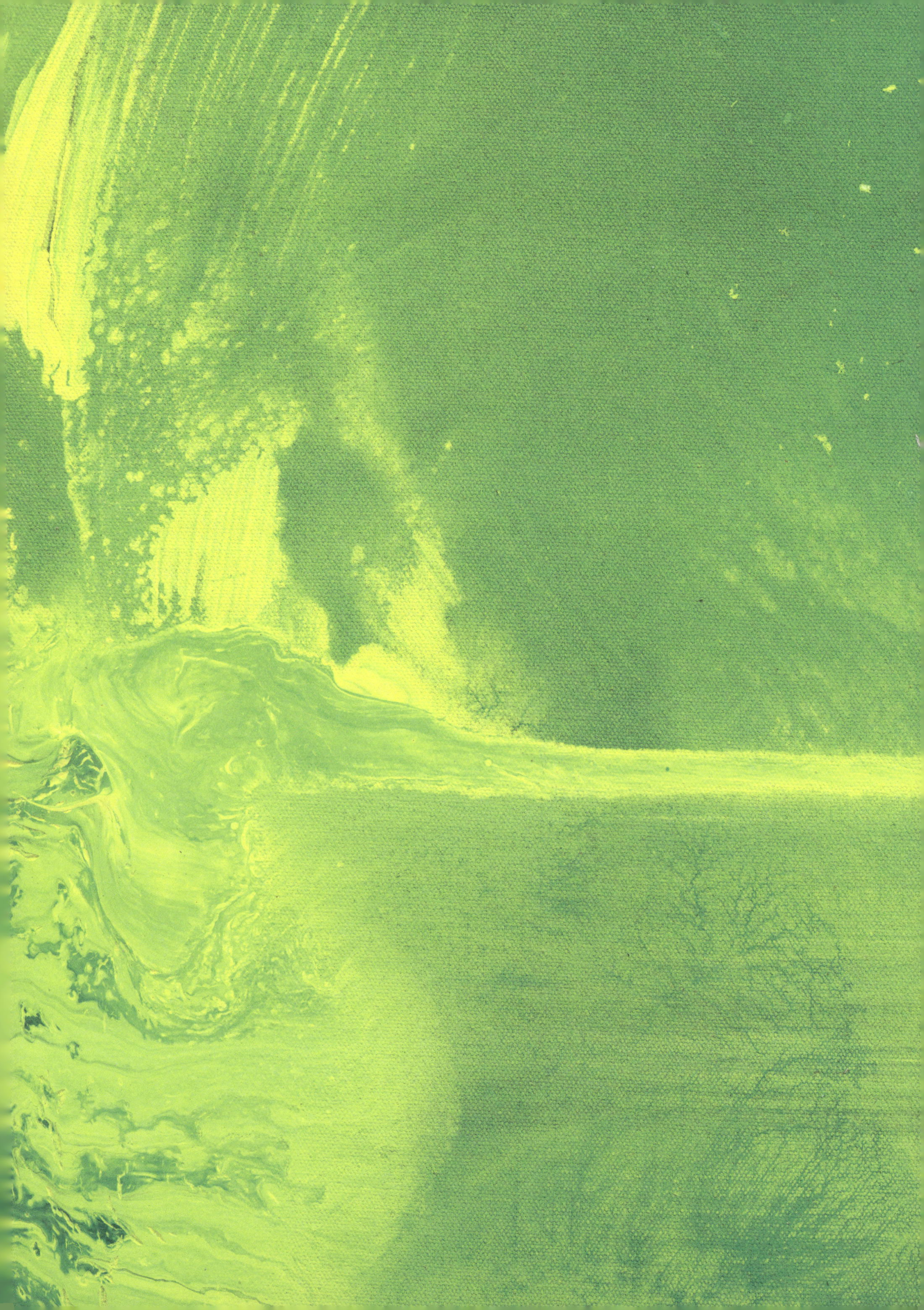

CLOUDED TURBIDITY

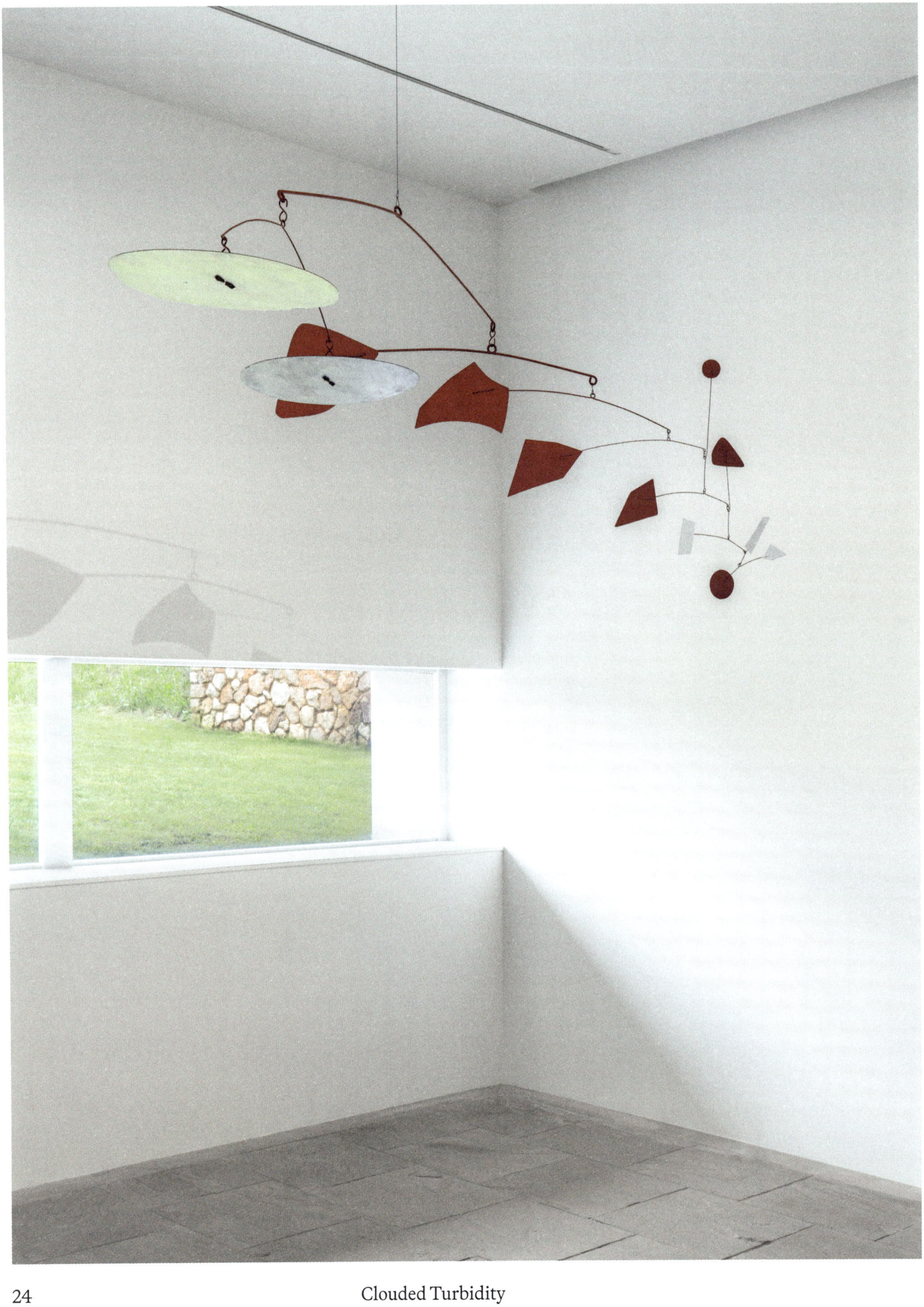

After the long descent downstairs, the introduction to *Vertigo* is immediately intangible: it consists of a dive into the atmosphere of a painting by Flora Moscovici. She sets aside the traditional medium of the canvas and applies, here, with a brush, colours that she associates with the rare solar phenomenon that Jules Verne describes in his book *The Green Ray* (1882) as "a green colour that no artist can obtain on his palette". The work of Flora Moscovici is an "environment" in itself: we find ourselves no longer in front of an isolated object on a wall, but in the heart of a colourful nebula whose sheer size submerges our field of vision (between approximately 110° and 130°). By surpassing the usual dimensions of a painting, the artist immediately dissolves any clear motif and the surrounding architecture. The energy of the aquatic landscape, reinforced by an effect of atmospheric mist, intrudes into the construct and destabilises its geometry.

In this first section, floating above our heads, a large *Mobile* by Calder, with gentle and polychrome forms, dances and renders the invisible air-flow perceptible. Like us, it is surrounded by paintings, themselves animated by an ambiguous fluidity. The eye, brought back to its most primal function of light and motion capture, is perturbed here by subtle or vigorous turbulence. The canvases, mounted on frames and agitated by both chromatic and gestural currents, present a painting that seems to have been restored to its initial liquid state. We feel ourselves floating as we contemplate it, mentally projecting ourselves into the panoramic format of Helen Frankenthaler's painting.

The technique that the artist instigated in the early 1950s, immediately after Jackson Pollock's drippings, consists of painting onto a canvas laid flat on the floor, sometimes with a squeegee, using particularly diluted pigments to exploit the fluidity and spread it through saturation, streaks and stains.

Like many of the paintings brought together in *Vertigo*, this practice resonates with the notion of "Trübe" (turbidity) formulated by Goethe, which refers, on the one hand, to an aquatic milieu whose clarity has been disturbed by the stirring up of all kinds of sediments and, on the other hand, the origin itself of new colours forming in space and time. In Frank Bowling's work, just as these particles move about through the effect of contradictory currents, our gaze dives into the endless space of a monochromatic wash, caused by a directed flow of liquids charged with pigments. With Gerhard Richter, we again find the conception of a murky world, agitated by the incessant molecular movements of coloured matter – here, a solar storm or a nuclear explosion, whose powerful winds would obliterate a landscape. This approach conveys these artists' refusal of a stable form whose semantic identification would provide a reassuring anchor, an illusory refuge in the face of the chaotic vertigo of reality. "When I die", Claude Monet reportedly said, "I'd like to be buried in a buoy."

Previous page: Helen Frankenthaler, *Petroglyphs* (detail), 1990, acrylic on canvas, 116.8 × 299.7 cm
Opposite and following pages: Alexander Calder, *Mobile*, 1970, painted metal, 95 × 305 cm

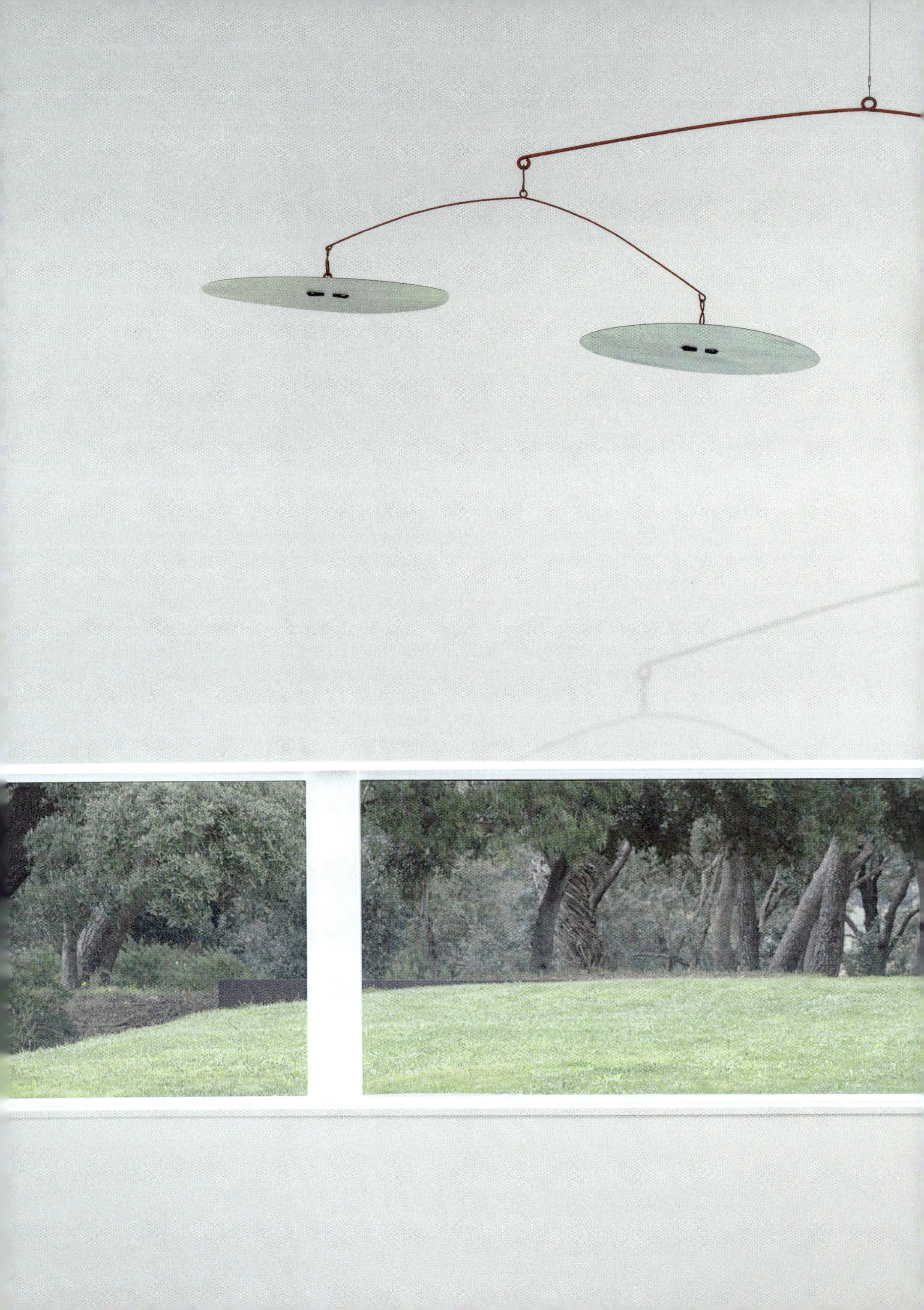

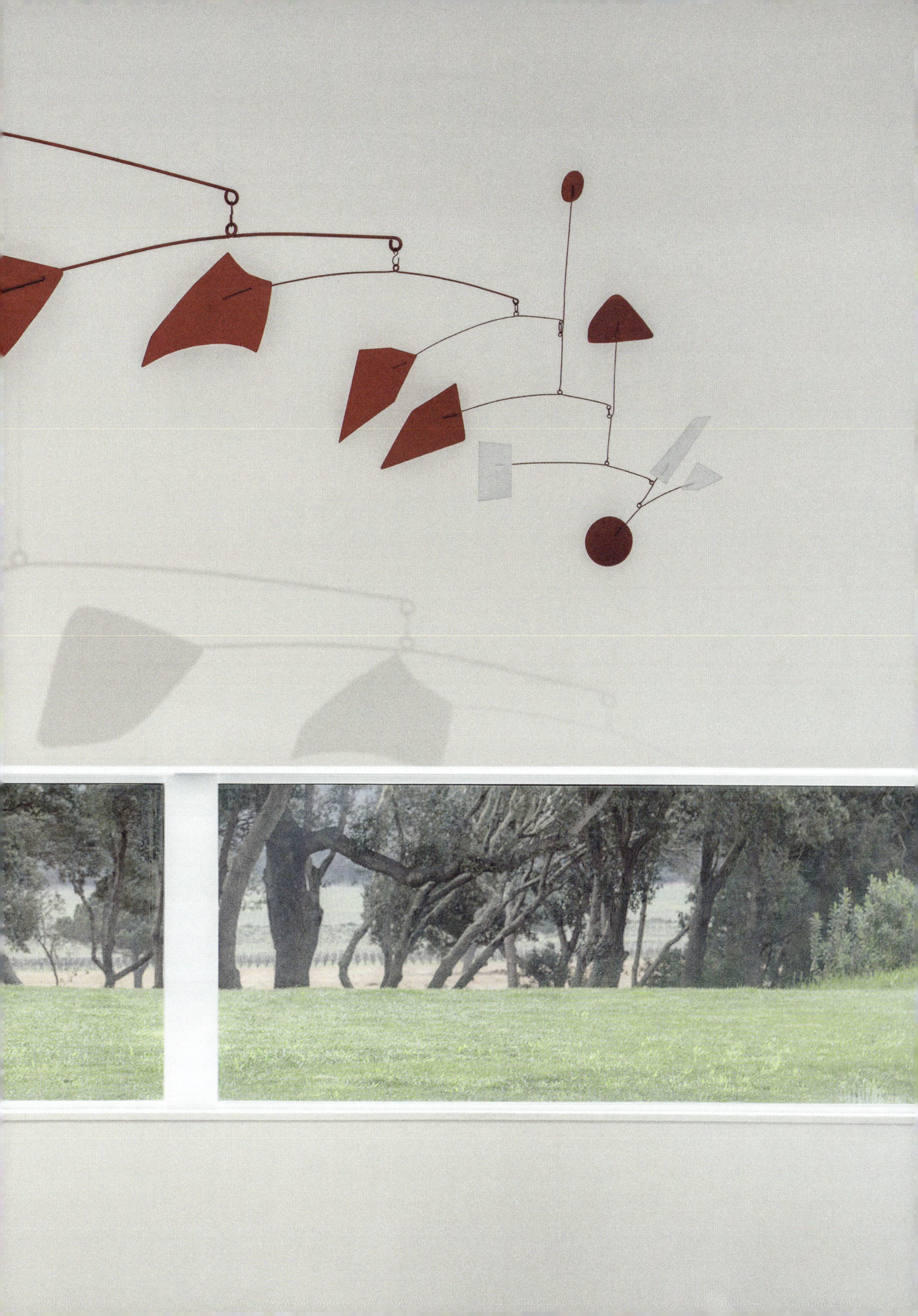

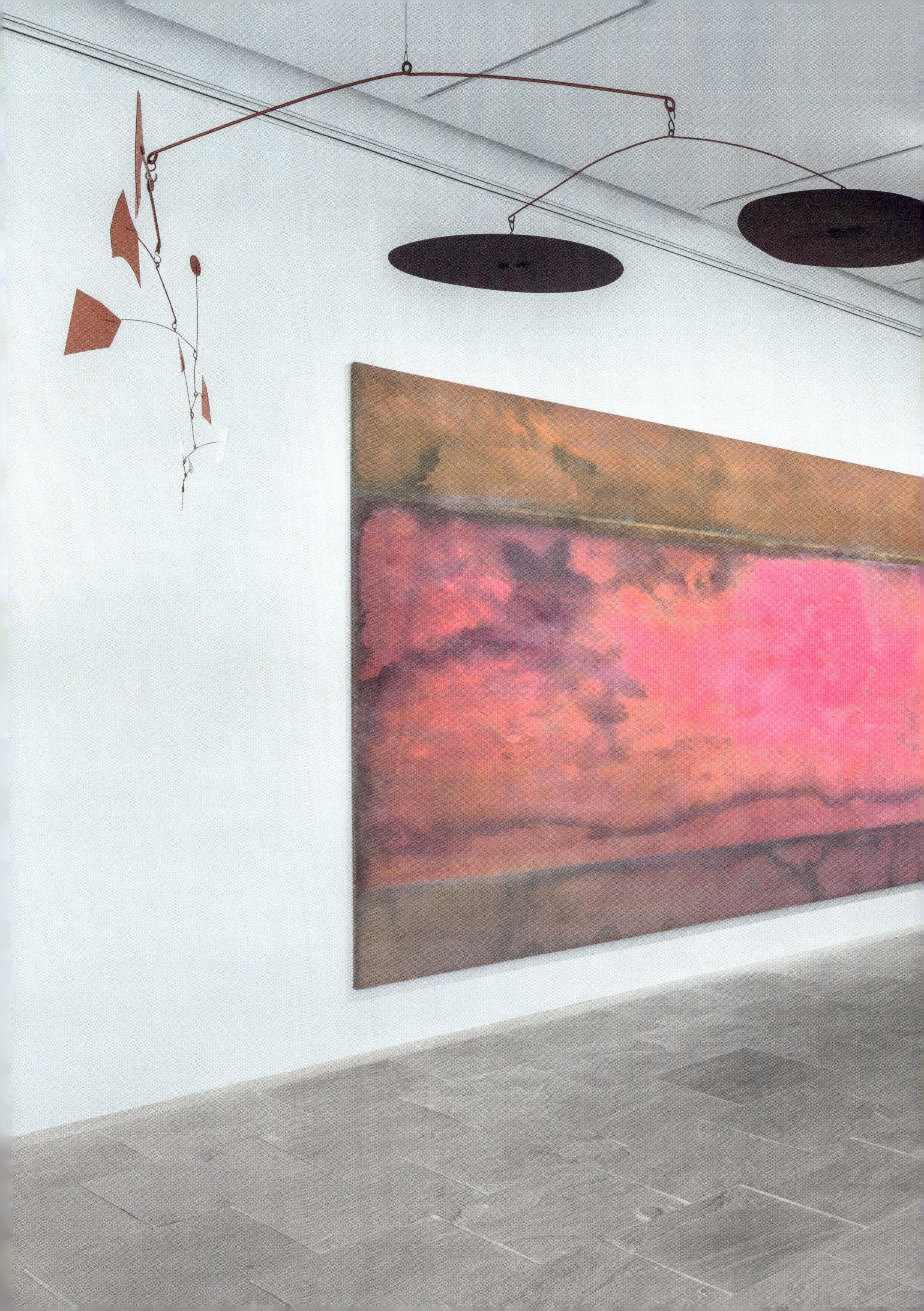

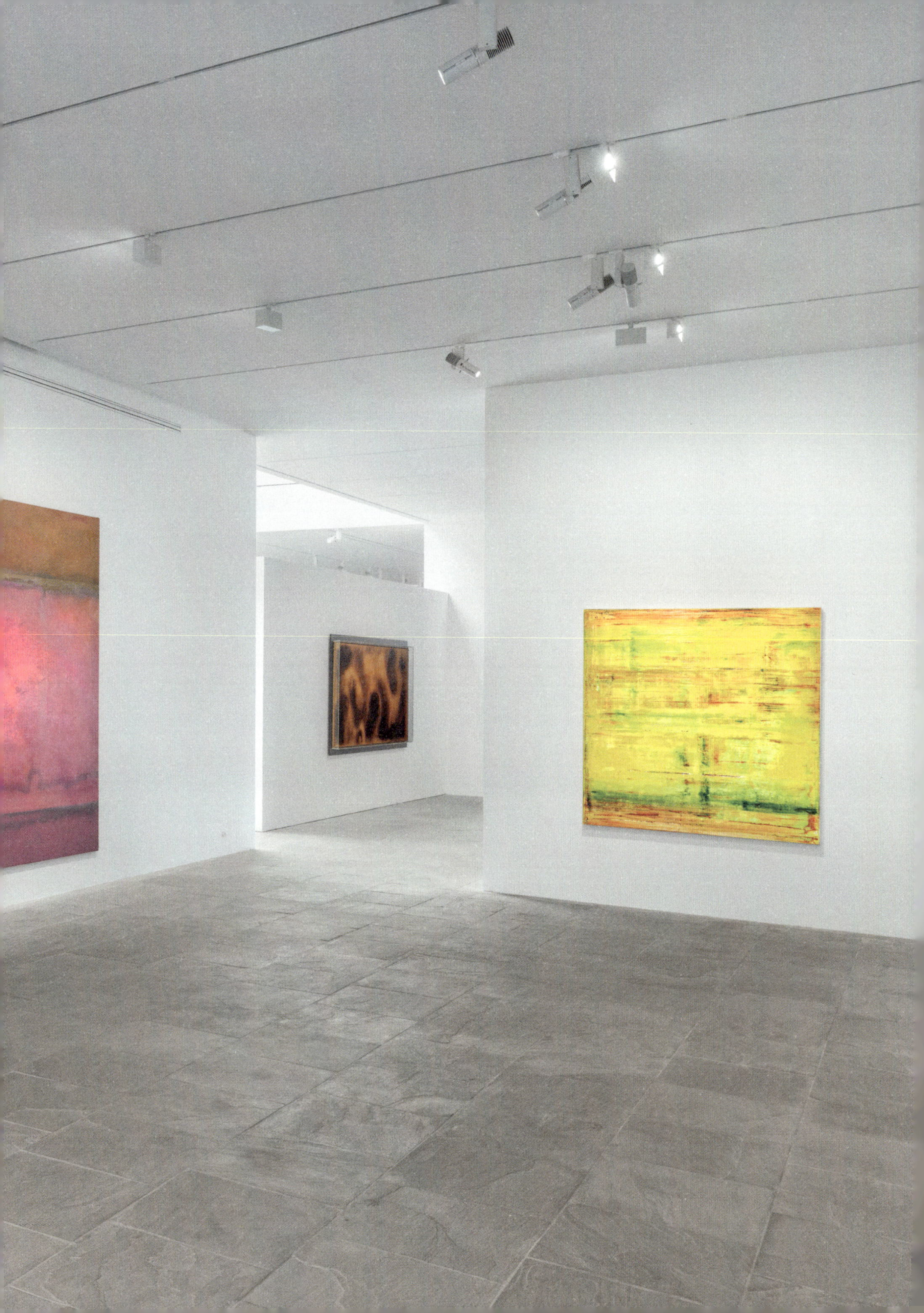

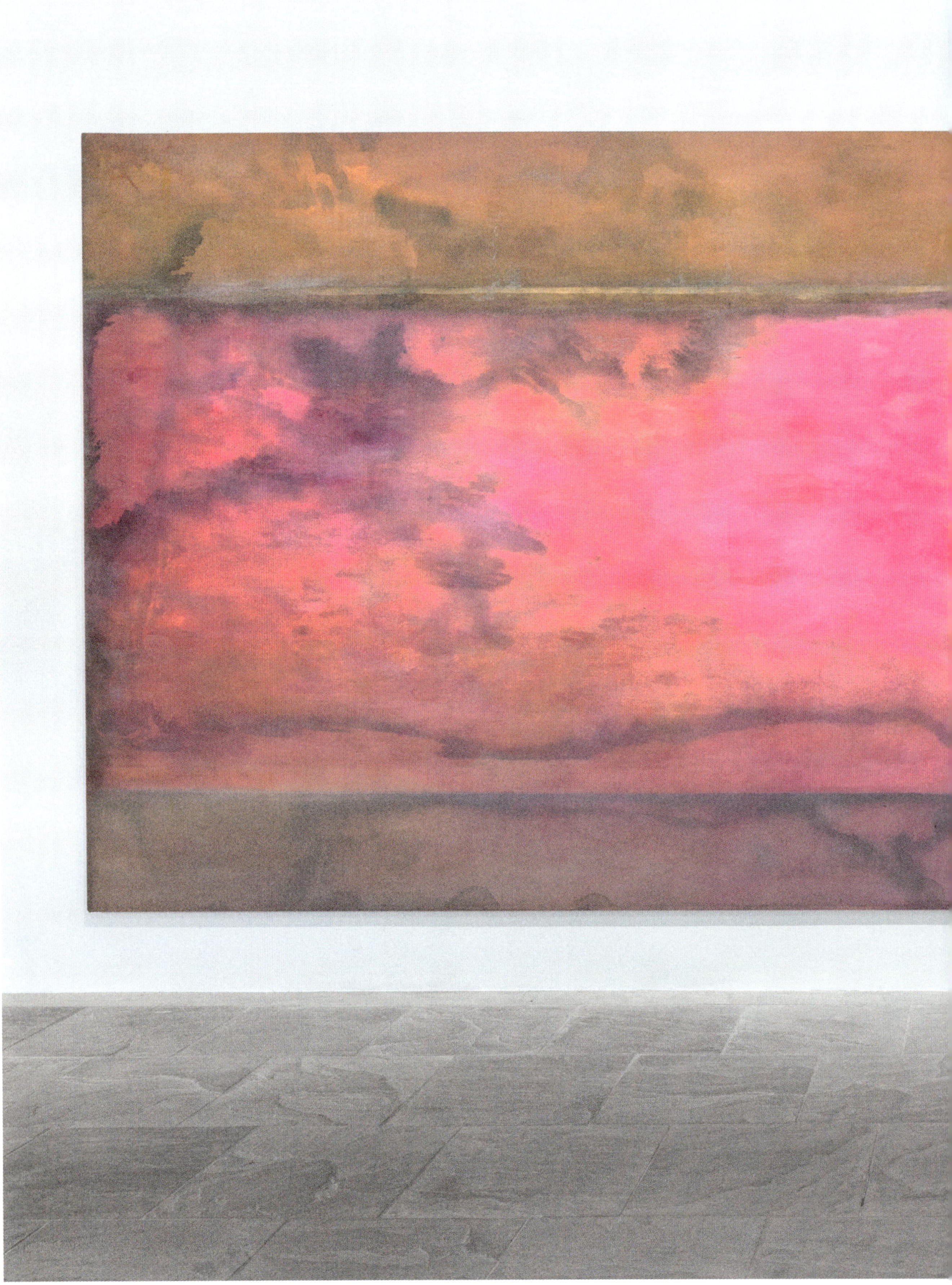

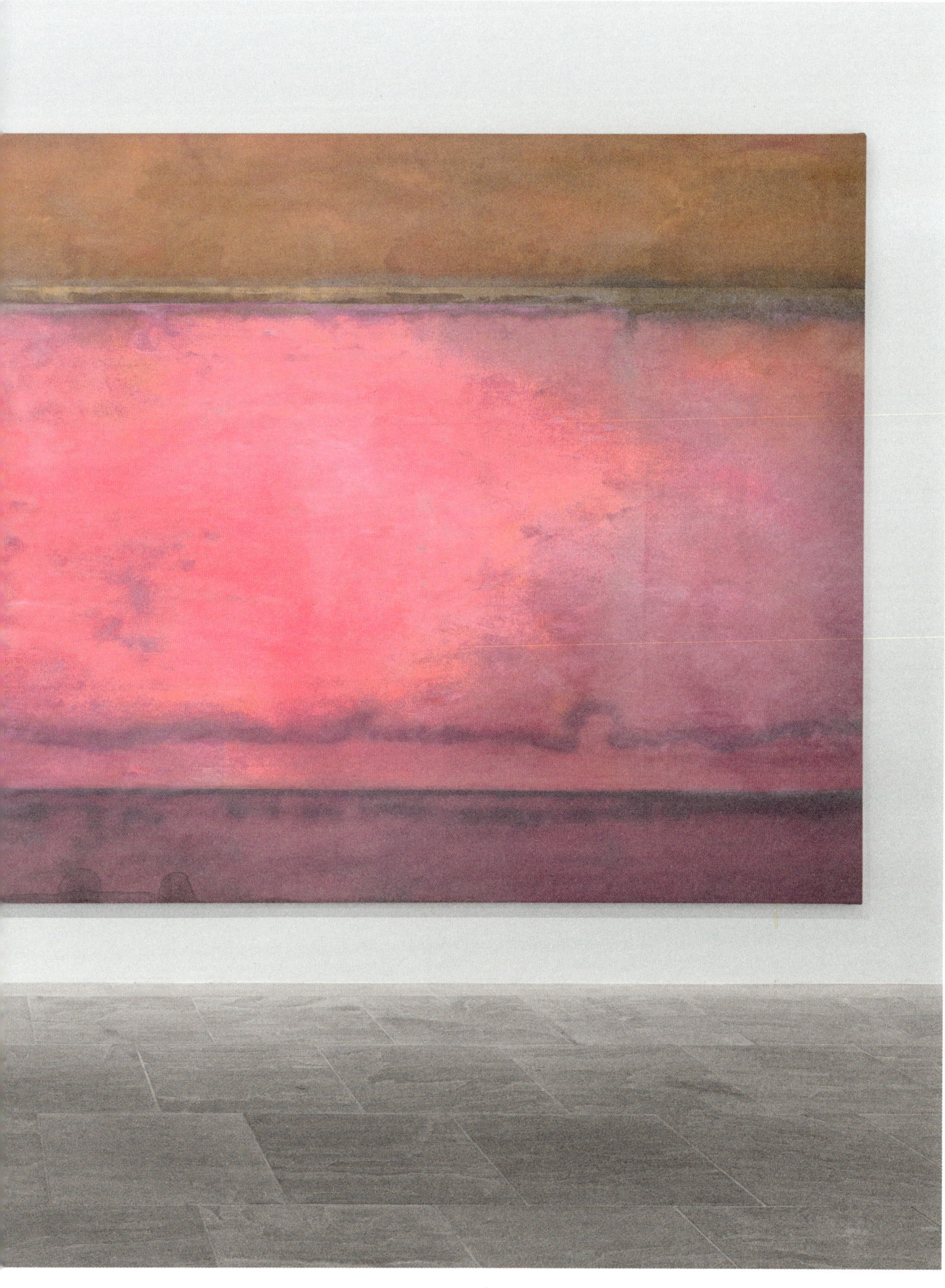

Frank Bowling, *Hello Rosa New York*, 1973, acrylic on canvas, 286 × 693.5 cm

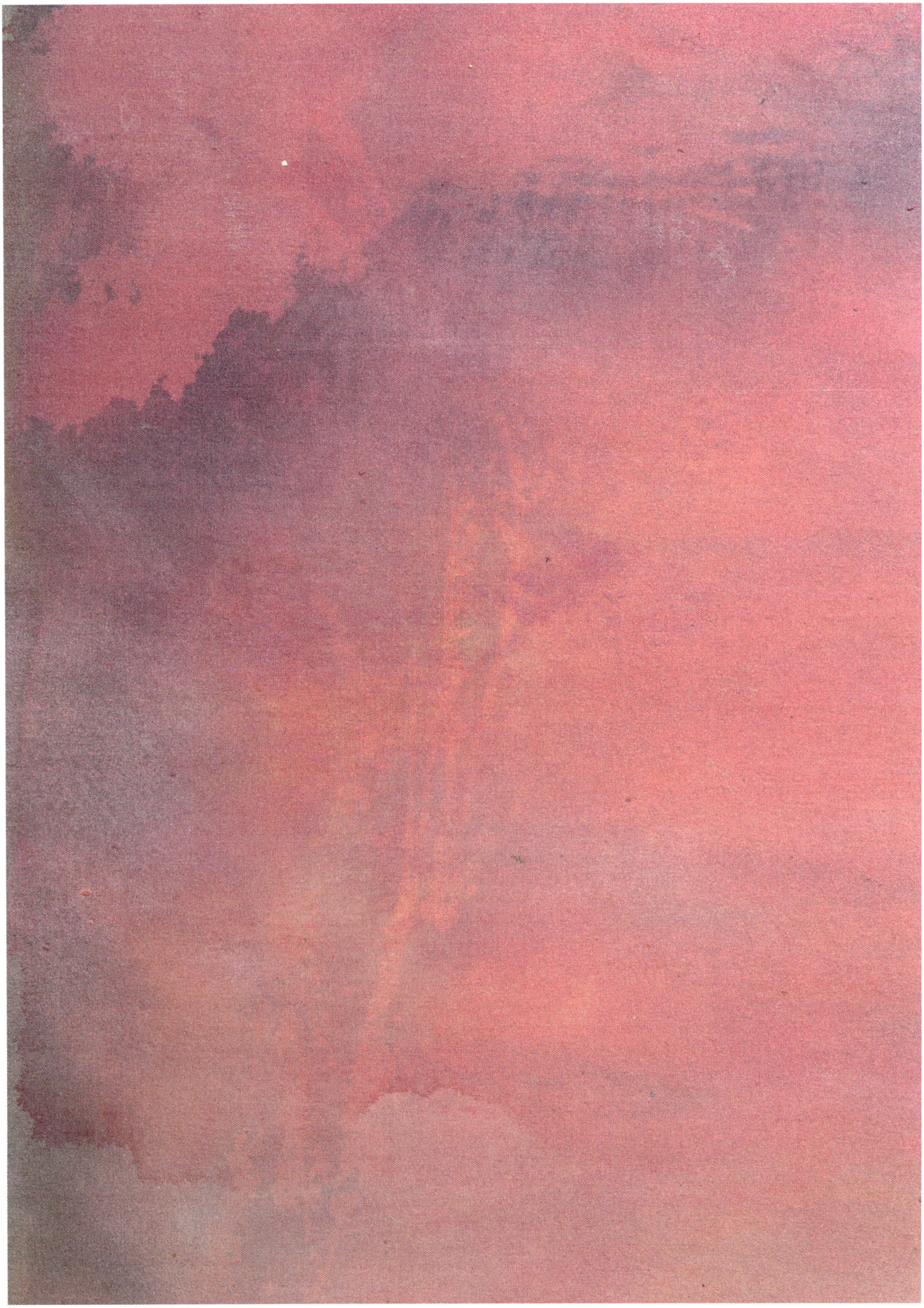

FRANK BOWLING

(Guyana, 1934)

Hello Rosa New York, 1973

Acrylic on canvas
286 × 693.5 cm

This outsized painting invites the viewer's gaze to swim in a vast swathe of pink framed by two strips. The bands are the result of happenstance carefully controlled by the artist: the marks were left by the floor of his New York studio when the canvas was placed on it horizontally. This "found geometry" led to an organic structure where Frank Bowling enjoyed working with the liquidity of his material, as if to swallow up the viewer entirely.

Hello Rosa New York is representative of his shift to abstraction, reflecting his research on colour and his work on its atmospheric, almost translucent qualities at a point in his career when he was close to the Color Field movement. The painting creates an impression of permanent flux. It was named after the art historian Barbara Rose, who in 1960 helped define one of the schools of minimalism.

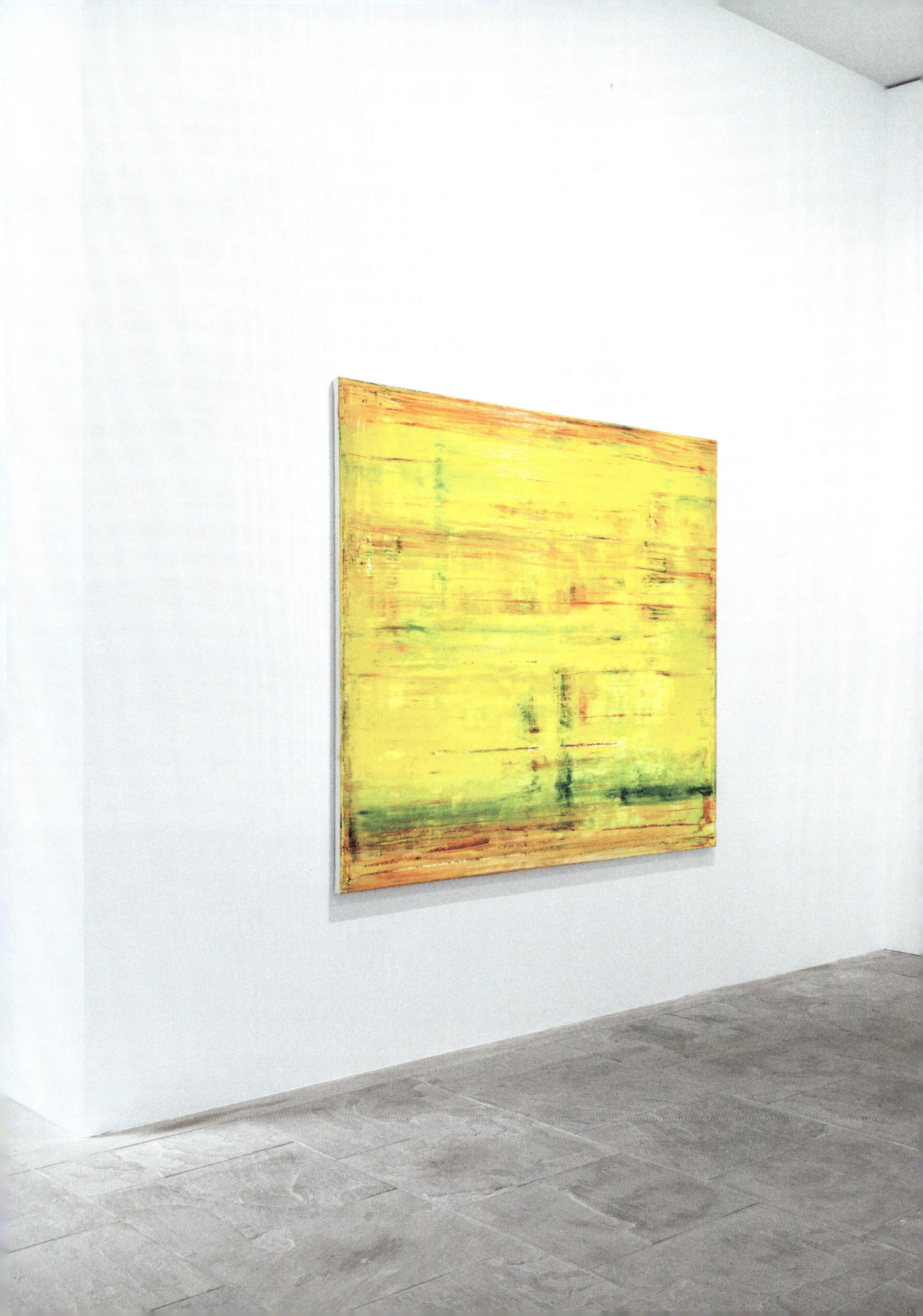

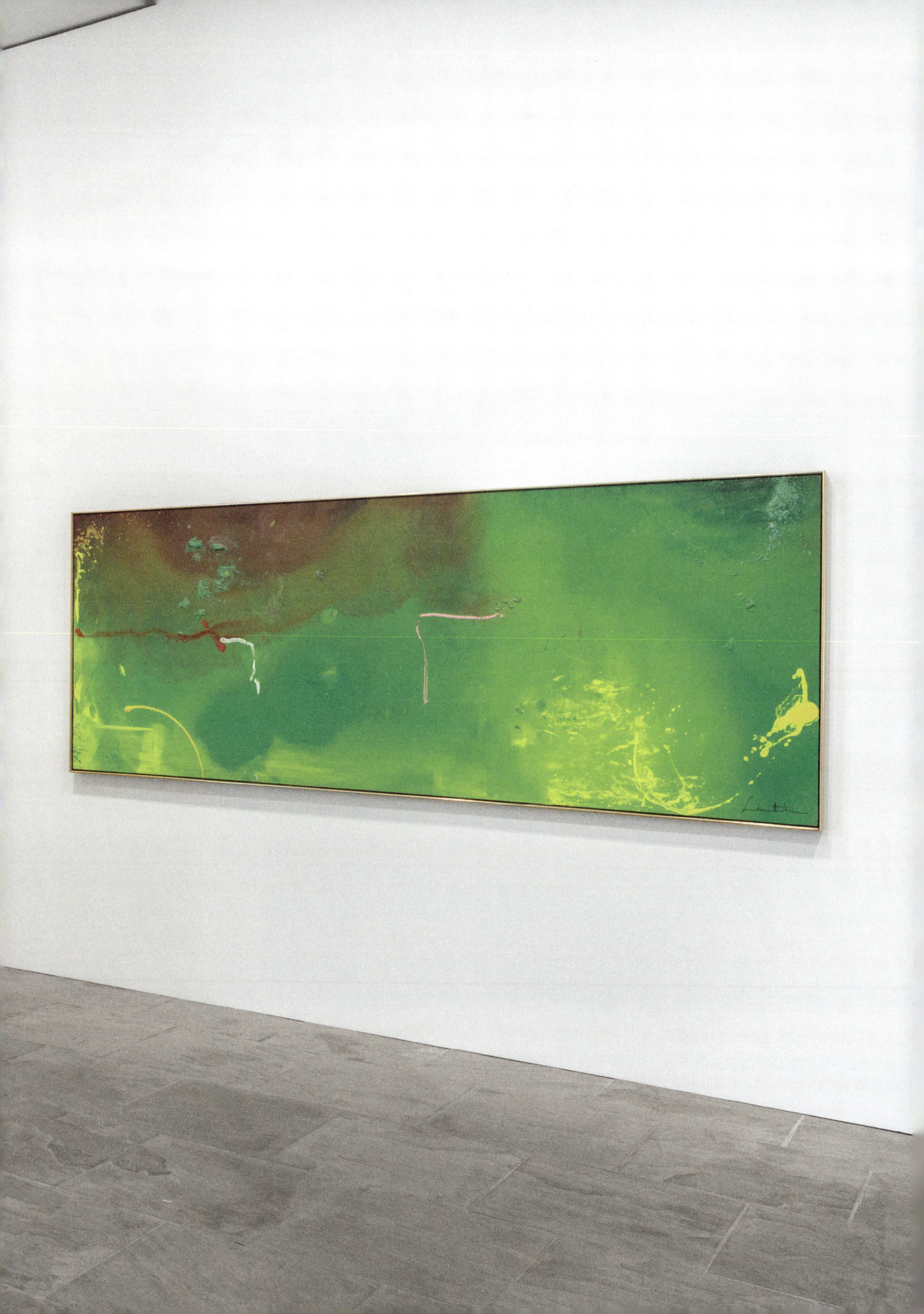

HELEN FRANKENTHALER

(United States, 1928–2011)

Petroglyphs, 1990

Acrylic paint on canvas
116.8 × 299.7 cm

This work takes its title from a type of cave art in which designs were etched or rubbed into stone. A sense of energy is injected into the swathe of green by projections of red, yellow, white and pink paint, generating what the artist has called "abstract climates". Helen Frankenthaler's paintings are full of movement and a sense of texture in spatters and raised reliefs, evoking a murky, swirling liquid landscape. Her soak-stain technique, which involved covering a canvas in highly diluted paint sometimes spread by hand, brought her acclaim in fields of abstraction expressionism such as the Color Field movement. Helen Frankenthaler's paintings shake off the constraints of context and subject to extend beyond the canvas, coming to represent unresolved, meditative landscapes.

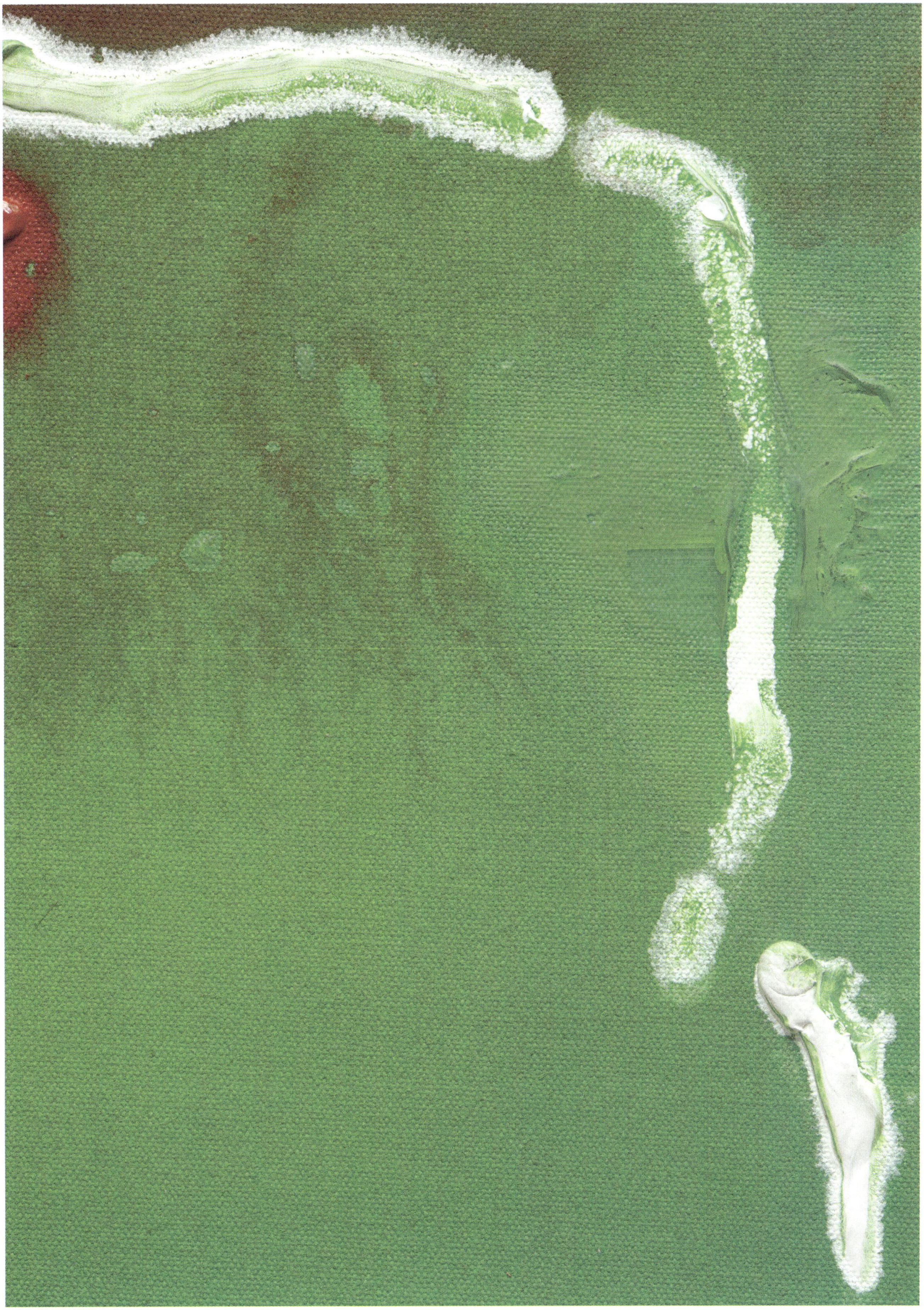

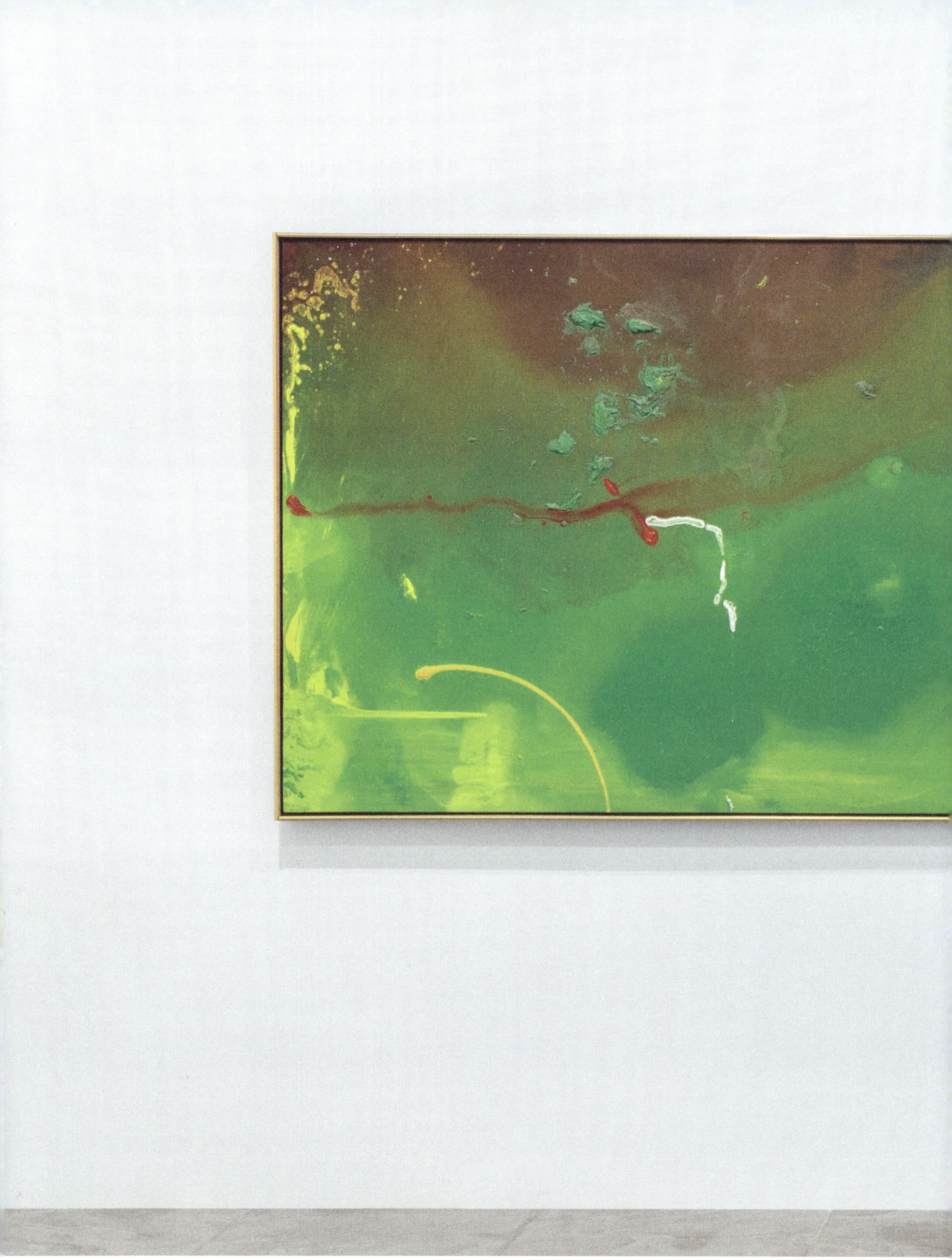

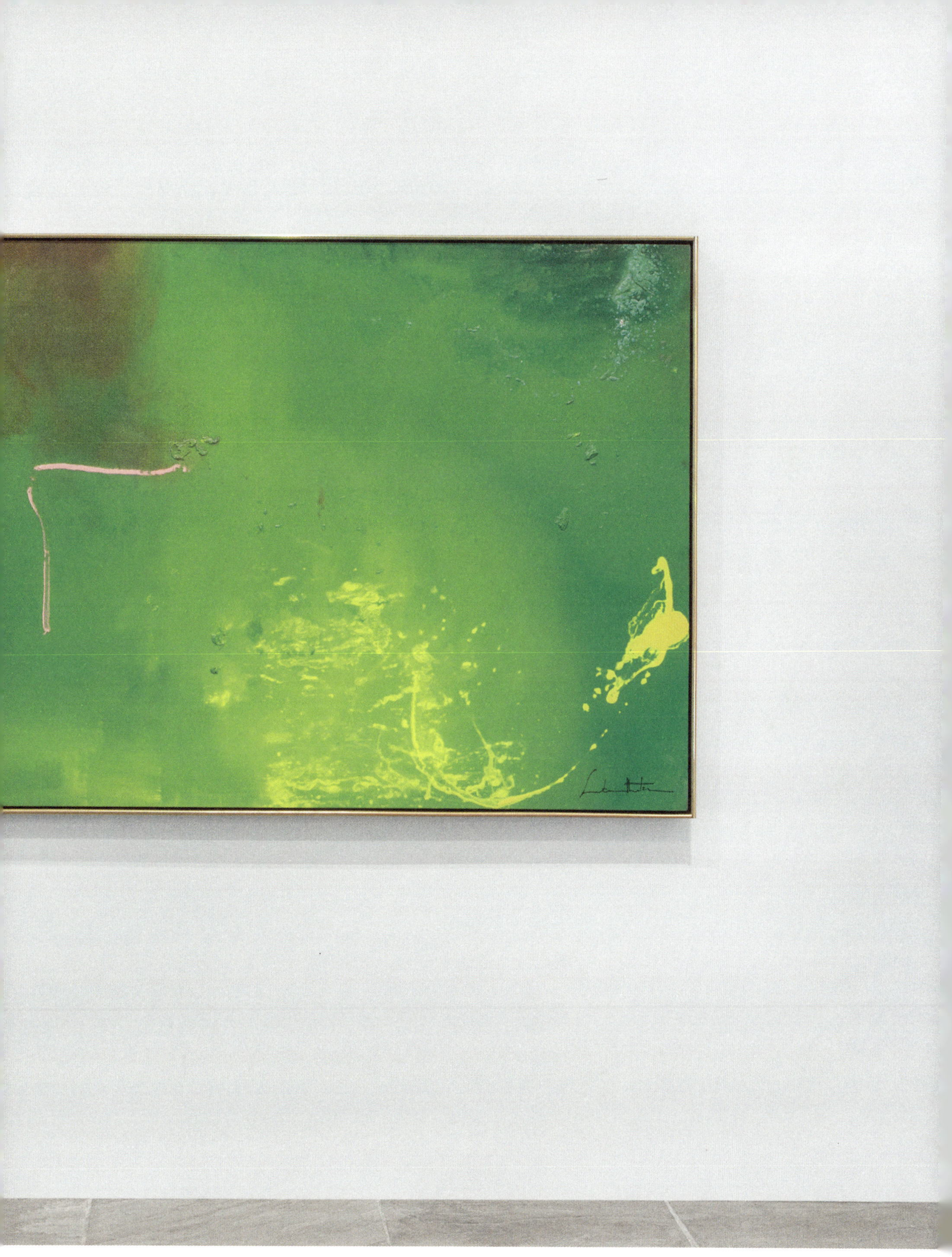

Helen Frankenthaler, *Petroglyphs*, 1990, acrylic on canvas, 116.8 × 299.7 cm

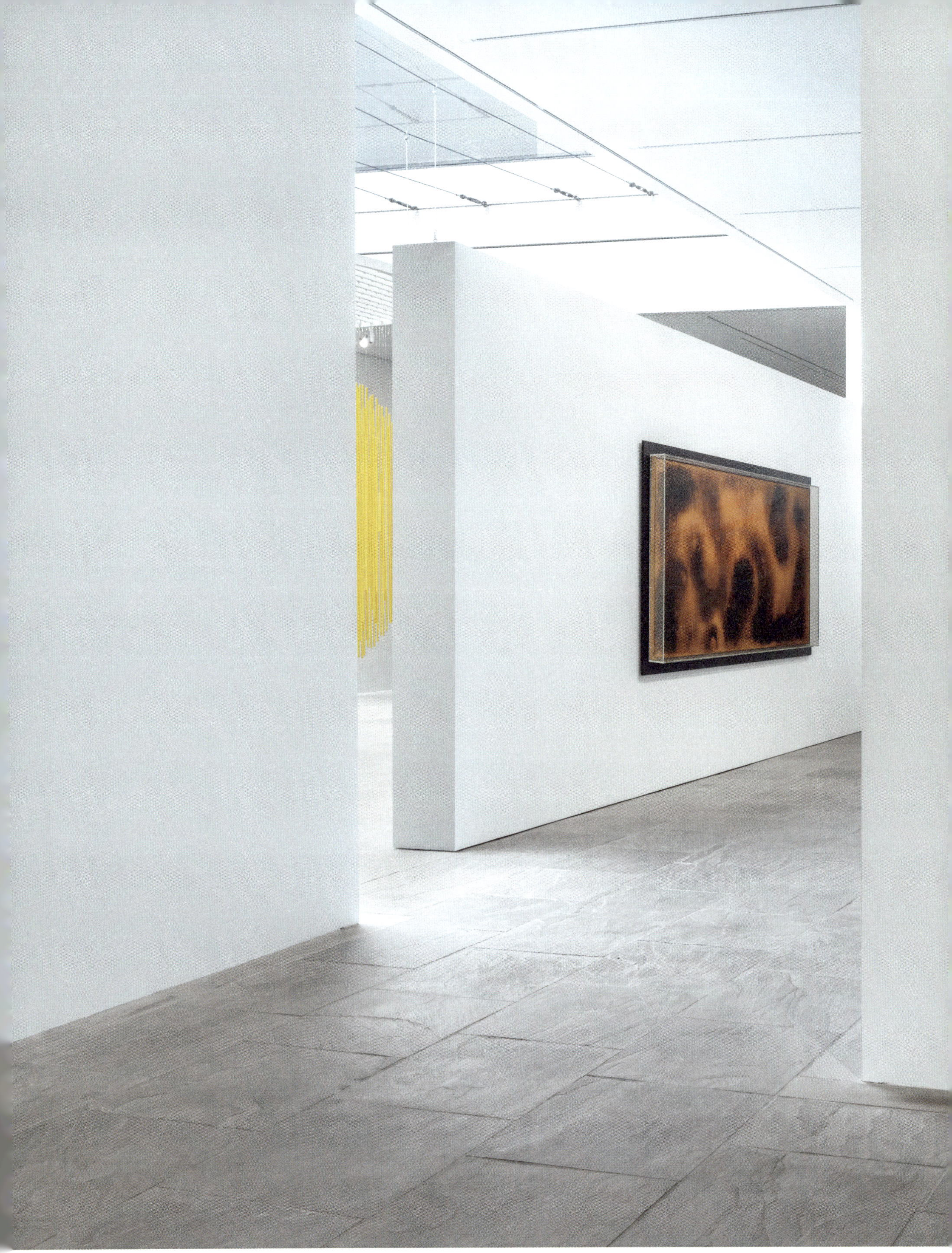

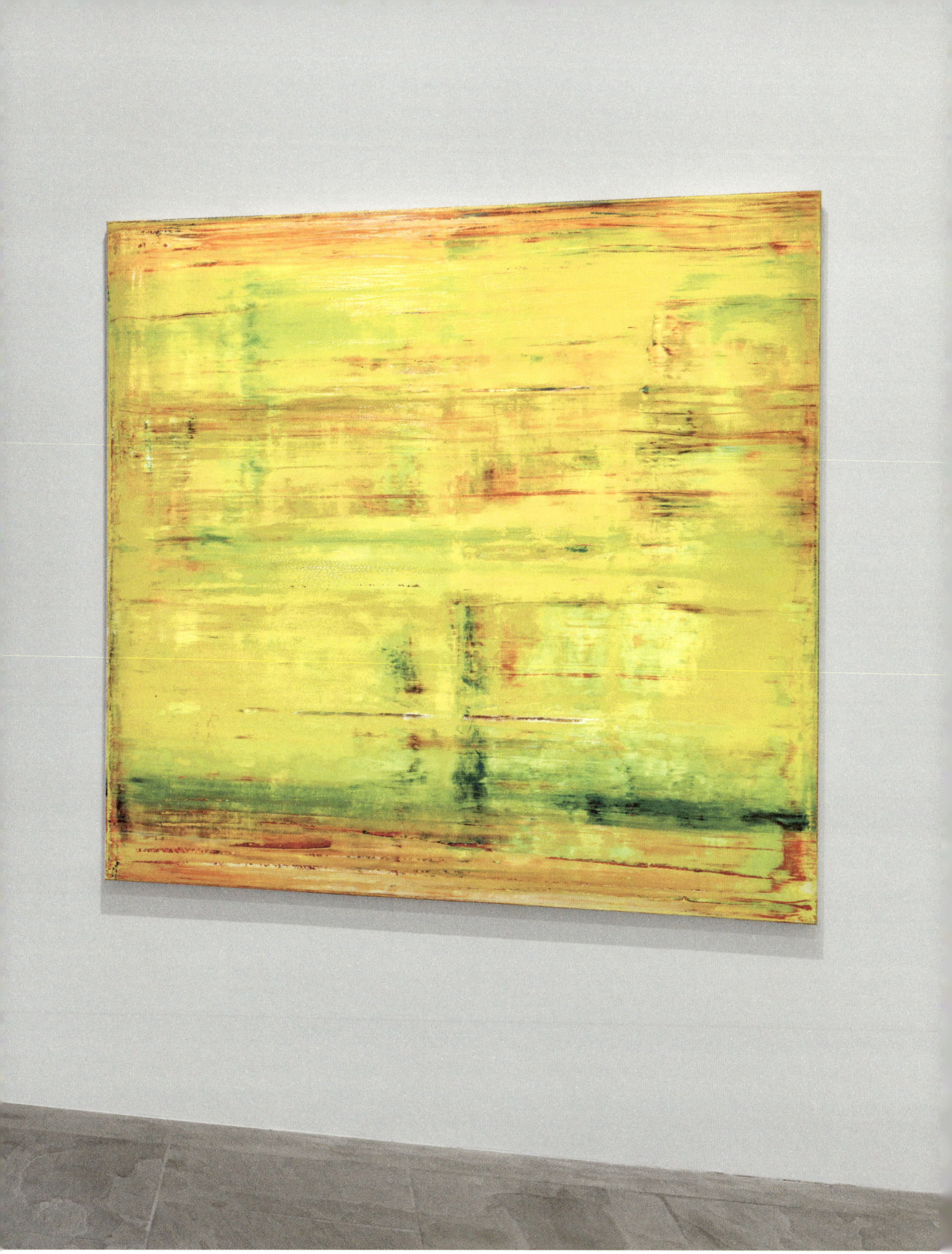

Gerhard Richter, *Abstract Painting*, 2009, oil on canvas, 180 × 180 cm

EVENT HORIZON

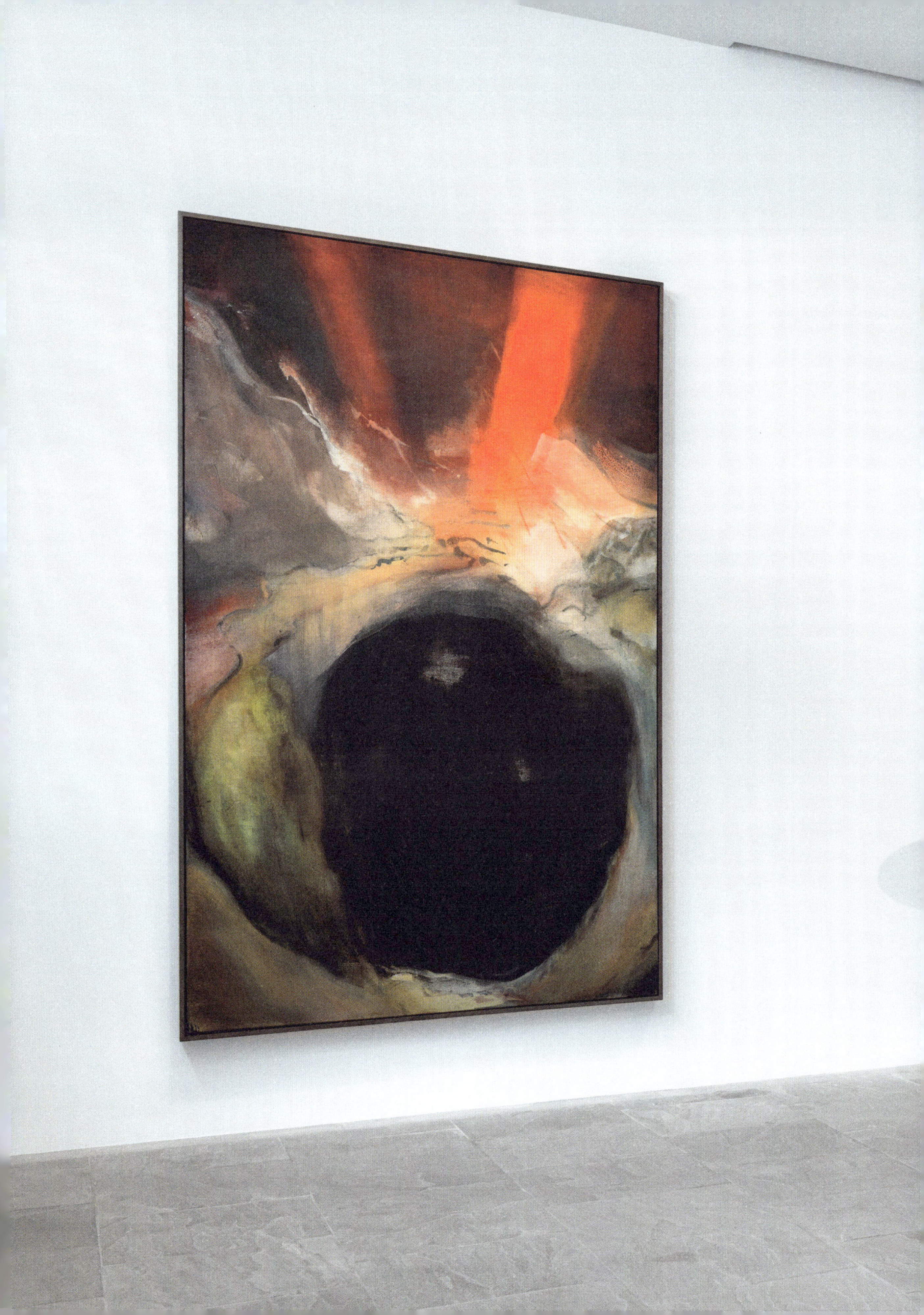

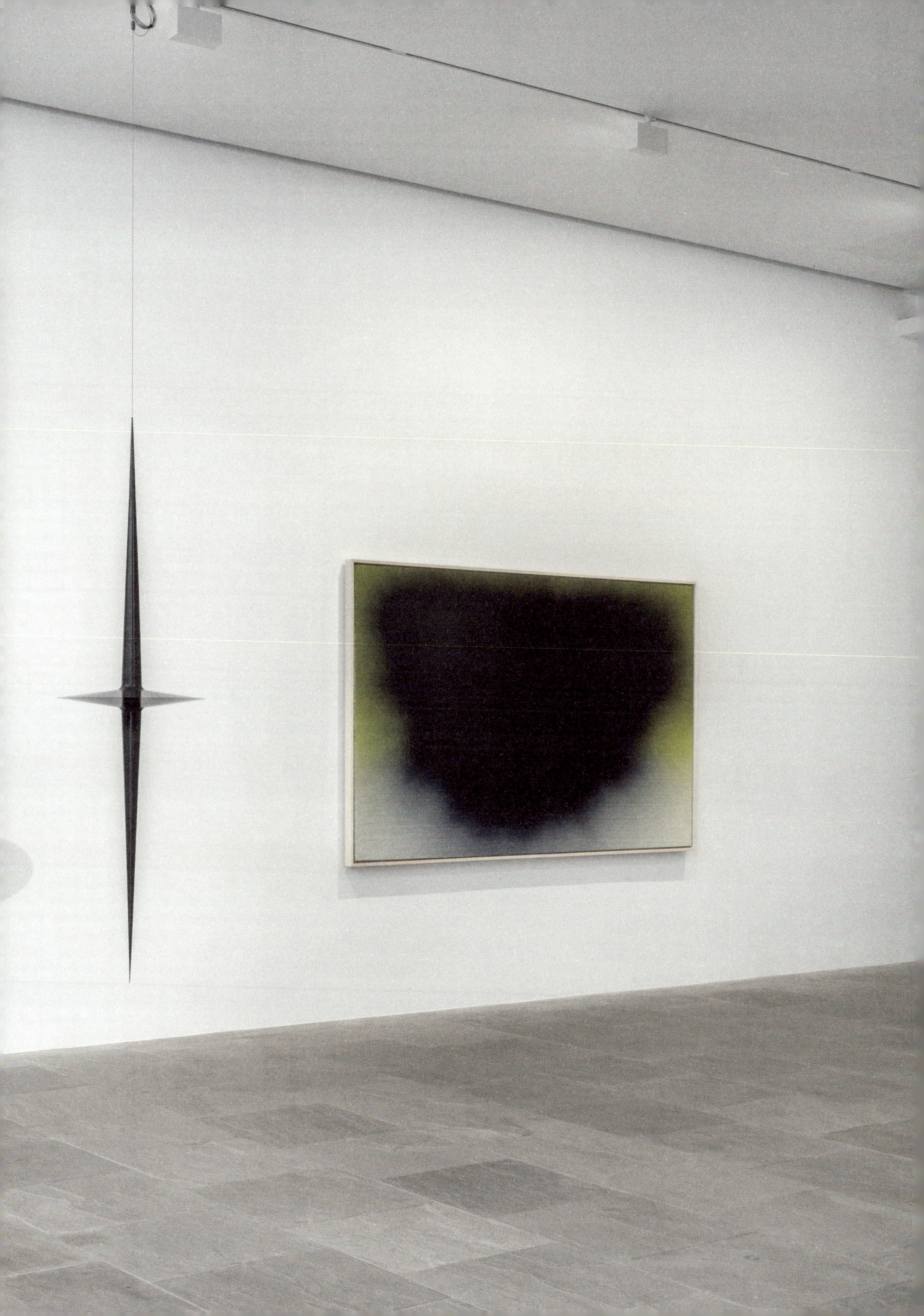

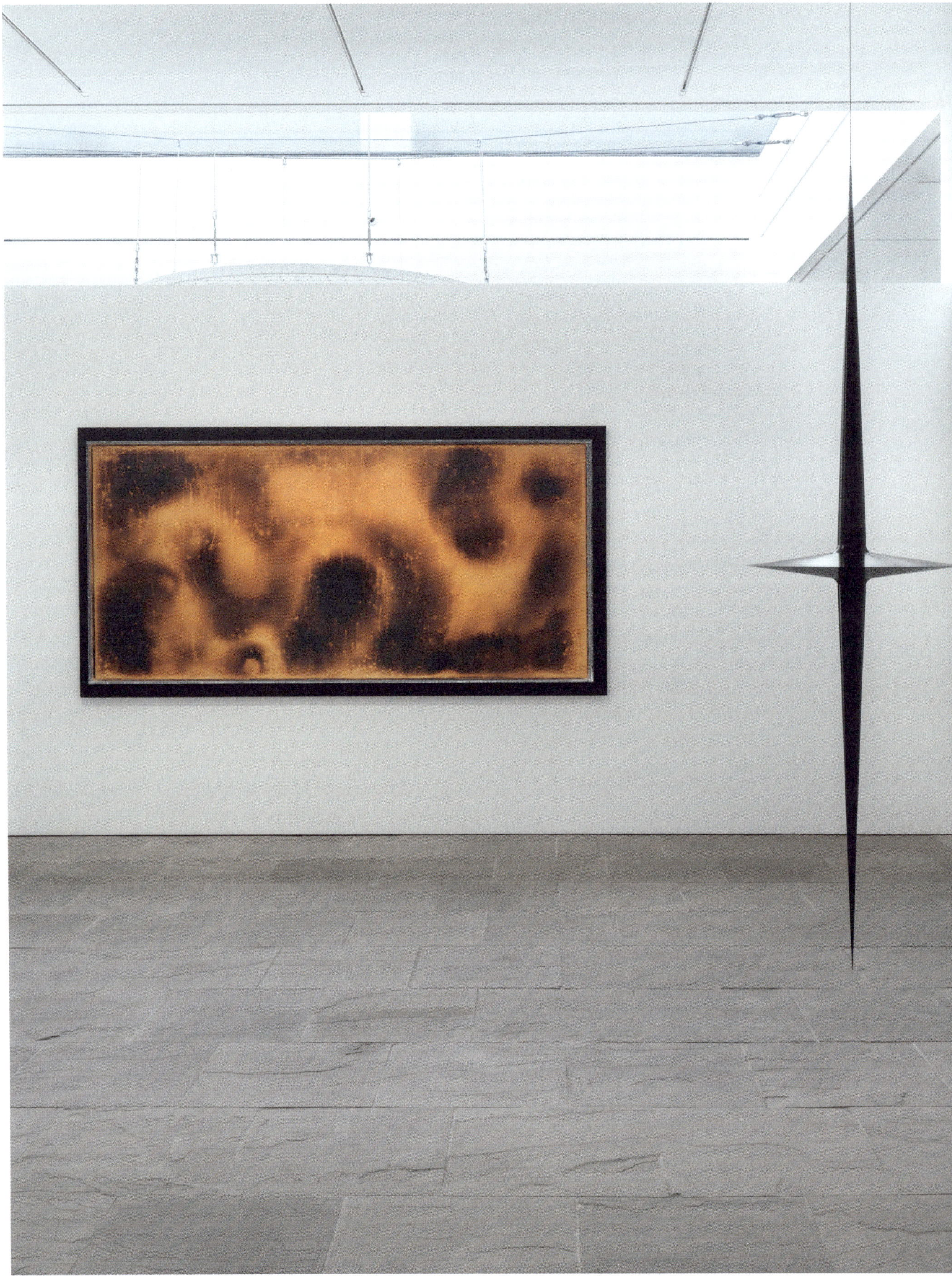

The planarity and calm of celestial and cosmic bodies are only skin deep: these visual fields are both boundless and constantly agitated by forces that defy all limits. Thus, by extrapolation, the macroscopic universe has been a source of inspiration since the early days of abstract art, notably for František Kupka. Artists connected to this aesthetic sensibility, but also many among us, have thus already had the experience of aerial vertigo, of traversing clouds and of the infinite sky. Our gaze thus wanders, attracted by erratic (or Brownian) movements, by a multitude of simultaneous, bright microevents in the environment of Otto Piene, one of the pioneers of the genre. This work is not comprised of paint, but a complex constellation of light projections at the heart of a dark patch, stemming from seven pierced boxes.

Yves Klein's *Peinture de feu* (Fire Painting) was made from a combustion directed and controlled by the artist, who was equipped for the occasion not with a paintbrush but with a flame thrower and fire retardant. The resulting spectral form is a blurry and complex halo of dancing and indecisive ectoplasmic forms, oscillating between flatness and volume, appearance and disappearance. The eye thus circulates between them without ever finding respite, as though it were trapped between these whirling entities.

Like a gargantuan wave, the spectral nebula by Caroline Corbasson seems ready to engulf us in its dark mass. It was taken from a cosmogonic form whose scientific image was initially formed by a digital data stream. The result, visually interpreted, is seen here reframed and expressed by the artist as an oversized screenprint. As for Thomas Ruff, he "composes" a cosmogonic cloud based on mathematic fractals, printed not on photographic paper, but on the fibres of an elegant velvet that plays with the light. The atomised composition catches the eye and draws it into its swirling spirals.

It is hard to situate ourselves spatially before the dark stars of Leiko Ikemura, Hans Hartung or Rotraut, given the extent to which "event horizons" or "black holes" suck the gazes and bodies that approach them into the void.
As for the sculpture hanging by a thread, by Artur Lescher, it came from the measurement made by one rotation of a pitch-black vinyl material. It unfolds like a line or a cross in the immaculate space and, like a sorcerer's pendulum, seems to point to the invisible magnetic currents surrounding us. Perfectly circular and incredibly elongated, extending upwards, it captures and traps our gaze within another black hole, in the manner of Lucio Fontana's *Concetto spaziale*. However, its numerous concentric grooves invite us to walk around it, to become its satellites; a visual dynamic that incidentally recalls the uninterrupted spinning top at the end of Christopher Nolan's film *Inception* (2010).

Yves Klein, *Peinture de feu sans titre* (F 24), 1961, burnt cardboard on wood panel, 139 × 299 cm
Artur Lescher, *Cardenal*, 2014, nylon, 220 × 60 × 60 cm
p. 42: Rotraut, *Éclipse* (detail), n.d., mixed techniques on canvas, 130 × 89 cm

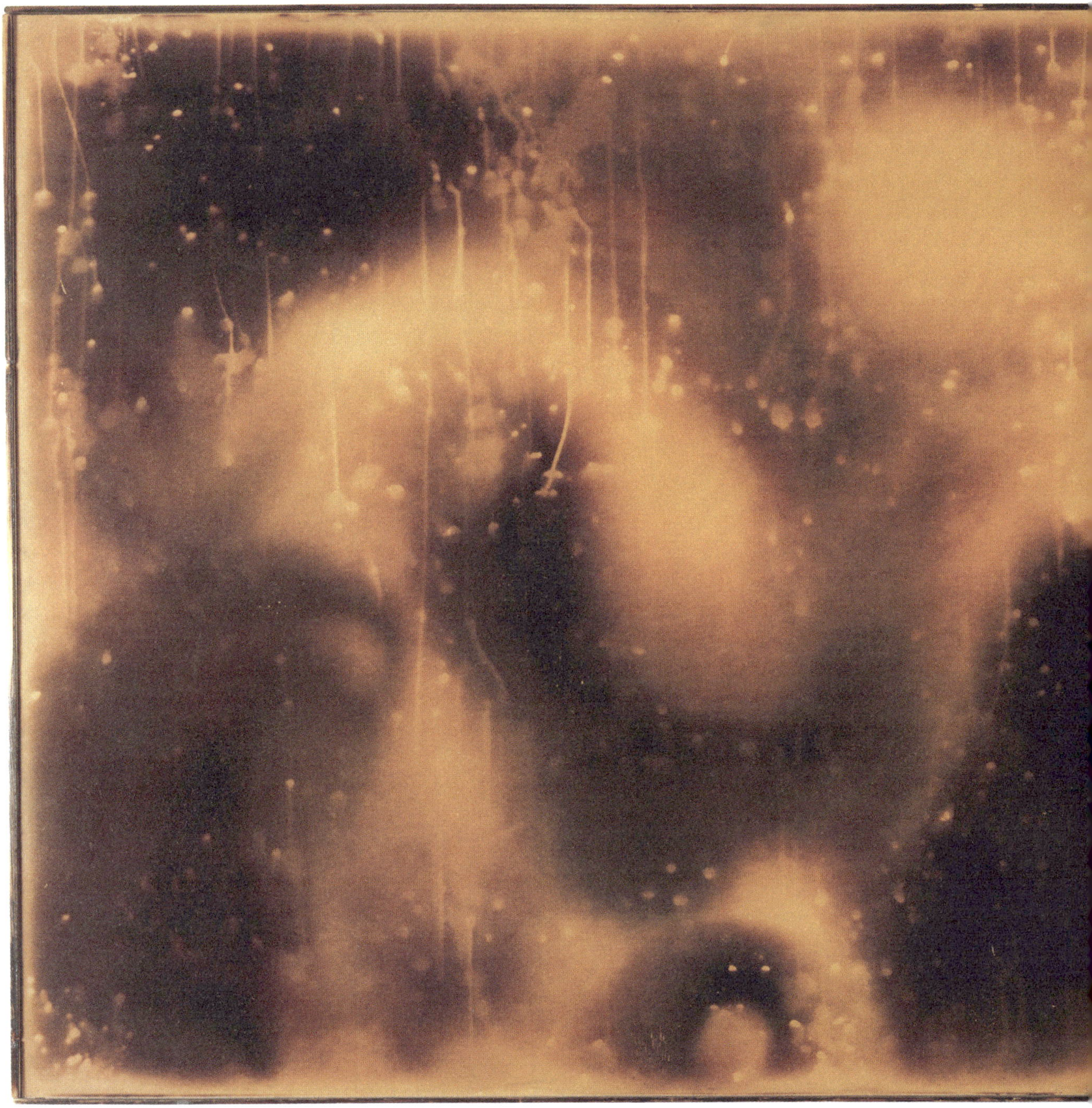

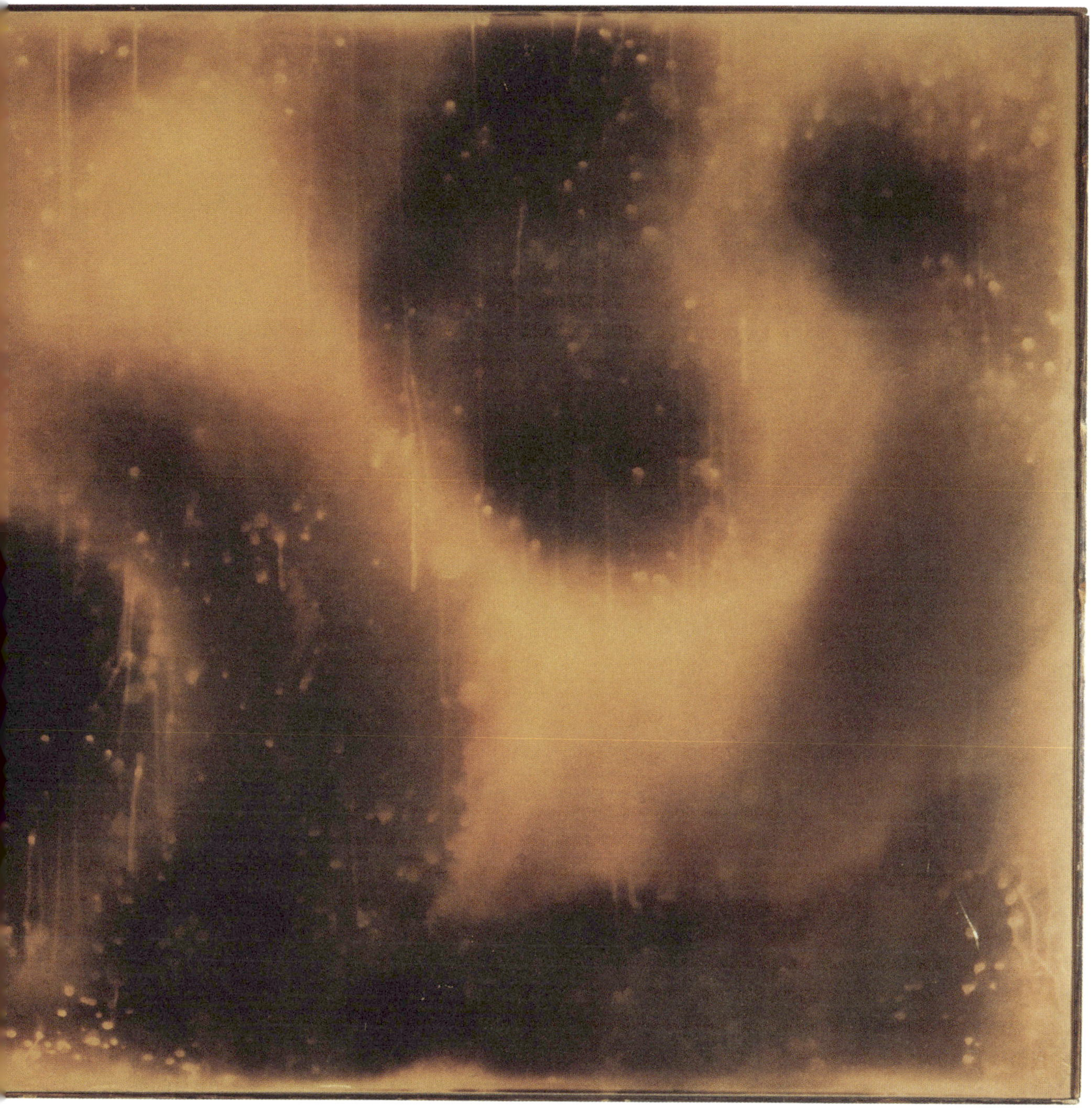

Yves Klein, *Peinture de feu sans titre* (F 24), 1961, burnt cardboard on wood panel, 139 × 299 cm

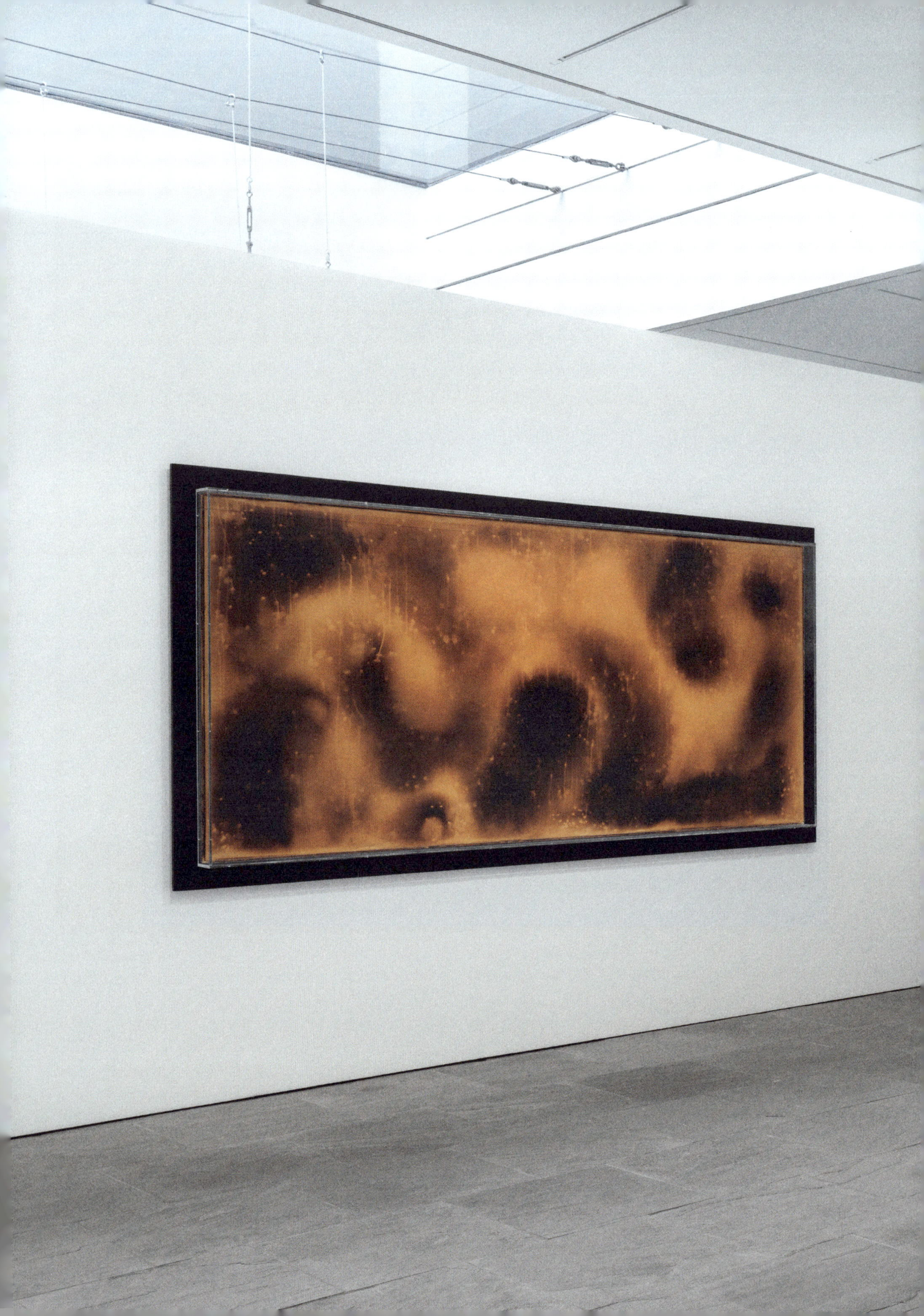

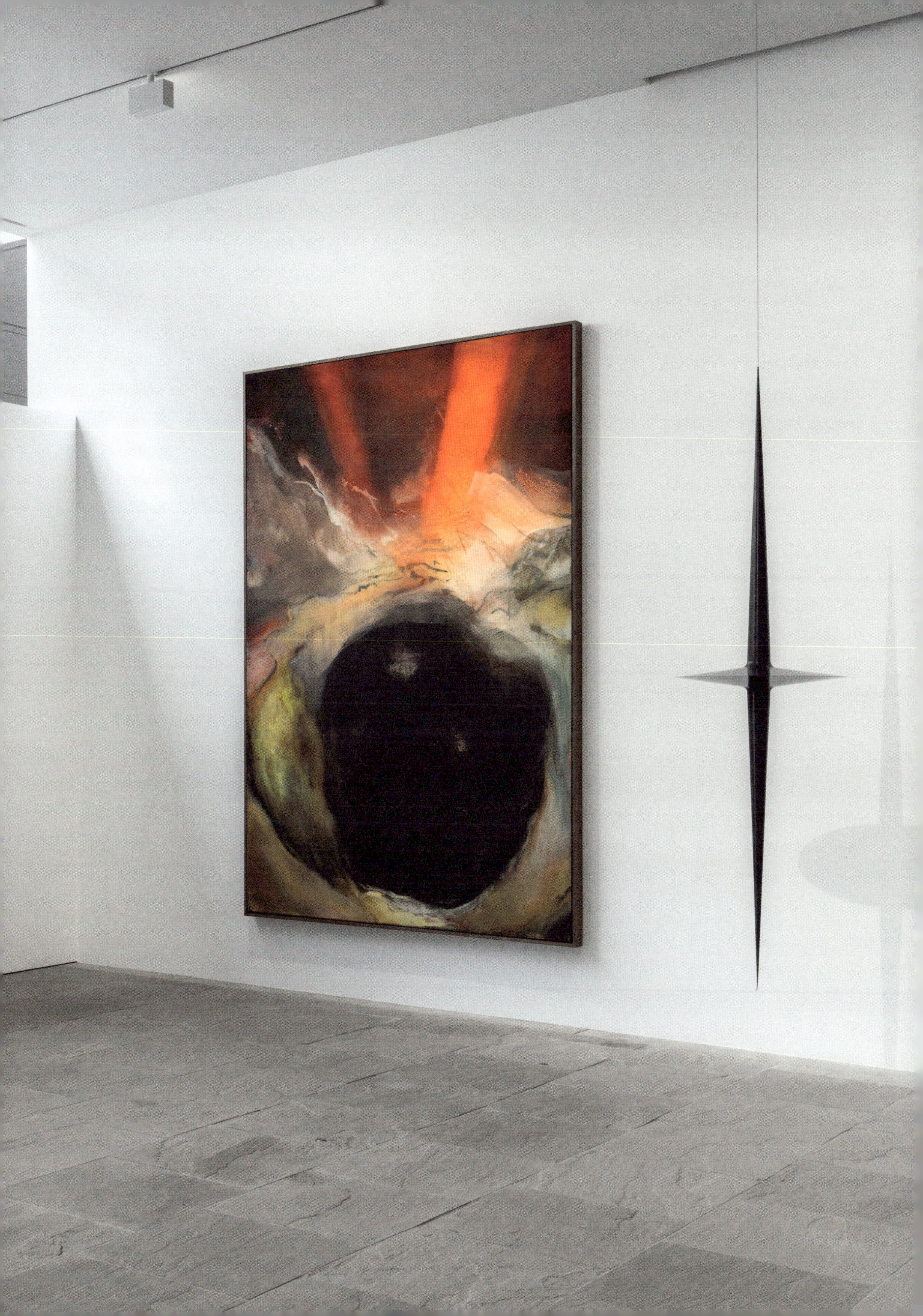

Leiko Ikemura, *Praise of Light II*, 2020, tempera and oil on jute canvas, 290 × 190 cm

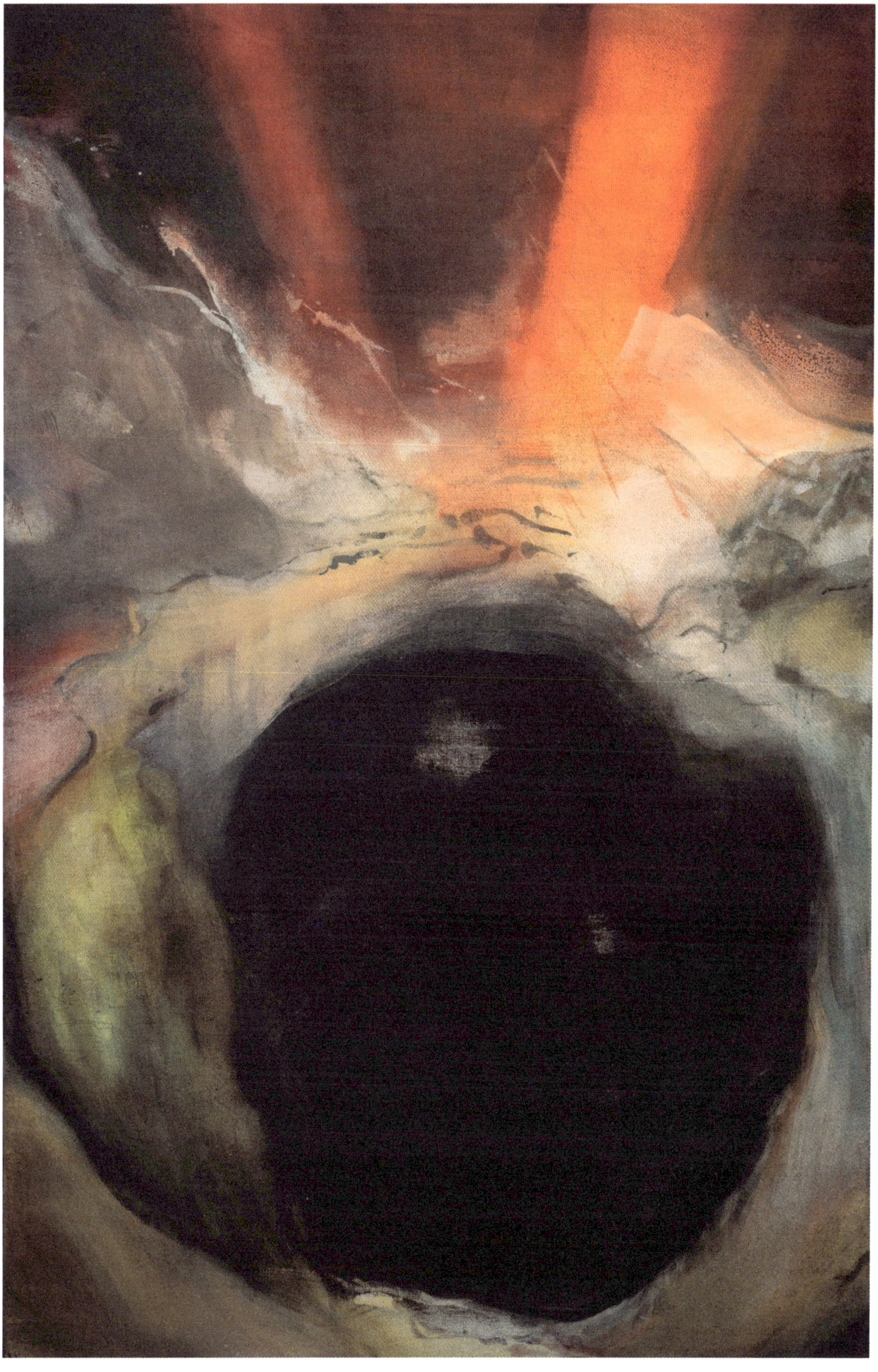

ARTUR LESCHER

(Brazil, 1962)

Cardenal, 2014

Nylon
220 × 60 × 60 cm

Suspended in the room like a gravitating black star, *Cardenal* is one of a series of minimalist geometrical 3D sculptures characteristic of Artur Lescher's art. The work, resembling an unidentified celestial object, instantiates Lescher's research on shapes and how they interact with space. Cut from deep-black vinyl, it unfolds like a cross or a magnetic needle, drawn to a flux invisible to the naked eye. *Cardenal* invites visitors to contemplate it in the round, evoking a spinning top, a compass or a pendulum, reacting to forces that lie beyond human perception.

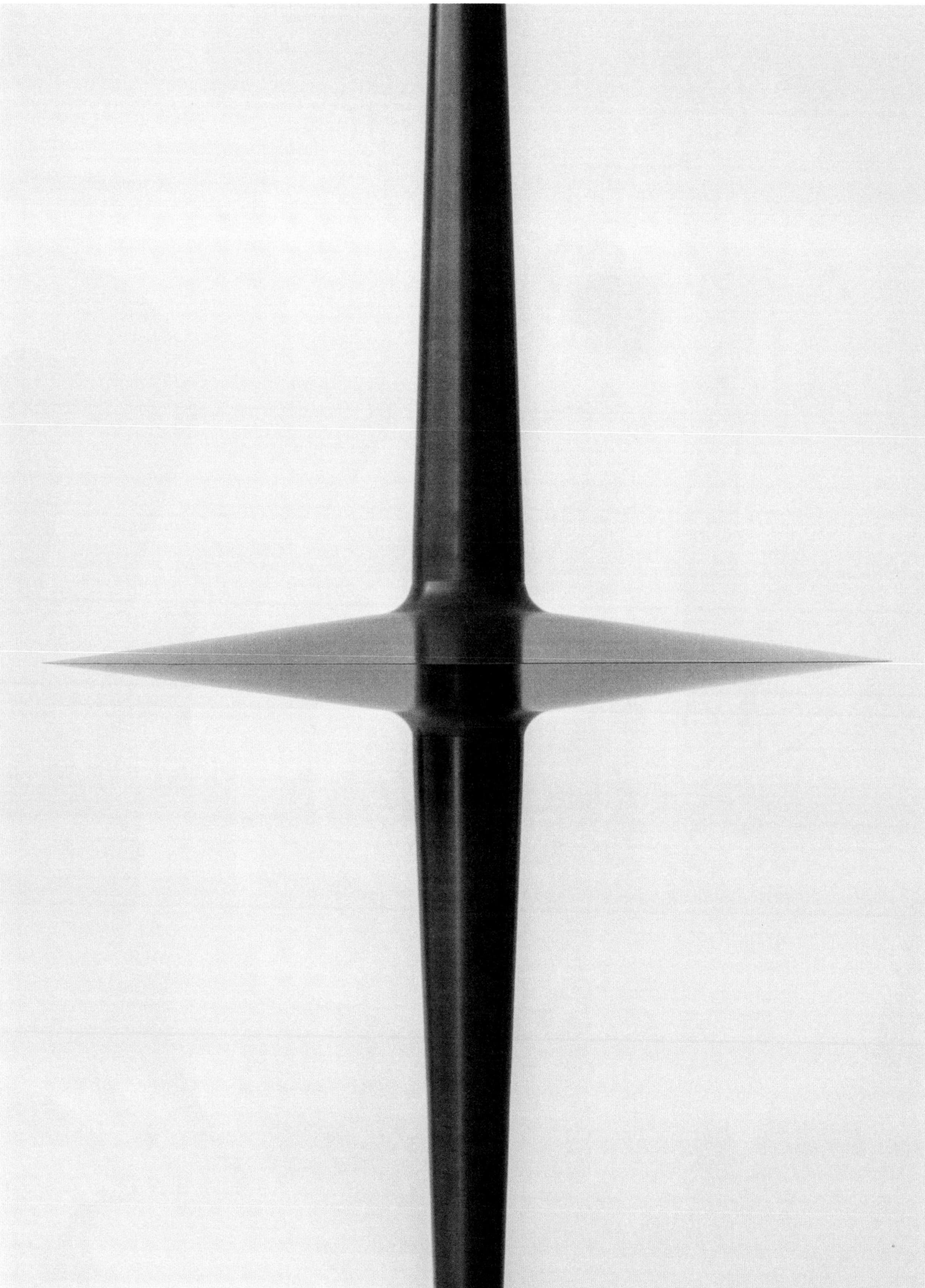

Hans Hartung, *T1967-H22*, 1967, vinyl paint on canvas, 154 × 250 cm

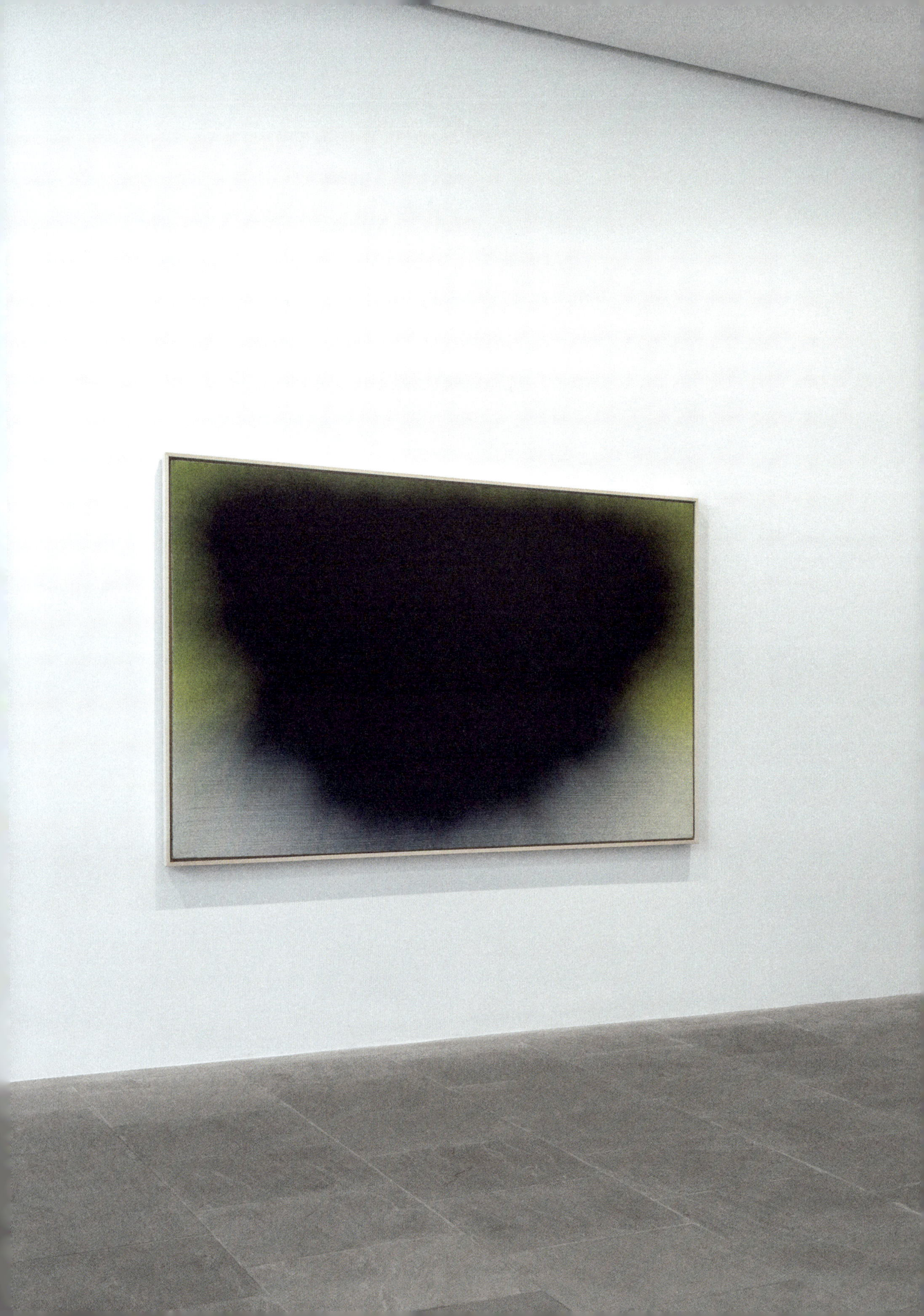

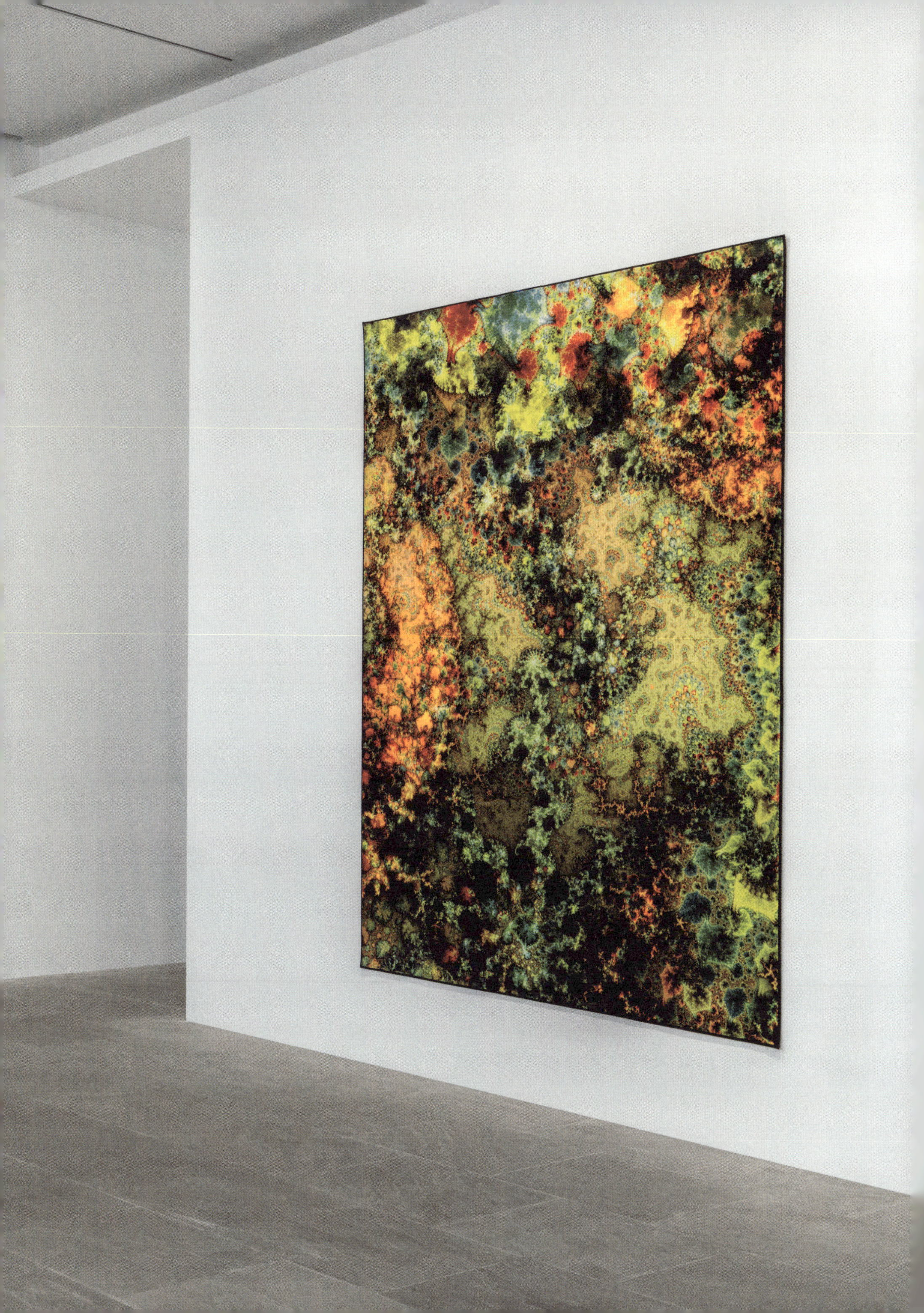

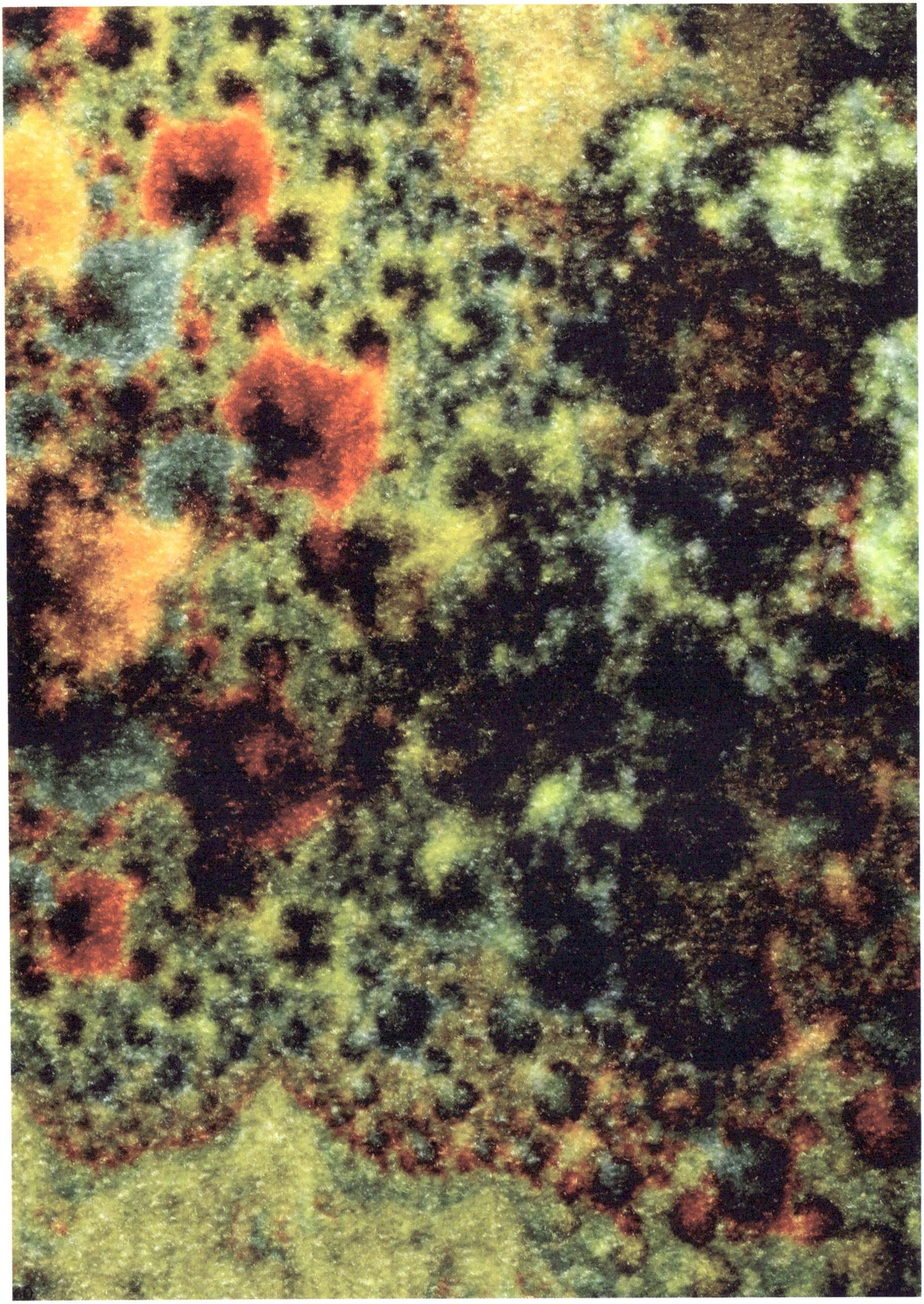

THOMAS RUFF

(Germany, 1958)

d.o.pe.05, 2022

Colaris on velvet carpet
267 × 200 cm

Aldous Huxley's 1954 book *The Doors of Perception*, exploring the use of psychedelics to heighten the senses, was a key inspiration for the *d.o.pe.* series that presents visitors with invisible, hallucinatory realms. Thomas Ruff sweeps us into an infinite landscape of repeated motifs, a headrush of brightly coloured senses rooted in science, like Caroline Corbasson's work displayed alongside this piece.

Ruff's research into the aestheticisation of complex mathematical formulas led to *d.o.pe.05*, a visual translation of the principle of fractals in which each unit shares the same shape as the whole, like a snowflake or Romanesco broccoli. The work is suffused with 1970s aesthetics, inviting us to forego our usual perceptions and drift into the depths of an infinitely fractured pattern.

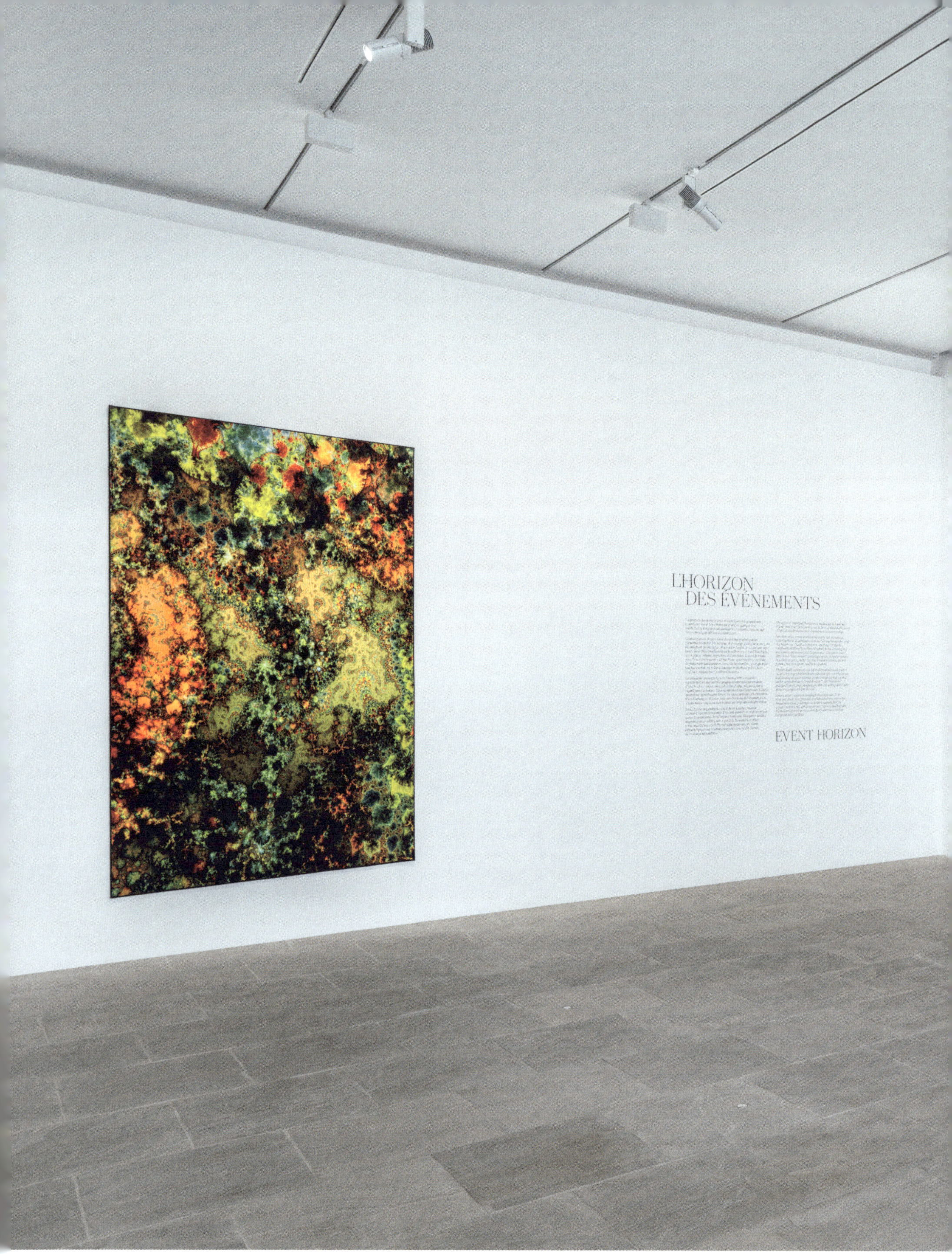

Thomas Ruff, *d.o.pe.05*, 2022, colaris on velvet carpet, 267 × 200 cm

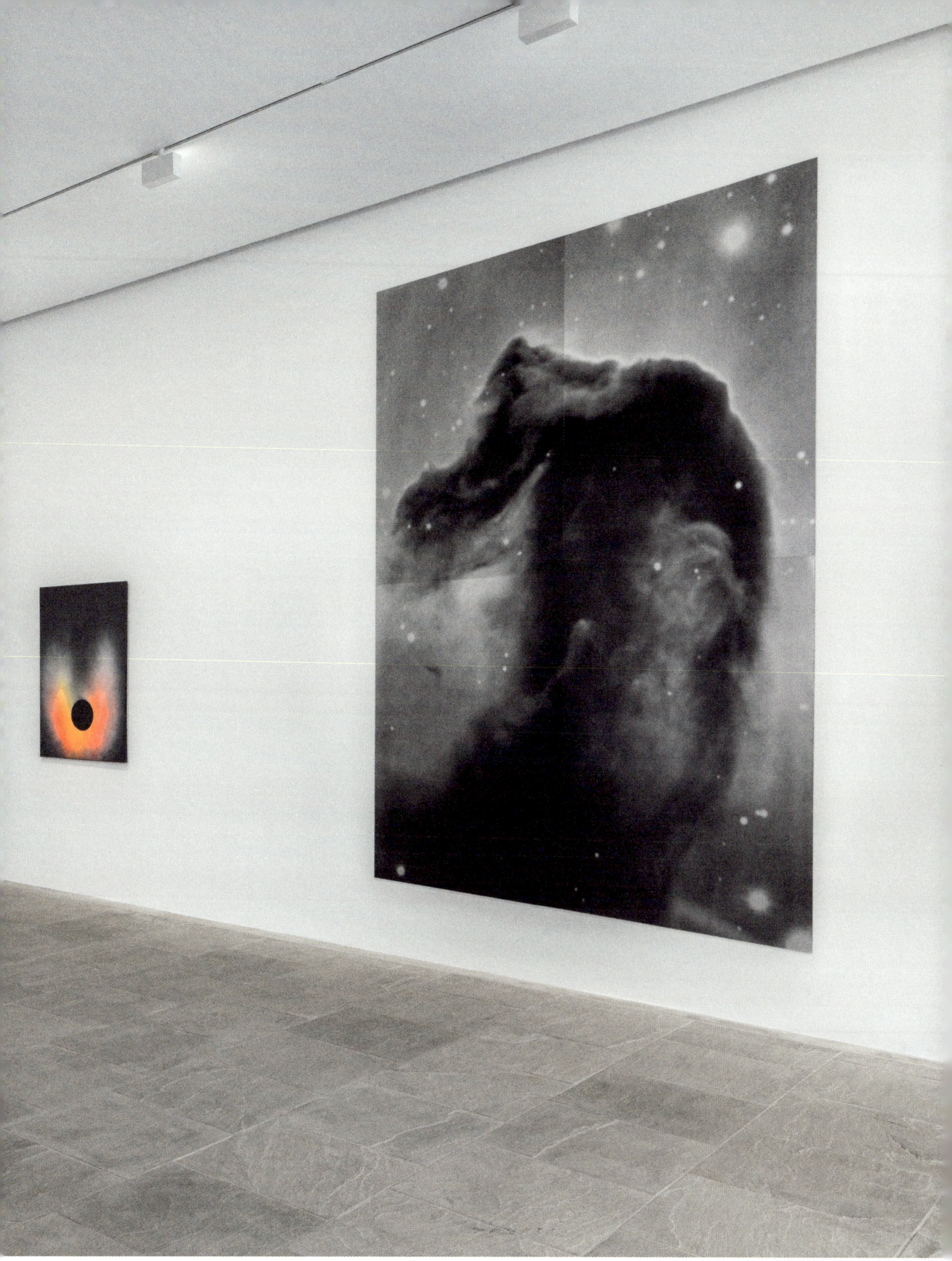

Rotraut, *Éclipse*, n.d., mixed techniques on canvas, 130 × 89 cm
Caroline Corbasson, *Collapse*, 2017, serigraphy with chrome ink on aluminium black Dibond, 350 × 260 cm

Rotraut, *Éclipse*, n.d., mixed techniques on canvas, 130 × 89 cm

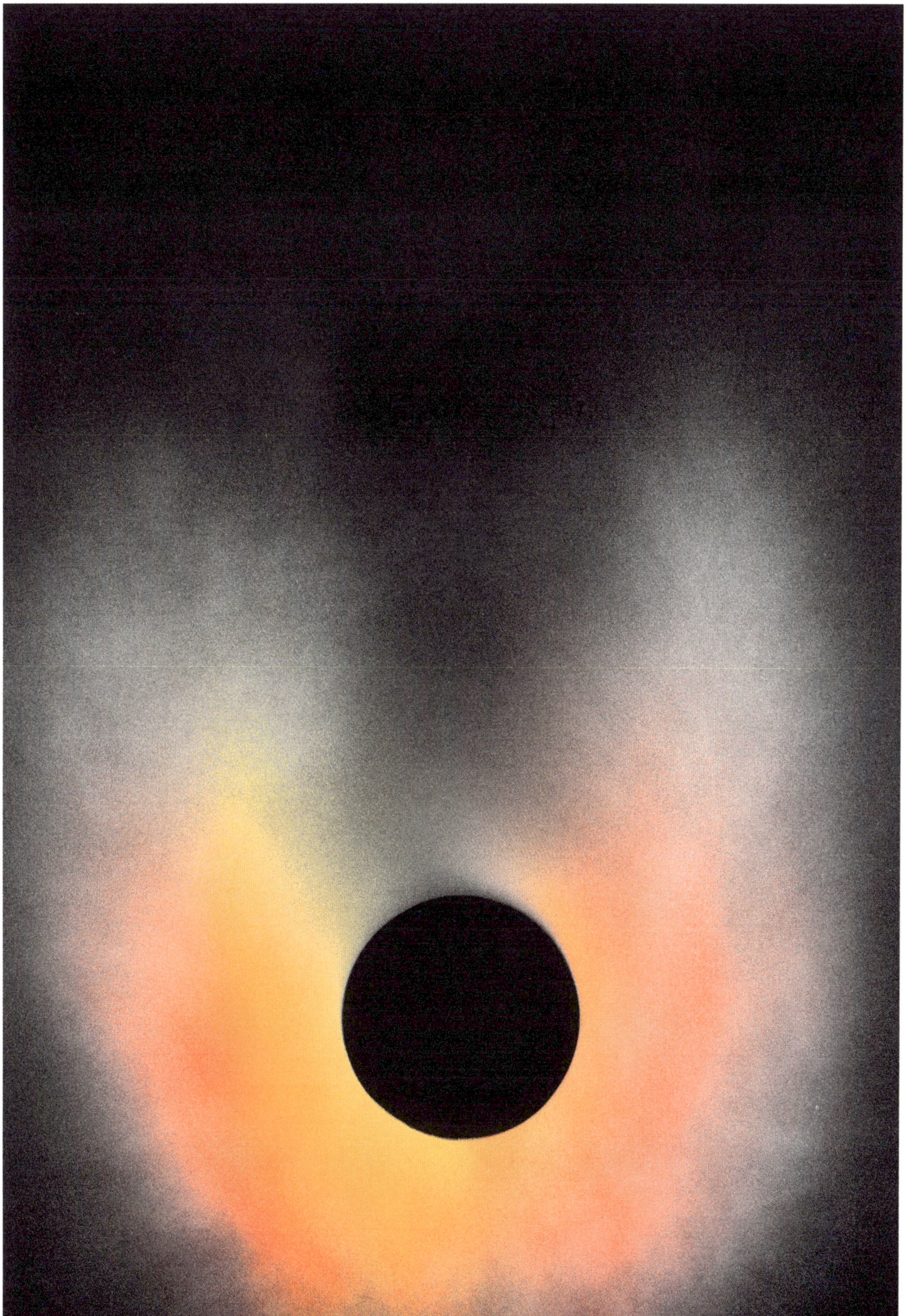

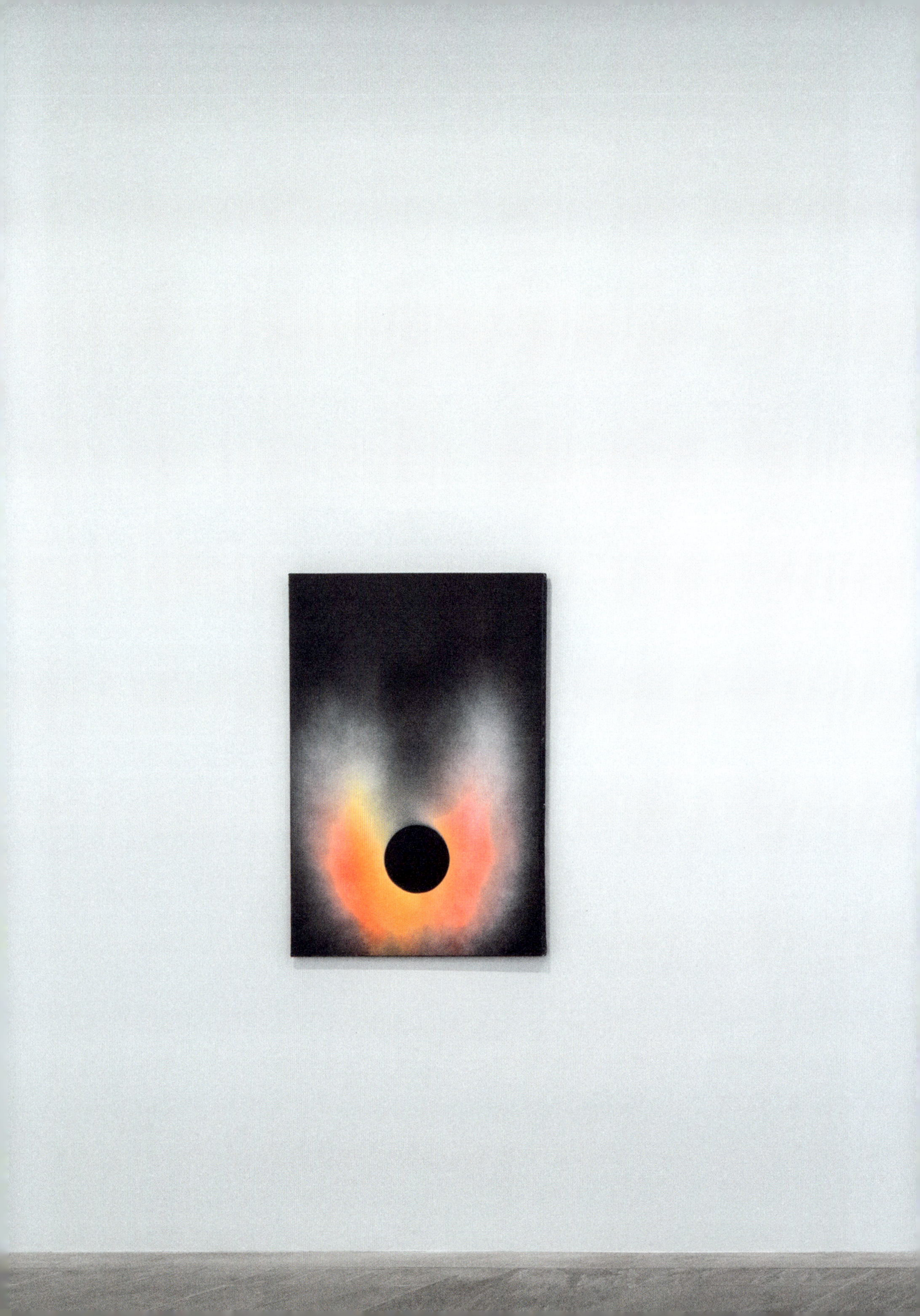

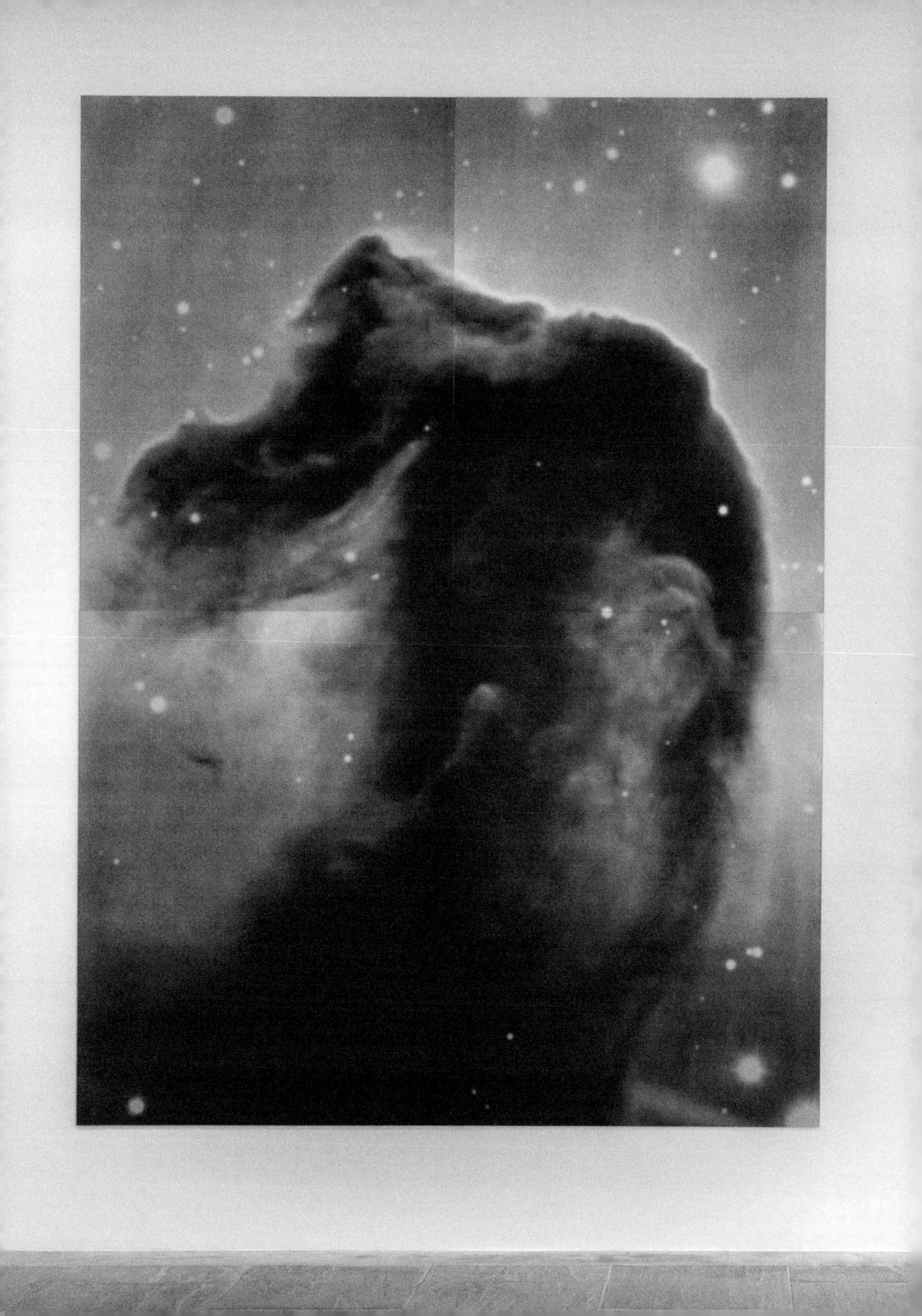

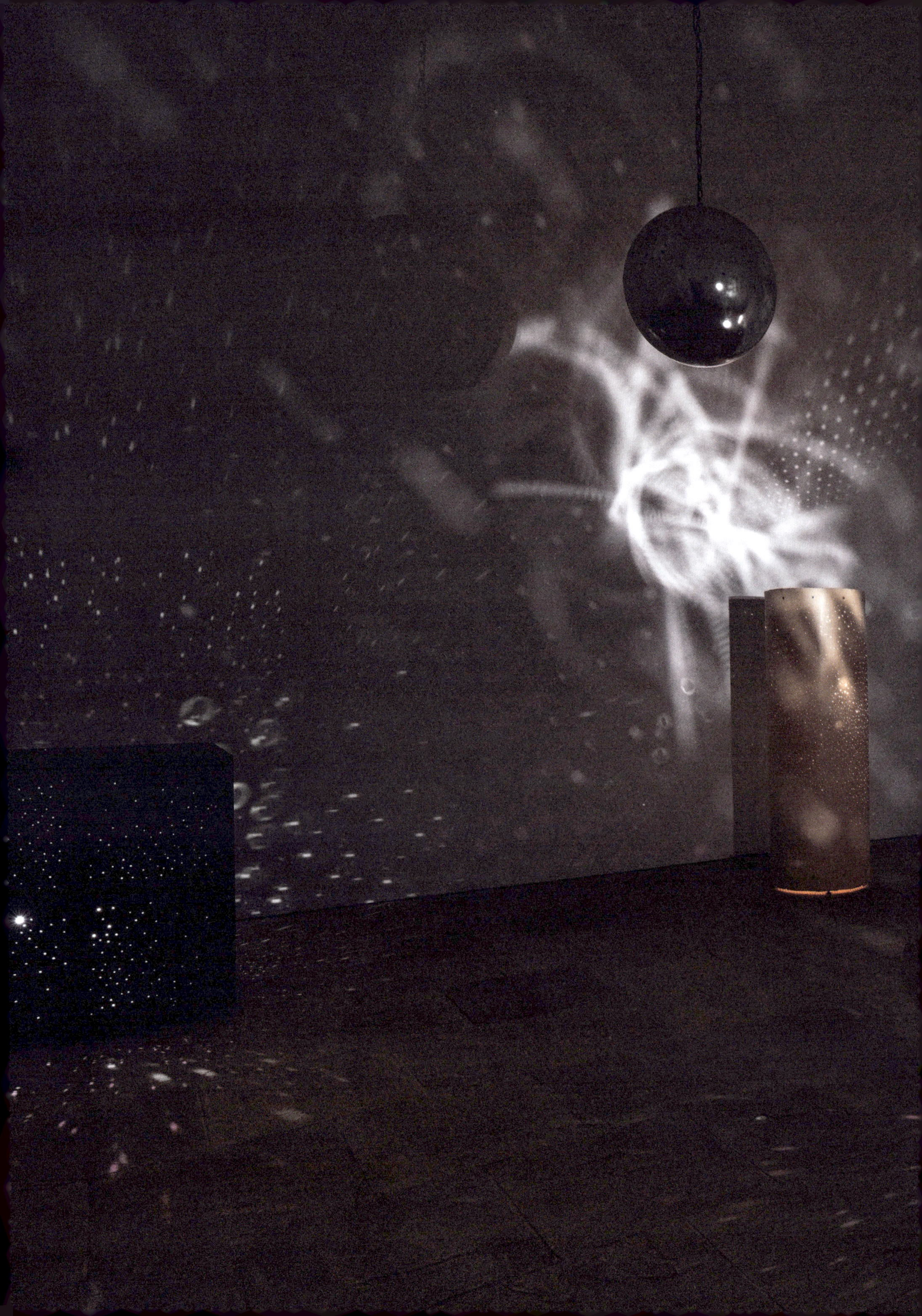

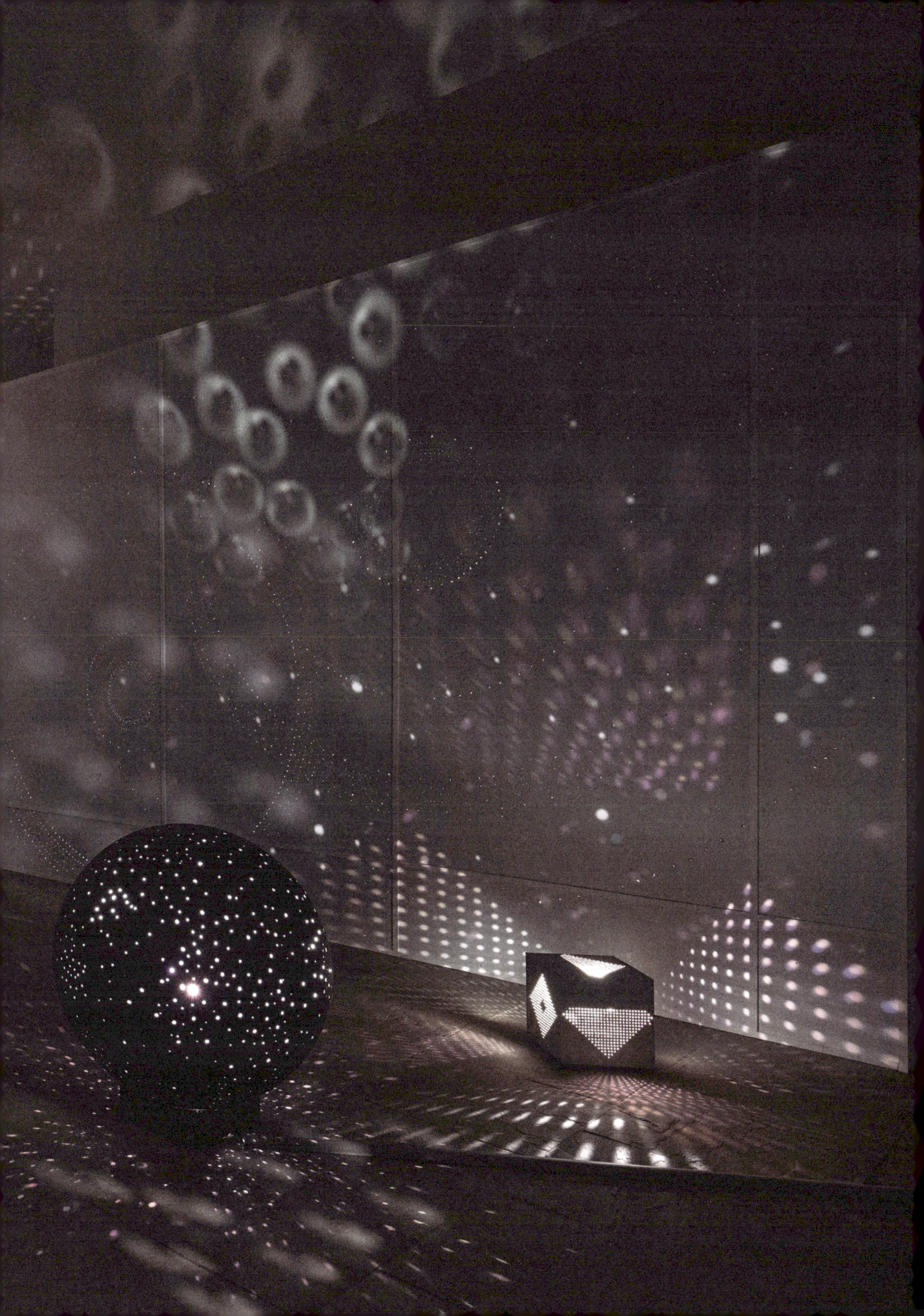

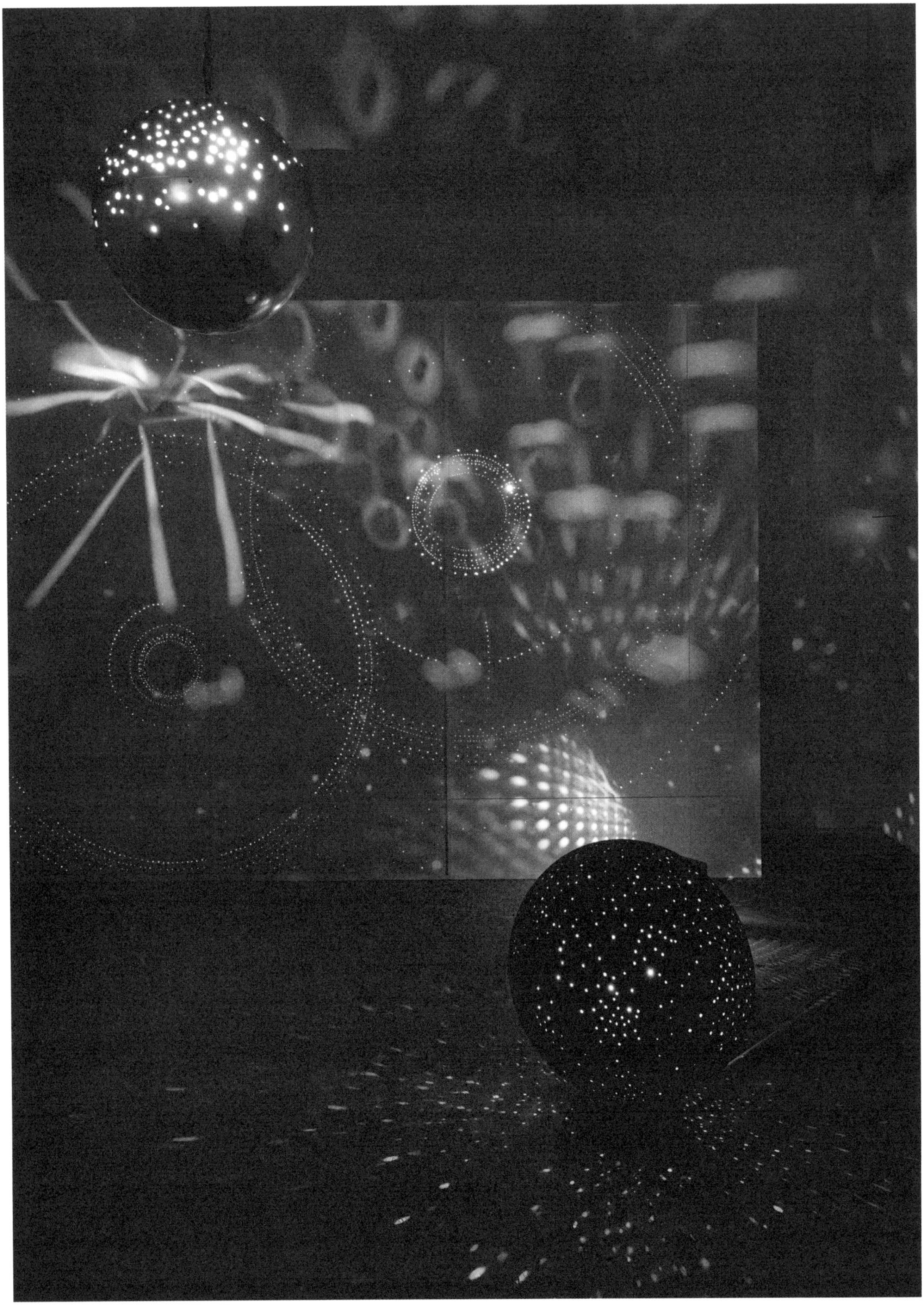

OTTO PIENE

(Germany, 1928–2014)

Lightroom with Mönchengladbach Wall, 1963–2013

Cardboard, wood, metal, motor, light
Variable dimensions

The immersive installation *Lightroom with Mönchengladbach Wall* invites us into a dimly lit space featuring geometric shapes of various dimensions, projected from multiple light sources. The shimmering galactic constellations, which Otto Piene called his *Light Ballet*, reflect his early 1960s ambition to choreograph light. As co-founder of the ZERO Group and inventor of Sky Art, Piene long sought to link his art with advances in technology. During the US–USSR space race, he thought of light as a creative force that could embody post-war technological progress. The *Lightroom* he designed encapsulates the world's vibratory, immaterial energy, enveloping viewers and connecting them to the fundamental, unifying pulse of the cosmos.

ATMOSPHERIC TURBULENCE

The sky is a scene that, even when seemingly empty, is made up of highly variable phenomena. It is a deep and complex visual field, alive with energies. Its atmosphere is anything but an inert void: it is a host of gaseous and luminous phenomena that transform perception. If this exhibition was a planetary system, the large yellow sphere by Jesús Rafael Soto would be its sun. Each viewer, drawn by its optical magnetism, by walking around it and through close observation, will note that its suspended mass is not so much comprised of painted metal rods – which is, in material terms, the case – as infused with a palpitating energy. The trace, nevertheless inert, of the creative act seems to preserve and convey to the viewer the impetus that sparked this creation. Emily Kraus's painting stems from a procedure inherent to printing, transposed to pictorial logic; it appears to divide, multiply and accelerate a landscape fragment, based on the chronophotographic method admired by the futurists over a century ago.

Philippe Decrauzat's shaped canvas is a vast painting whose superimposed fluid curves and lines, in glimmering blue, derive from geometric speculation. This procures the illusion of a deep relief and even echoes a snowy mountain range, vibrant with light. It needles our gaze towards optical habits and immerses it in undulating air currents. As for Bridget Riley's canvas, it echoes Henri Matisse's paper cutouts and the vibrational principle of neo-impressionism: its atmosphere comprises colourful, rhythmic and disjointed sections. Other artworks abolish the hierarchy of elements in the visual field in favour of a gradual, gentle modulation of light, as in the large glasses in iridescent layers by Ann Veronica Janssens; but also, on a pictorial plane this time, in the nebulous and polychrome painting by Jean-Baptiste Bernadet, in which the pigment seems to detach itself from the canvas and float in the air, like the pollen of a thousand flowers blown by a gentle breeze. This is the case of the relief in aluminium with embossed surfaces, by Heinz Mack, which springs to life at our slightest movement; or of Carlos Cruz-Diez's *Physichromie*, which fragments its vast palette of colours into multiple vertical sinews. All of these scenarios make the viewers the very source of the transformation, as they bring their own energy to them. Our merest movements are effectively enough to activate their visual phenomena, to cause them to palpitate in real time and space, in their lumino-chromatic atmospheres. To paraphrase Jesús Rafael Soto, our eye is the real driver of movement.

Previous page: Jean-Baptiste Bernadet, *Untitled (Feelings)* (detail), 2021, oil on canvas, 205 × 390 cm
Opposite: Philippe Decrauzat, *newwave* (detail), 2025, acrylic on canvas, iridescent blue, 2 sections: 204 × 250 cm; 204 × 500 cm (overall)

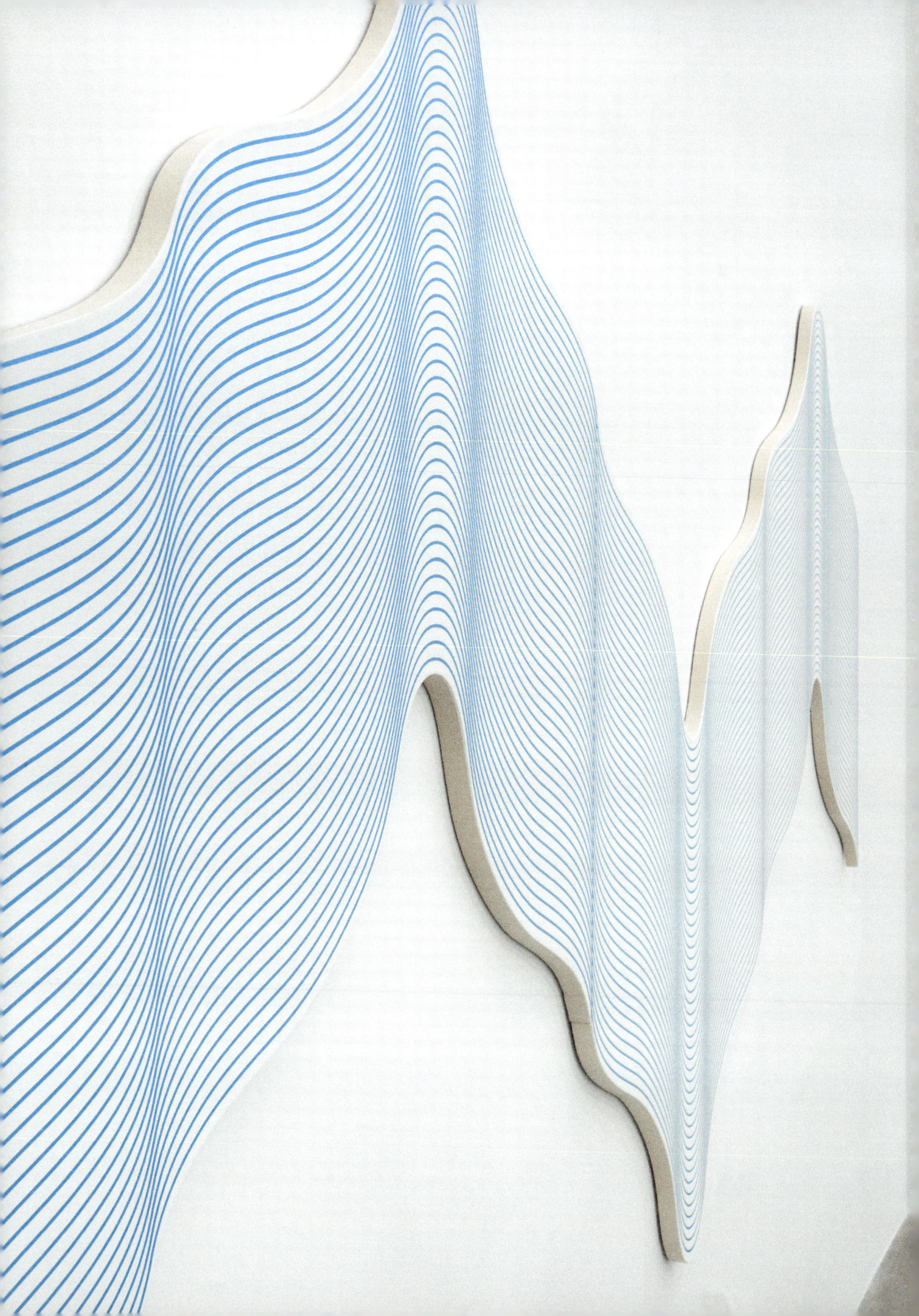

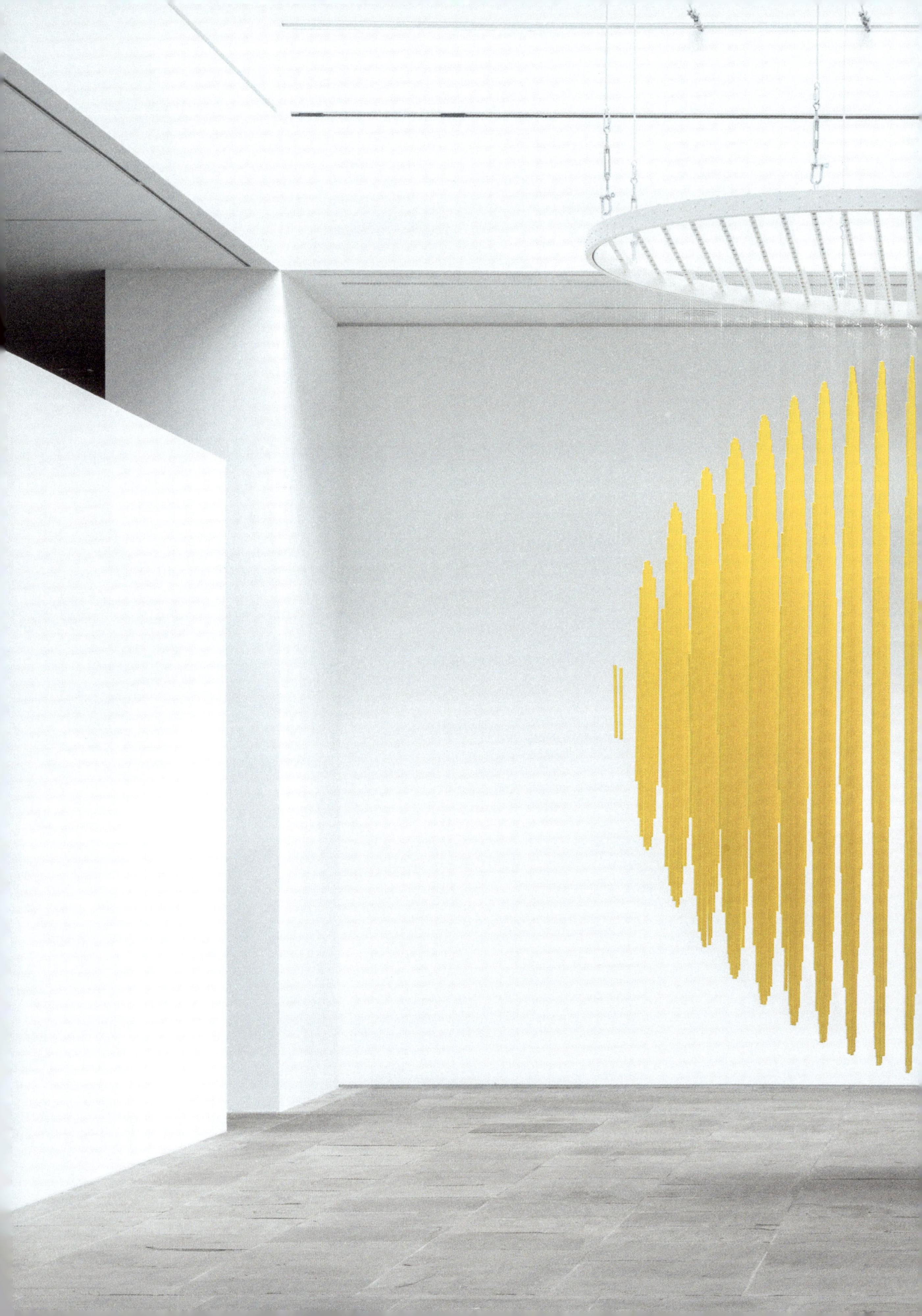

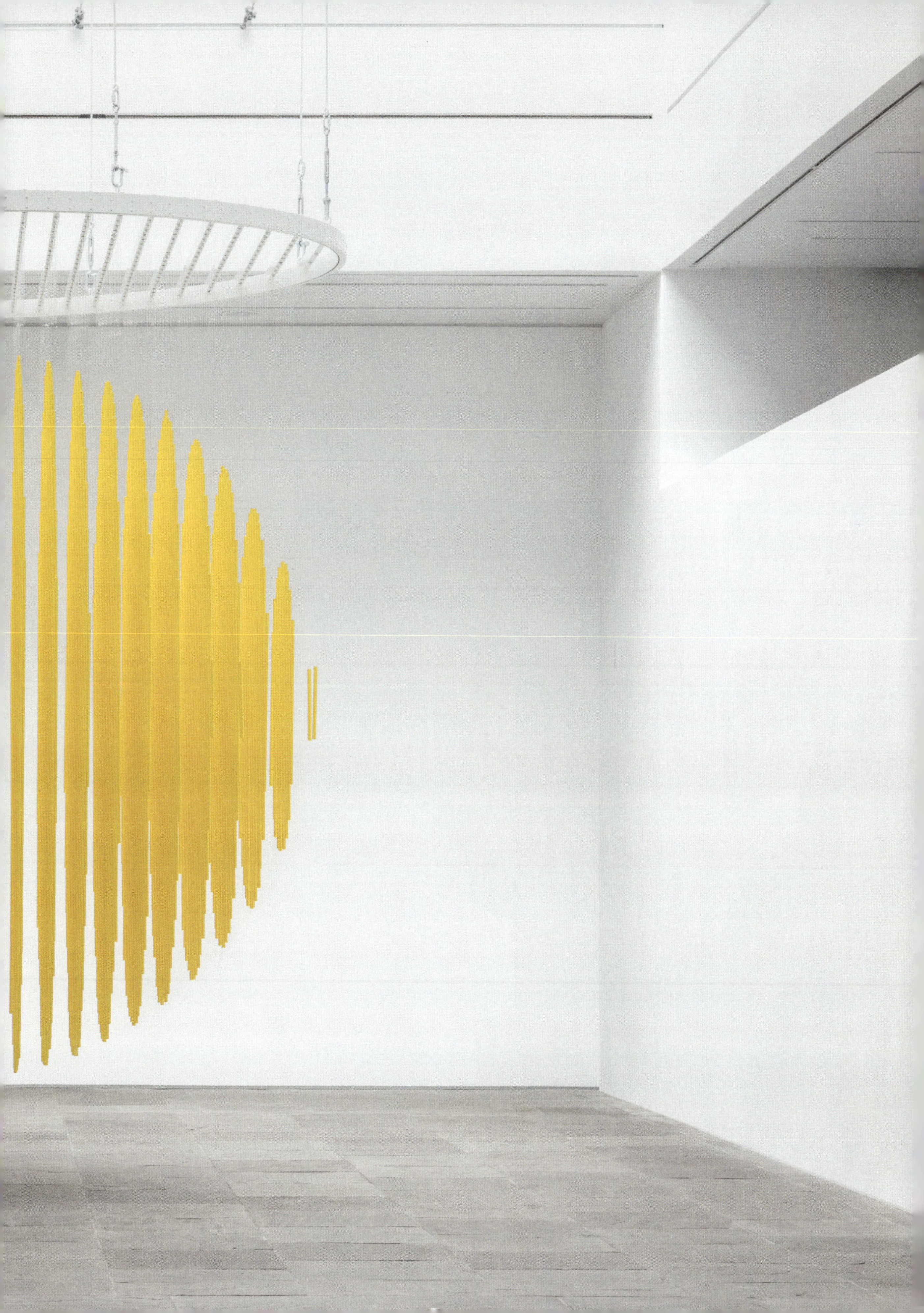

JESÚS RAFAEL SOTO

(Venezuela, 1923–2005)

Esfera Amarilla, 1984

Painted metal and nylon thread
300 × 300 × 300 cm

Jesús Rafael Soto's 1984 work *Esfera Amarilla* is a yellow sphere suspended from the underside of the Villa's central water ceiling, brightening the *Atmospheric Turbulence* space with its sunny presence. The 453 metal tubes, all painted the same colour, seem to pulse as we move round it, an effect similar to walking past rows of vines in a vineyard. The sensation, created by the parallax effect, is amplified by the shimmering light of the water ceiling overhead. Soto was a key figure of op art and kinetic art. Here he invites us to stroll around his work to grasp its materiality, alternation of empty and occupied space, shards of light, interplay with its surroundings, colour, and movement. For Soto, the relationship between work and audience foregrounds the world's "matter-energy" and lets us feel mobility and invisibility.

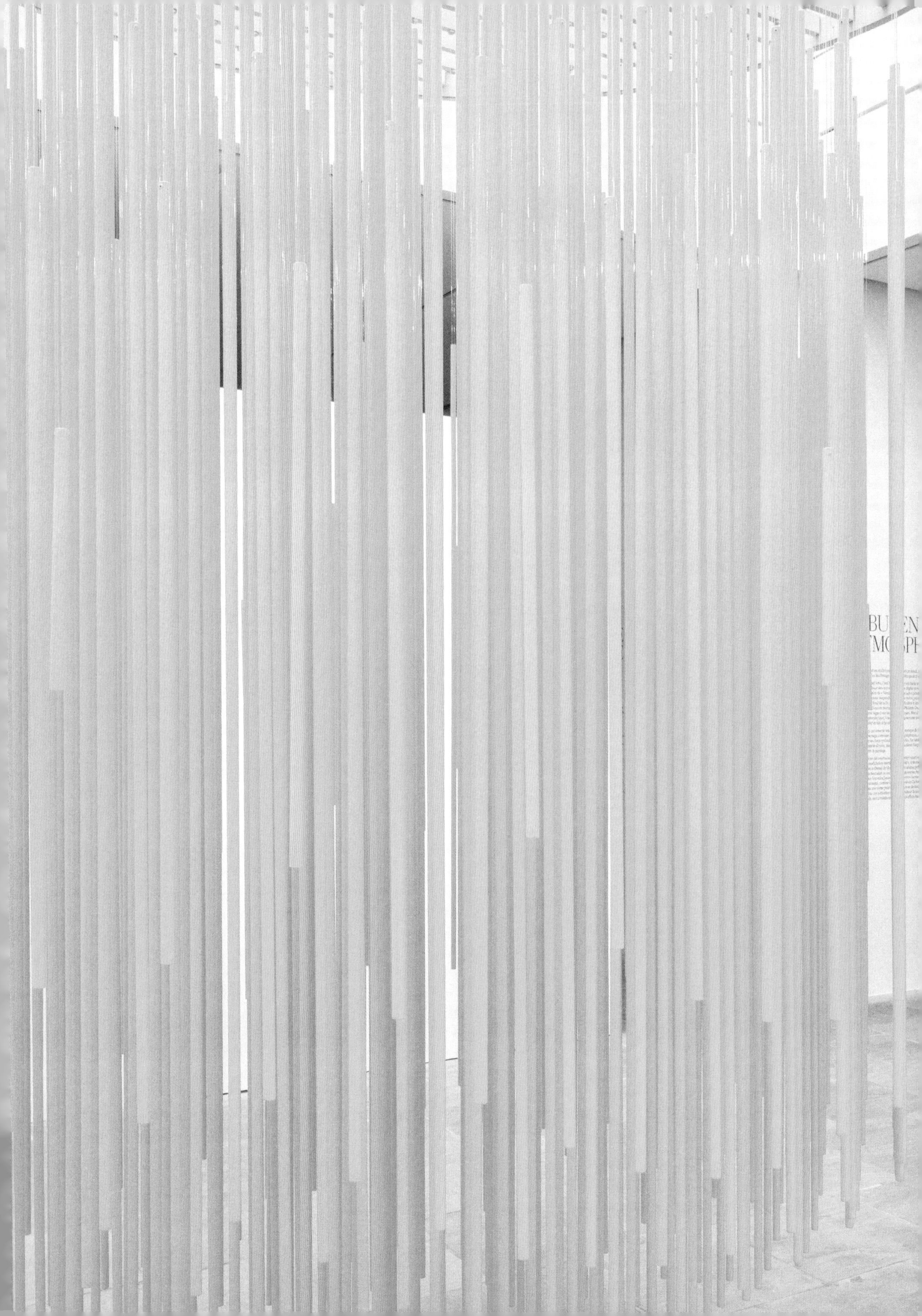

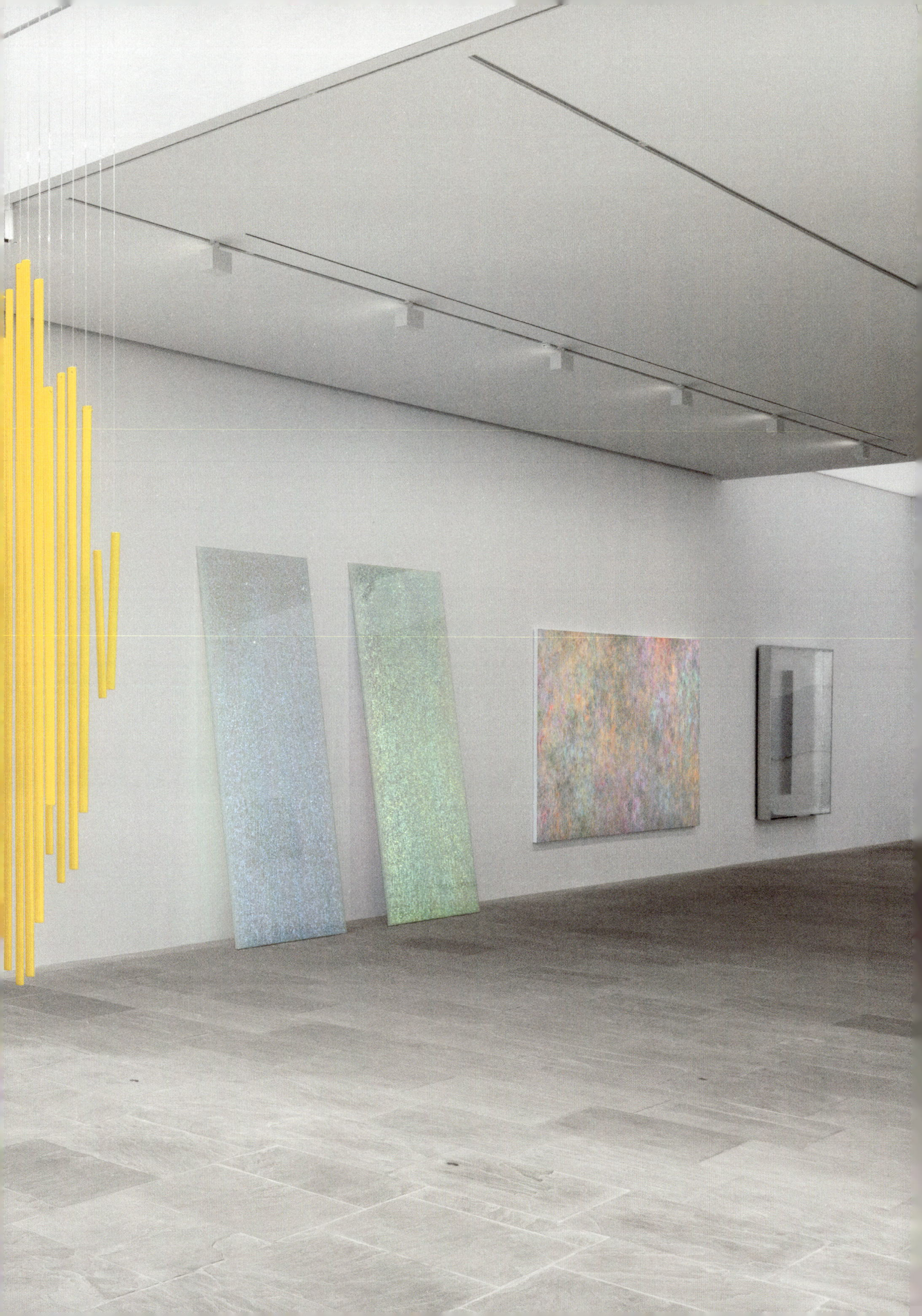

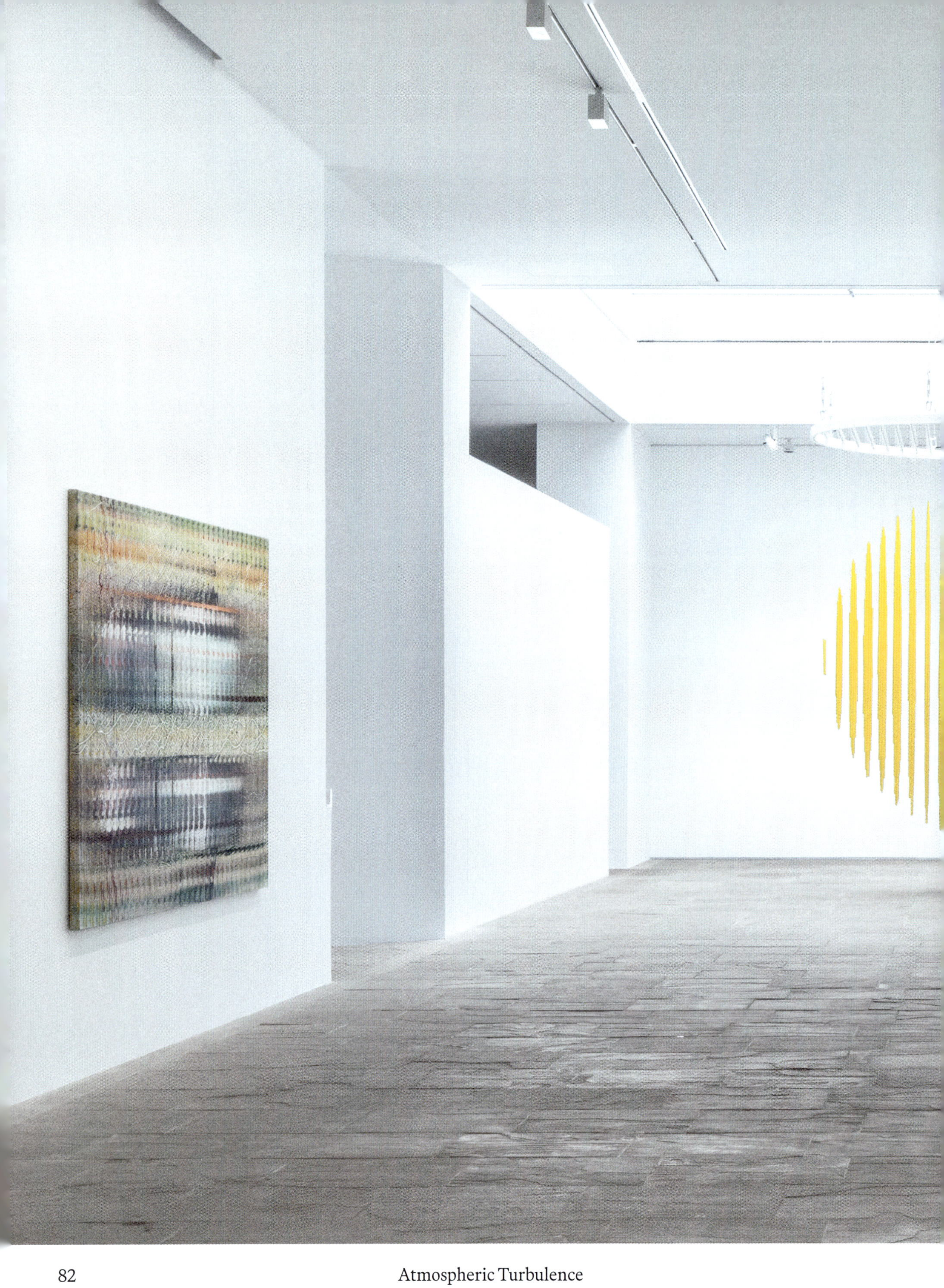

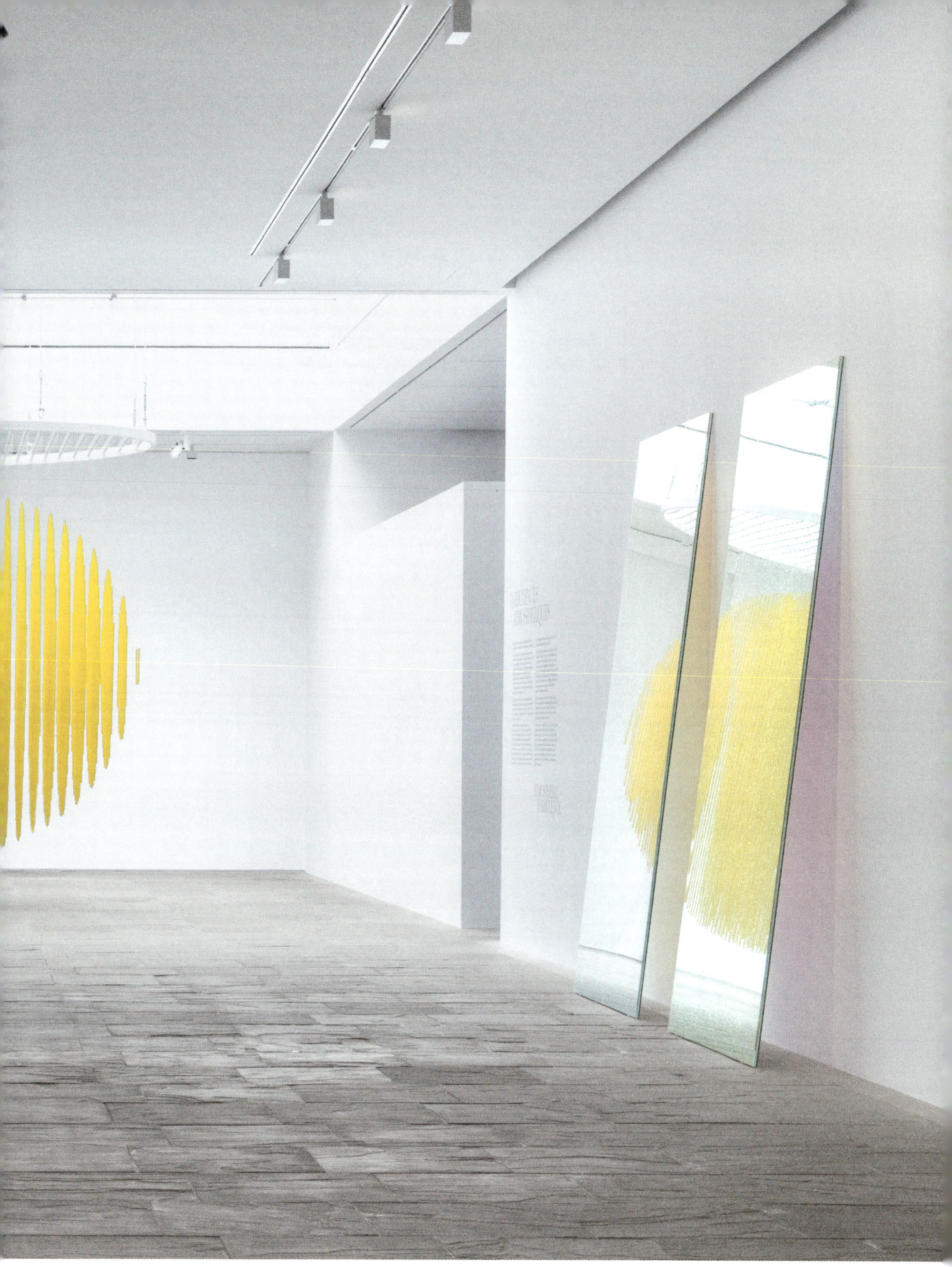

ANN VERONICA JANSSENS

(United Kingdom, 1956)

Magic Mirrors (Pink & Blue), 2013–2023

Dichromic laminated glass made of shattered glass, float glass and gelatin filters
300 × 150 × 1.8 cm each

Ann Veronica Janssens describes her work as "using the properties of light, refraction and reflection to explore various perspectives on colour. The instability and mutability of *Magic Mirrors (Pink & Blue)* calls the very nature of art into question: is it a material articulation or the experience of its interaction with the world and the self?" She begins by creating a controlled accident, shattering the glass with a single sharp tap at the top of the sheet, to reveal an entire world pinioned between illusion and reality. As we move around the artwork, the light and our own reflection oscillate in delicate hues of blue and pink generated by a dichroic membrane that diffracts the spectrum of light. *Magic Mirrors (Pink & Blue)* bears witness to the ineffability that Janssens often strives to capture in her art.

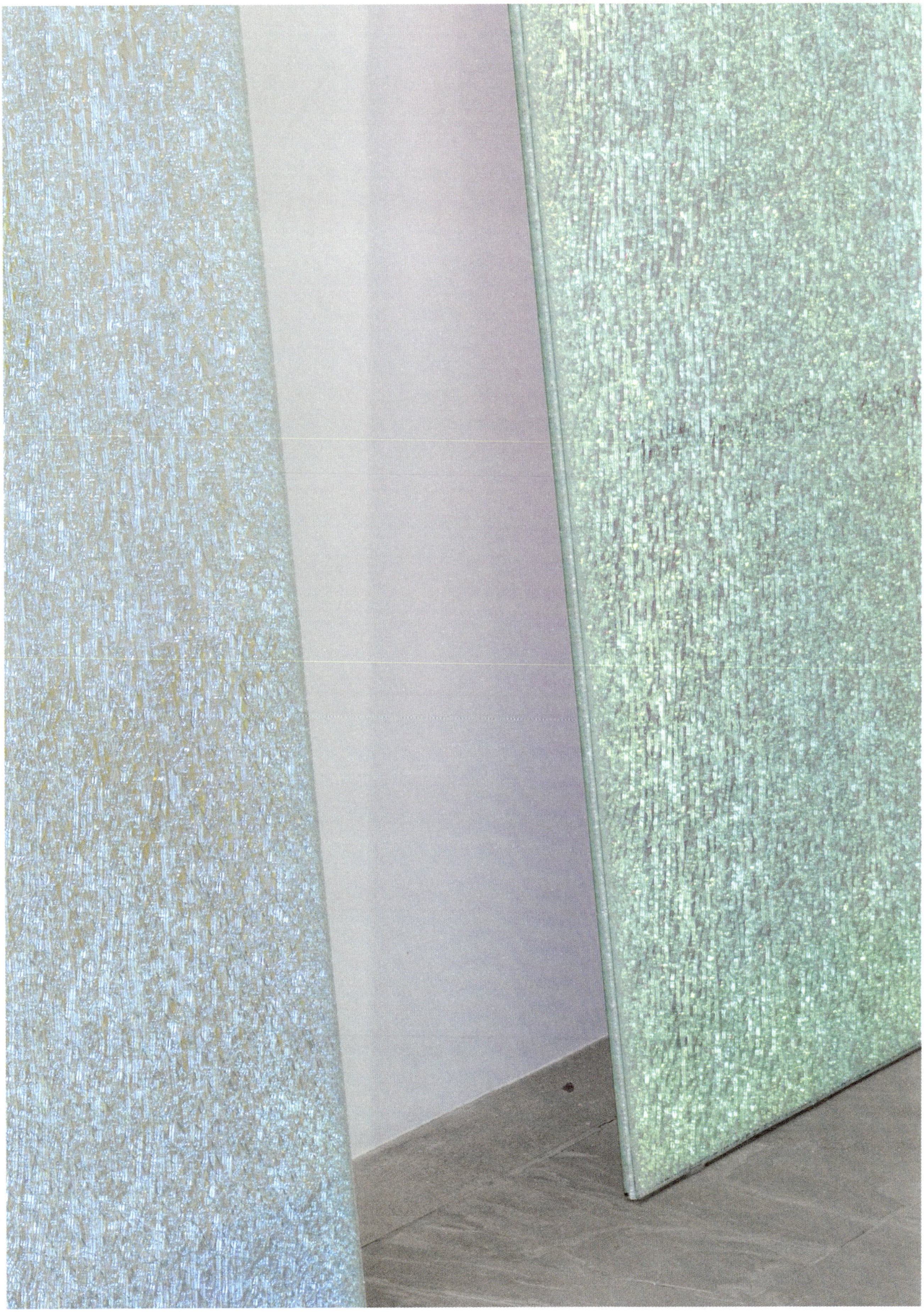

Riccardo Venturi

BLURRING PERCEPTION

A CONVERSATION

with Ann Veronica Janssens

Why do landscape paintings
reach such a ripe old age?
Wondered a philosopher painter.
It is because the mist and clouds provide
them with sustenance.

WALTER BENJAMIN, *PEINTURES CHINOISES À LA BIBLIOTHÈQUE NATIONALE*, 1938[1]

Ann Veronica Janssens strives to escape what she calls the tyranny of objects. She therefore uses very simple, non-enduring, preferably performative forms, that is, forms in constant flux, animated by natural phenomena like light or artificial like induced "fog". *Vertigo* offers us the chance to reflect on certain aspects of her artistic practice.

A TRANSPARENT ARCHITECTURE

Riccardo Venturi
It seems to me that architecture, sculpture and painting are intertwined in your work. To proceed in order, beyond a biographical question (your father is an architect), your first installation of coloured smoke (*Blue, Red and Yellow*, 2001) was exhibited on the esplanade of the Neue Nationalgalerie in Berlin, in a direct confrontation with the architecture of Mies van der Rohe. Where did this initial and constant need to confront architecture come from?

Ann Veronica Janssens
My first "constructions" actually date back to the second half of the 1980s and constitute spatial extensions of existing architecture. They were grafted to them, to form and open up what I called "Super Spaces"; then, there was notably the *Super Space* project, divided into twelve interventions in Utrecht, dotted all over the city. Visitors received a map on which the various locations of my interventions in urban space were indicated.

For this occasion, I'd created spatial extensions in order to present and feel the world differently, by working with light and in real time, but also on the threshold between visitors' mental space and the physical space.

At the Neue Nationalgalerie in Berlin, the *Blue, Red and Yellow* pavilion adopted a minimalist structure, placed on the museum's terrace, in conversation with the transparency of the architecture and the interventions that I'd devised for the interior. What interests me about architecture is its ability to accommodate the transparency of air and light, silence, noise, spaces to penetrate… this is how the immateriality of air became one of my preferred materials.

1. Walter Benjamin, *Peintures chinoises à la Bibliothèque nationale* (1938), in *Écrits français* (Paris: Gallimard, 1991), 262. All translations are our own unless otherwise stated.

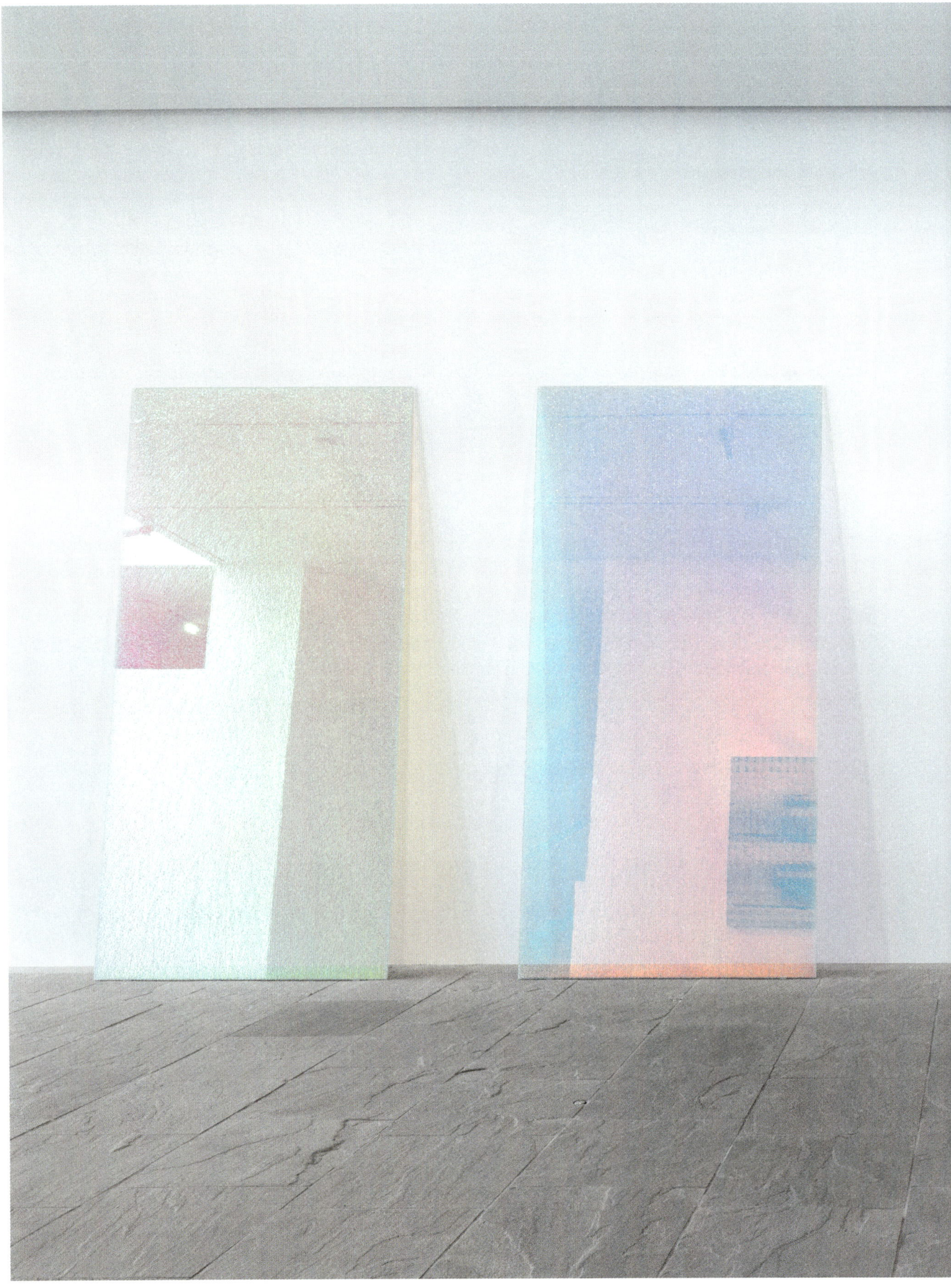

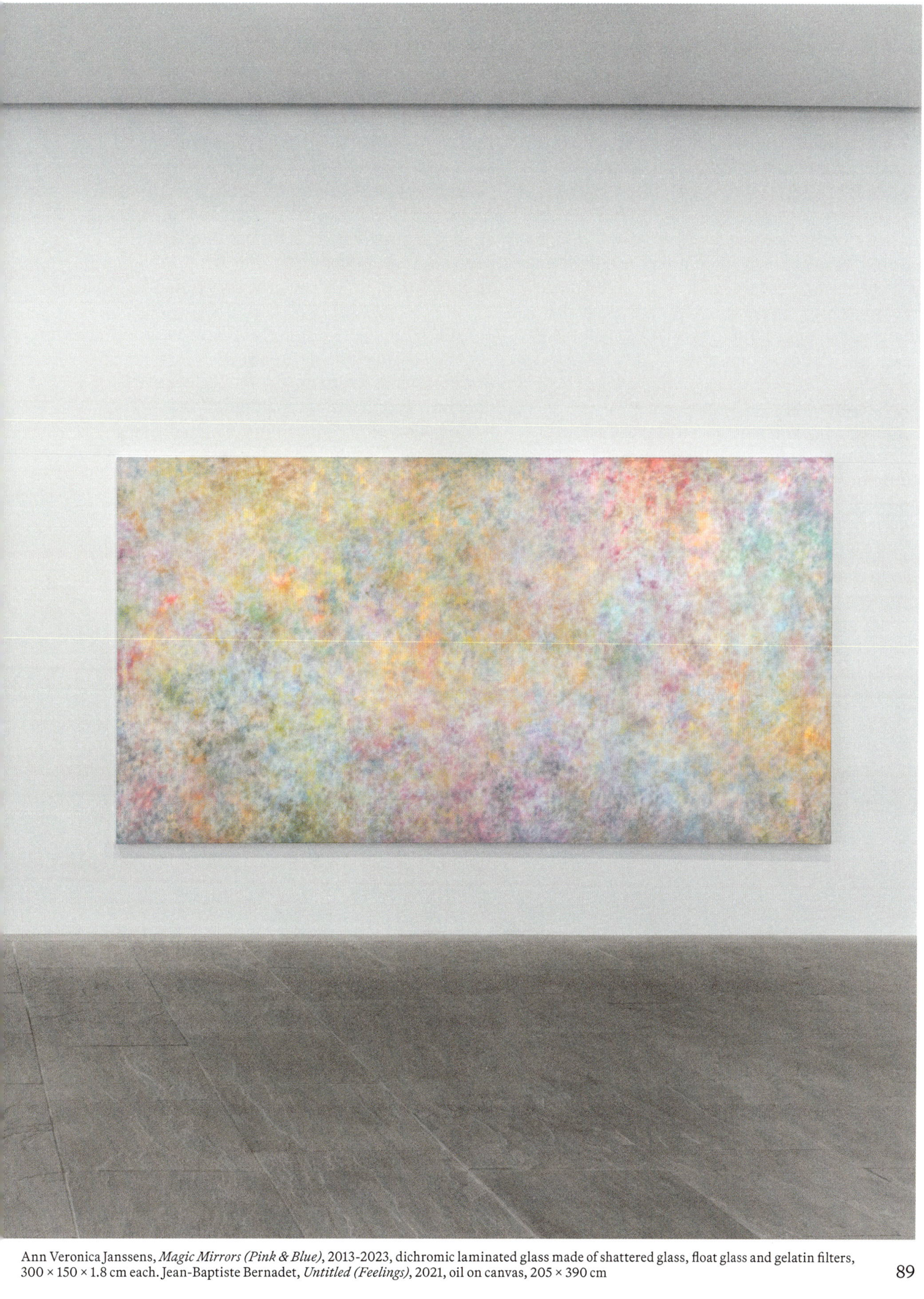

Ann Veronica Janssens, *Magic Mirrors (Pink & Blue)*, 2013-2023, dichromic laminated glass made of shattered glass, float glass and gelatin filters, 300 × 150 × 1.8 cm each. Jean-Baptiste Bernadet, *Untitled (Feelings)*, 2021, oil on canvas, 205 × 390 cm

A TEMPORAL SCULPTURE

R.V.

Viewing your sculptures, we are confronted by at least two paradoxes: they are ephemeral, and here I'm thinking of Aerogel, a material unlike anything else, which enables you to test the limits of sculpture as an object; they become milieus, penetrable spaces far from any volume and substance. The result is a very fragile structure – a sculpture made of air, like a piece of sky – which reveals an extreme state of the material: are we still able to call this sculpture?

A.V.J.

I'm interested in the medium of sculpture, but even more so in its extension, its potential expansion towards psychology, consciousness, senses, unstable situations and new temporalities that give us access to an experience of disintegration. This is how I find inspiration among those I'd call sculptor-researchers, evenif they often remain far-removed from my practice.

My sculptures do not impose themselves, they give form to limitrophe states of matter, such as fog, with the pulverisation of all substance that results from such states. They create space-times that render phenomena noticeable and also flag their temporal inscription.

A PERFORMATIVE PAINTING

R.V.

In front of or inside of your works, we have the impression of a colourful, intangible abstraction, a close-up inside the painting, as though we were walking within a patch of colour. As *Vertigo* clearly shows, there is an atmospheric quality to abstraction: "a process more than an end result", as Matthieu Poirier wrote. Yet your approach to painting remains very unique...

A.V.J.

You see, in painting, as elsewhere, I tend to fabricate or invent my own tools; in terms of painting, I do without pigment. I'm thinking, for instance, of my aquariums, which present the illusion of a colour floating at the surface of a transparent liquid; or a project I'm currently working on: structural colours.

Structural colouring produces colour through microscopically structured surfaces in layers thin enough to interfere with visible light. The interaction between the light and these surfaces is responsible for phenomena such as iridescence or rapid colour changes. By making films of melanin-dopamine and provoking a few incidents designed to cause the colours to vibrate, this research into biomimetic surfaces plays with chance and the little accidents that crop up during the process of emergence of colour. They are then deposited onto a non-porous material that maintains the vulnerability of the nanostructure. As with butterfly wings, touching the surface with a finger would definitively erase its colours.

While my questions sometimes still owe something to painting or pictoriality, I do not however make paintings. The same goes for drawing, which I practise in my own way, that is, non-traditionally. For instance, using the shadow cast by water rippled by a breeze – an animation made of light. The experience and knowledge of light allow us to discover new ways of approaching colour...

R.V.

Could we liken your idea of pictoriality to the atmospheric quality of modernist abstract painting?

A.V.J.

When I talk about pictoriality, I am referring to the modernist tradition, yes, but also to other, older traditions (suprematism, impressionism, etc.), not to mention primitive art and even prehistory. However, besides the history of art, for me the key element is time, or even better still, the perception of time, which is why I often insist on the continual modification of states of matter in my work. My artworks are transformed depending on the light or the person looking at them; they take on very different appearances. Hence their fragility, their ephemeral nature.

In other words, these artworks act, they unfold in a performance, which has one major consequence: you can't control them. And this is by no means a fault, I'm fascinated by this loss of control.

R.V.

When I look at *Magic Mirrors (Pink & Blue)* (2013–2023), exhibited at the Fondation Carmignac, I wonder if ultimately you consider the mirror as a way of painting via other means.

A.V.J.

In some ways, yes. Mirrors provide another way of experimenting with temporality, a sublime experience of vertigo and the abyss for visitors. Their texture and reflective quality offer a dilated view of volumes and events.

The *Magic Mirrors* that I exhibit make structure and pictoriality coexist. In the end, they stem from a very simple gesture or, at least, one that appears simple in the eyes of visitors, thanks to the precision of this gesture. By greatly increasing the reflection of light and colours onto the mirrored surface, *Magic Mirrors* creates a stream of golden light. Sticking with the theme of painting, the result reminds me of variations in the façade of the Rouen Cathedral painted by Claude Monet.

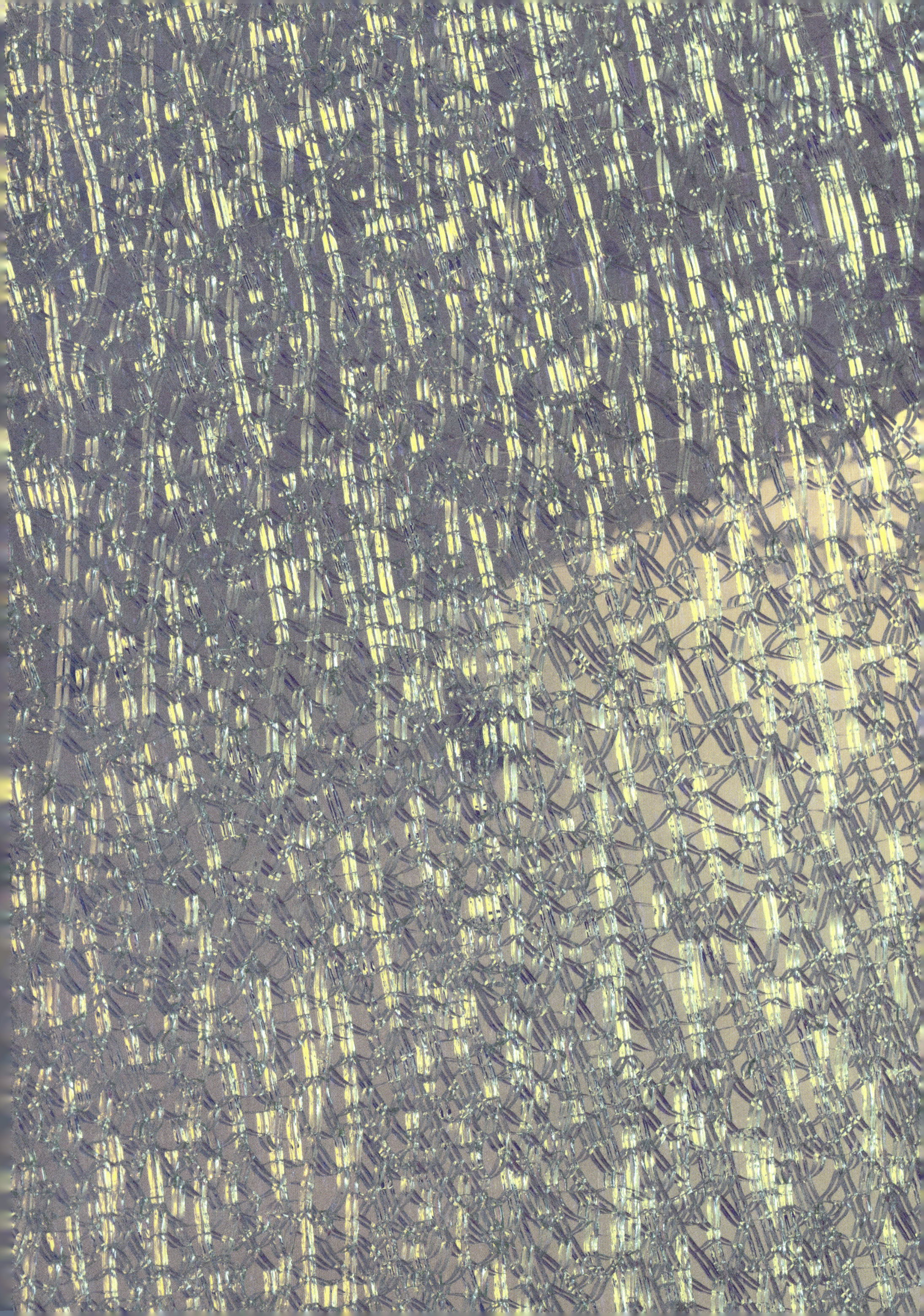

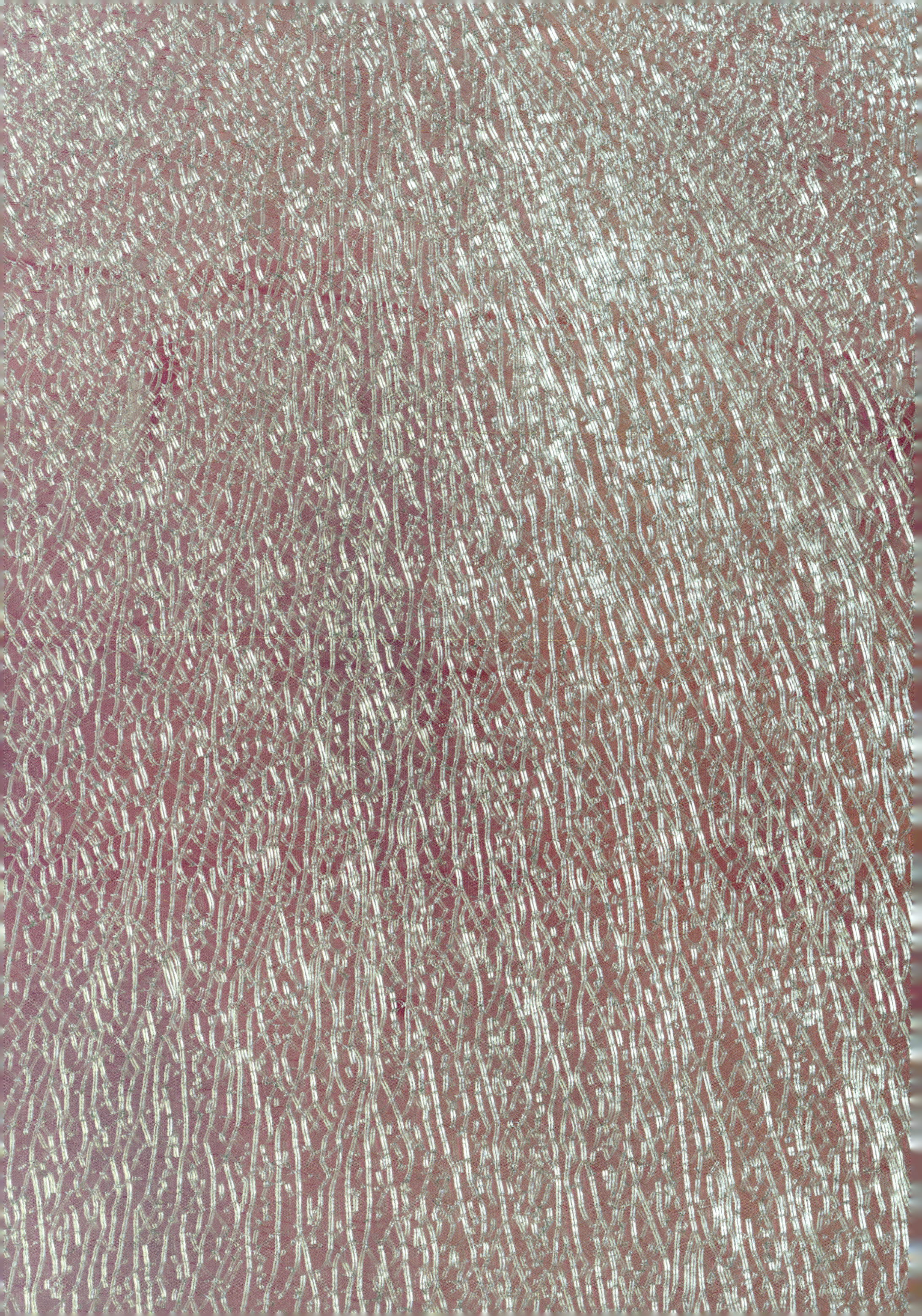

A COLOURED SCENE

R.V.
I feel like this attention to temporality is closely linked to theatre, which plays an important role in your work.

A.V.J.
Yes, the first coloured fog I made was designed for the stage, as part of the *Festival d'Automne* in Tours (2000), on the invitation of choreographer Pierre Droulers. With the help of scenographer Jim Clayburgh, I used the theatre's artificial lighting to create an enclosed space on stage filled with a coloured fog, reminiscent of the changing colours during a sunset, rotated by 45°.

Visitors were invited to experiment with the space and with their slowed down, choreographed movements. The frontal nature of the stage has always disturbed me. After this initial experience, I was lucky enough to meet choreographer Anne Teresa De Keersmaeker, with whom I have collaborated on several projects.

A TANGIBLE MILIEU

R.V.
In your coloured milieus, the cloud-like atmosphere becomes visible and tangible. Without a surface on which to settle, the colour is everywhere: it invades the space, but also our body, and it goes beyond that, being incorporated through our eyes and even our nostrils.

It makes me think of *Manger fantôme. Manuel pratique de l'alimentation vaporeuse* (Ghost Eating: A Practical Manual for Vaporous Food) (2018), by Ryoko Sekiguchi, devoted to aerial food, the polar opposite of food attached – just as we are – to the ground. Can we eat mist, which is tasteless, textureless, odourless and so "evanescent that it only takes shape in the words used to describe it, before it immediately disappears"?[2]

Besides vision, could food be seen to relate to your installations?

A.V.J.
I've never really thought of a possible correspondence with food. But I have a series of works with names of cocktails: *Cocktail Sculptures* (1992); the aquariums: *Pink Coco Lopez*, *Yellow Yellow*, *Golden Dream*, *Margarita*, *Acapulco Kiss*, *Sweet Blue*, *Green Day*, *Blue Hawaï*; in 2003 in San Francisco I made an installation from programmed light entitled *Donut*; and also a series of sculptures I called *Candy Sculptures*.

So yes, now that I think about it, there is undoubtedly a kind of appreciation for food that you could relate to my artistic practice, as if the idea was to eat colour!

I guess it's not really so strange, if you think of it as a shift to the heart of my artworks: we move from ordinary perception to a kind of mental vision, from the experience of an everyday space to its interiorisation, and perhaps, sometimes, we move from the gaze to the nose and mouth, as they are involved just as much.

2. Ryoko Sekiguchi, *Manger fantôme. Manuel pratique de l'alimentation vaporeuse*, (Paris: Les Ateliers d'Argol, 2018), 19–20.

BLURRING PERCEPTION

R.V.

Through your work on phosphenes and total solar eclipses, you not only associate natural light with darkness but also, which is even more fascinating, light with blindness. Being in the light but not able to see, being blinded by a dazzling colour: are these attempts to blur perception?

A.V.J.

The project on solar eclipses goes back to a film commissioned for the inauguration of the Centre d'art contemporain WIELS, which had just opened in Brussels. I wanted to pay tribute to the physician Joseph Plateau, the inventor of the phenakistiscope, which was an early precursor to film. It is a device that gives the illusion of movement due to persistence of vision.

Plateau had temporarily lost his sight after looking at the sun for too long. Incidentally, he had also worked on surface tension, a phenomenon that interests me too, and which led me to work on several different projects. I see the eclipse as both an astronomical phenomenon and a representation of the eye and its cone of vision.

From 2006 to 2020, I travelled the world to observe and film nine total eclipses of the Sun. During this rare natural phenomenon, the Moon passes in front of the Sun, totally covering it and casting a shadow on a narrow section of the Earth for several minutes, plunging the surrounding area into near-total darkness and creating a circle of fire around the Sun.

For one fragile and uncertain moment, solar eclipses provide us with an immersion at the scale of the universe, bathing us in shadow, colour and fire.

And as for my work on phosphenes, I like the idea that we all contain within us colour, light, movement and space.

Disrupting perception? Yes, no doubt. Even though sometimes it may have unexpected consequences. For example, many years ago in China, I exhibited a red fog; the visitors were frightened and quickly left, which hadn't been my intention. How can we perceive the imperceptible? How can we grasp what escapes us?

These are the questions that lie at the heart of my artistic approach.

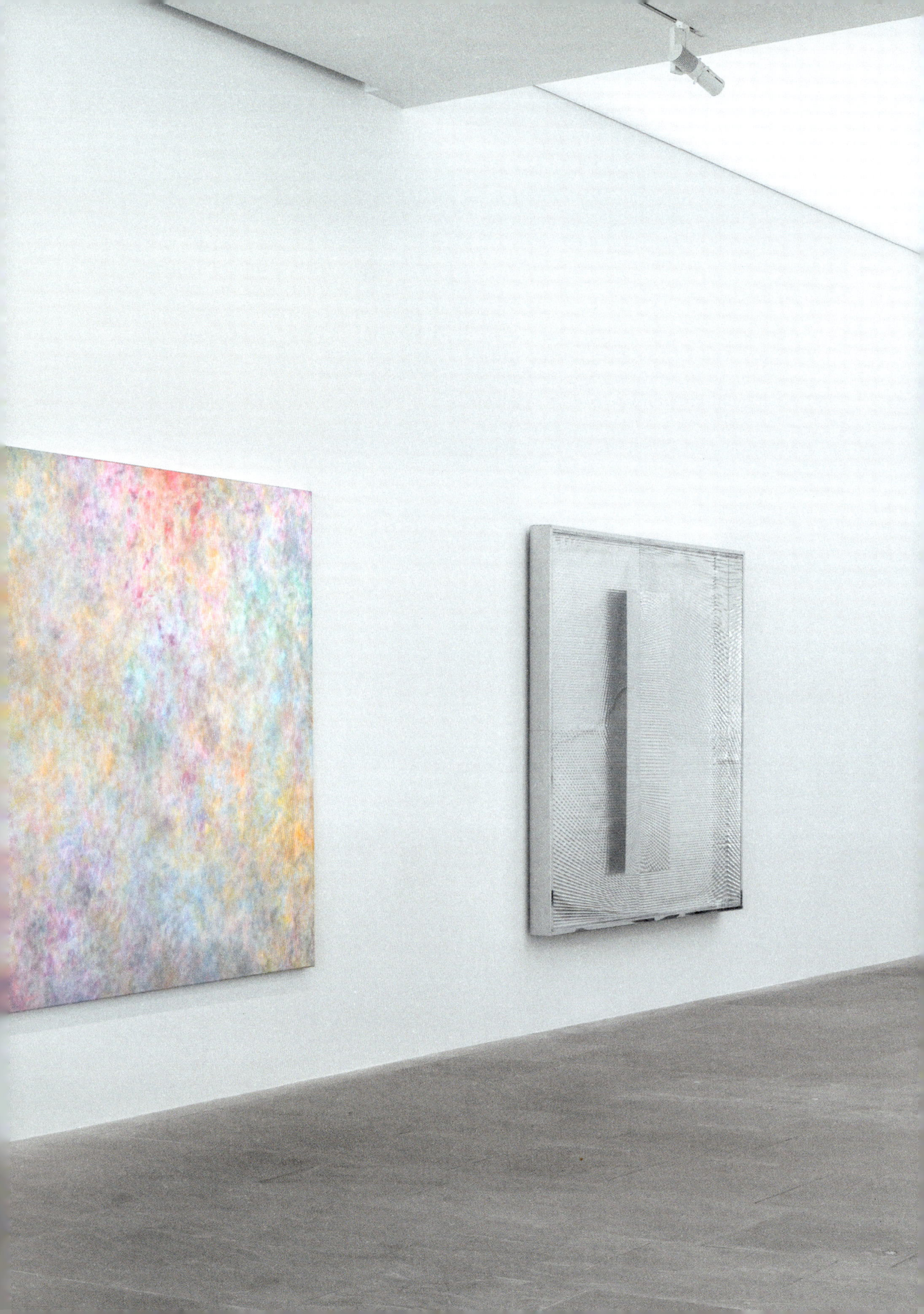

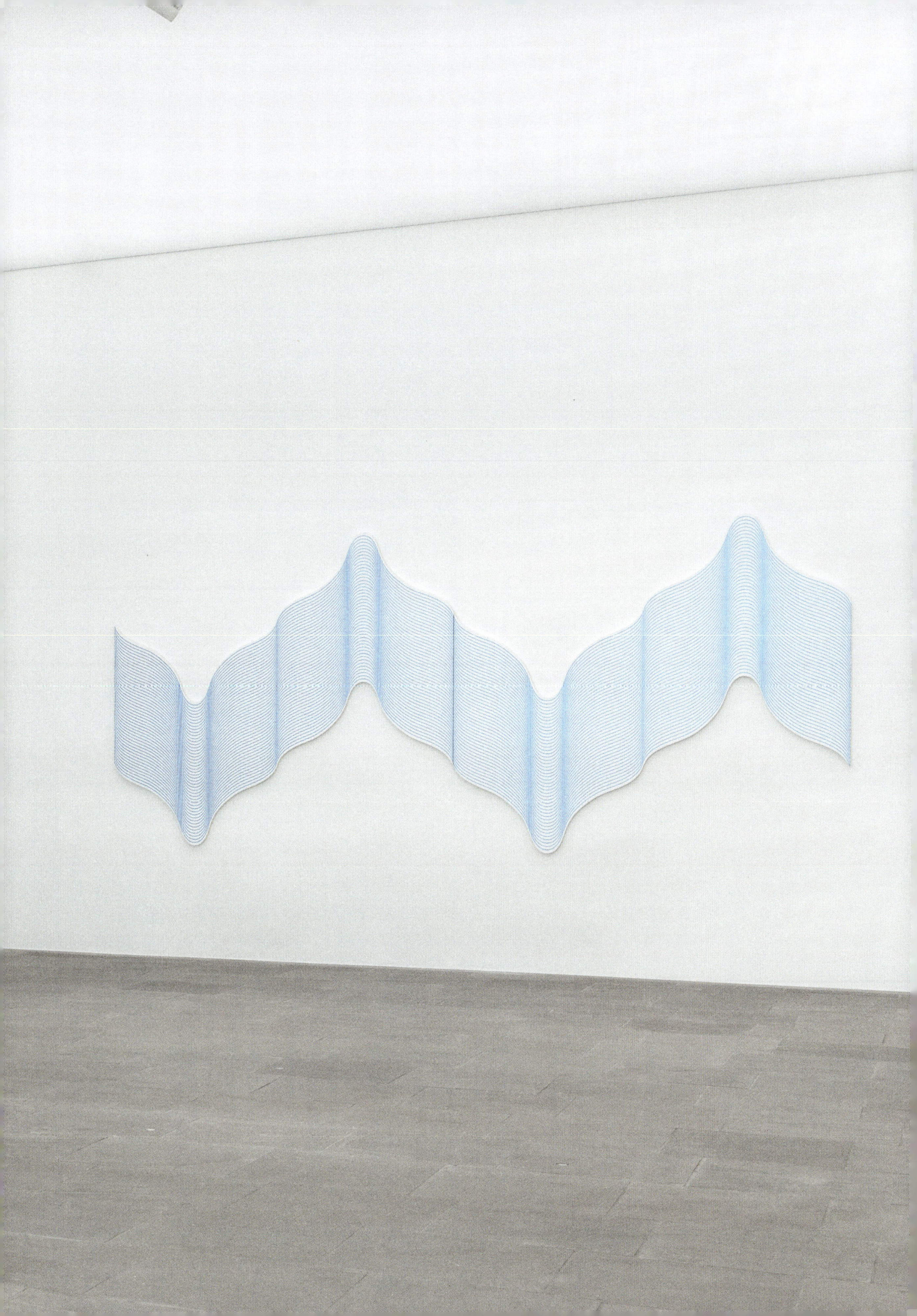

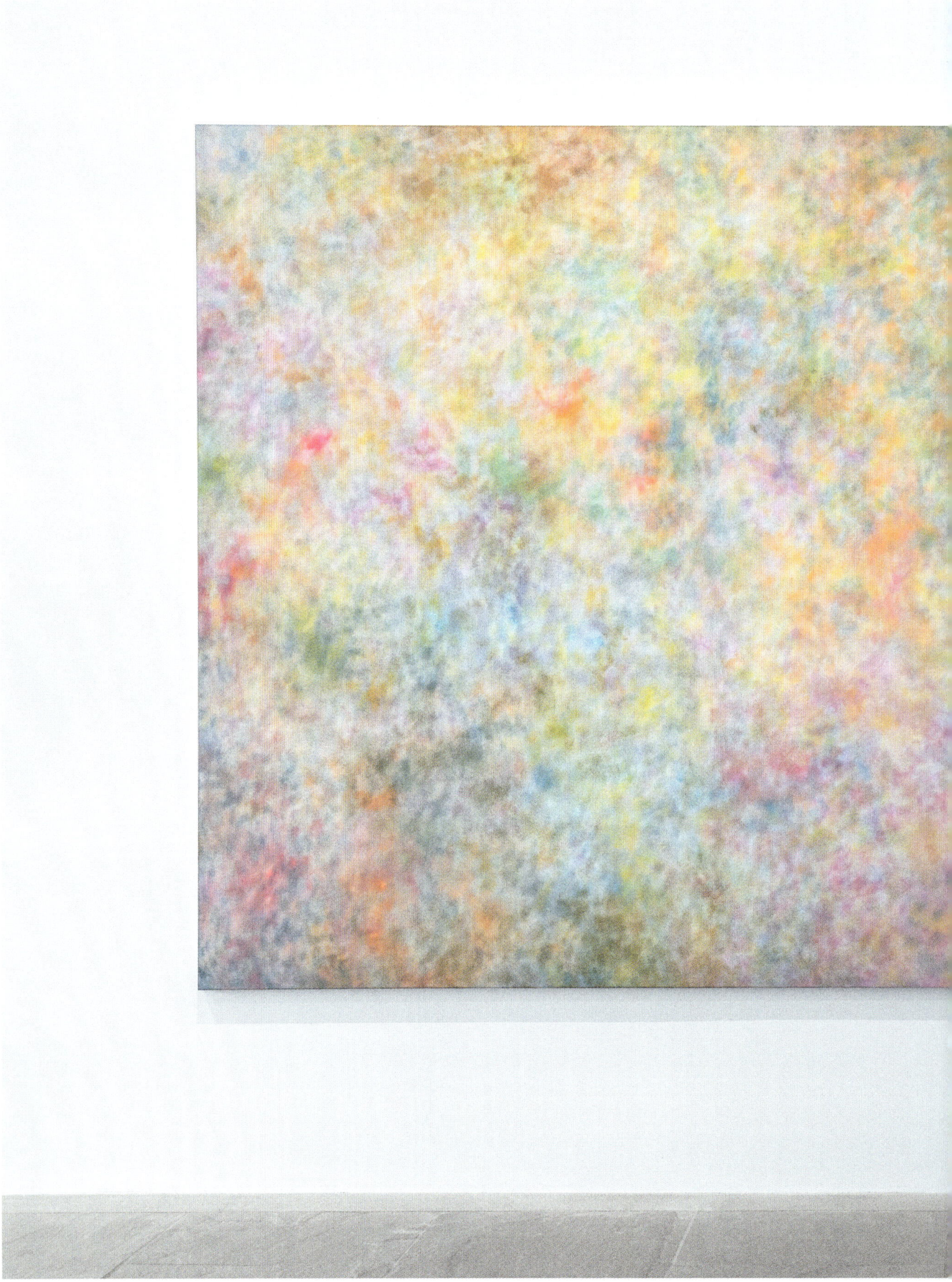

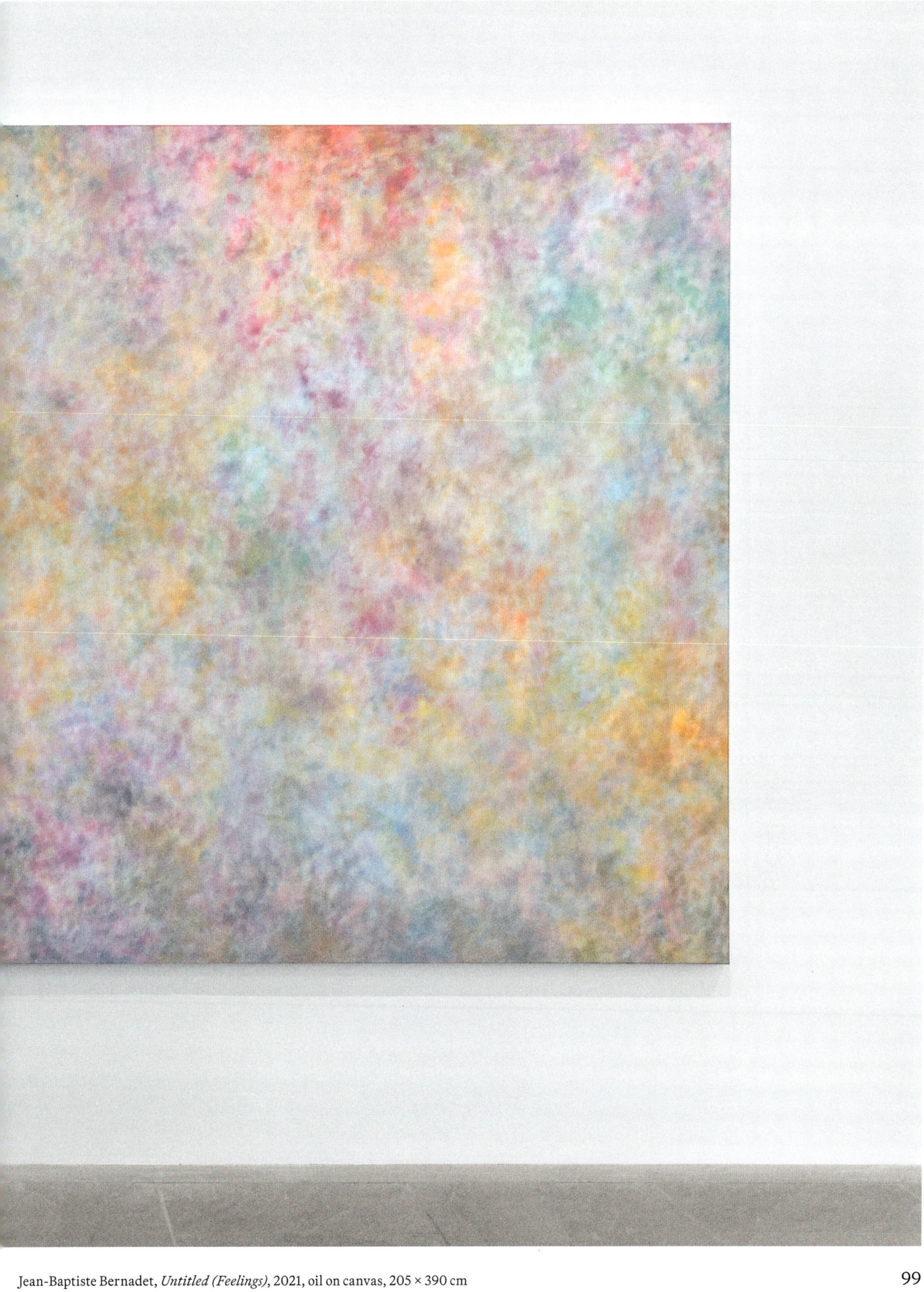

Jean-Baptiste Bernadet, *Untitled (Feelings)*, 2021, oil on canvas, 205 × 390 cm

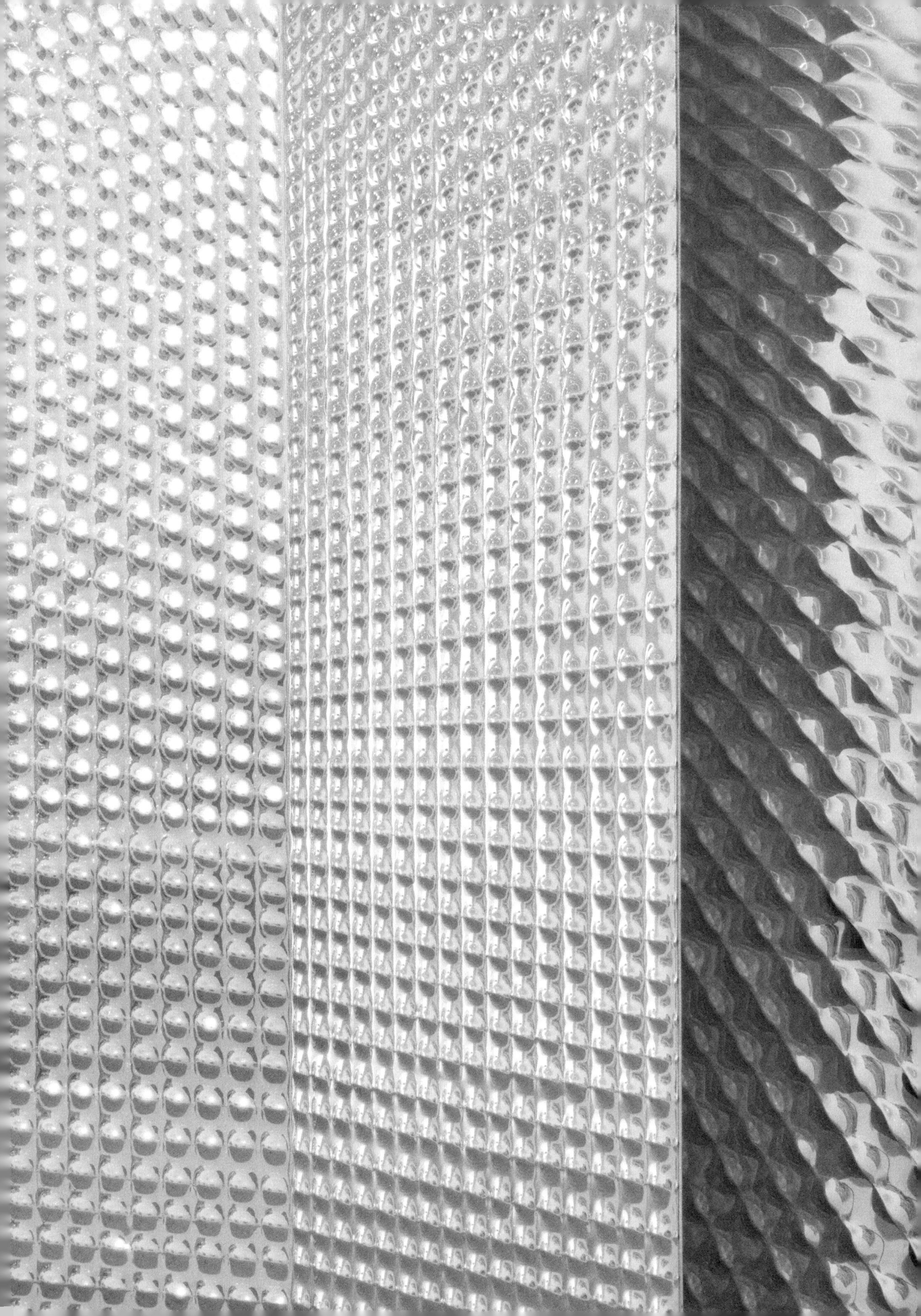

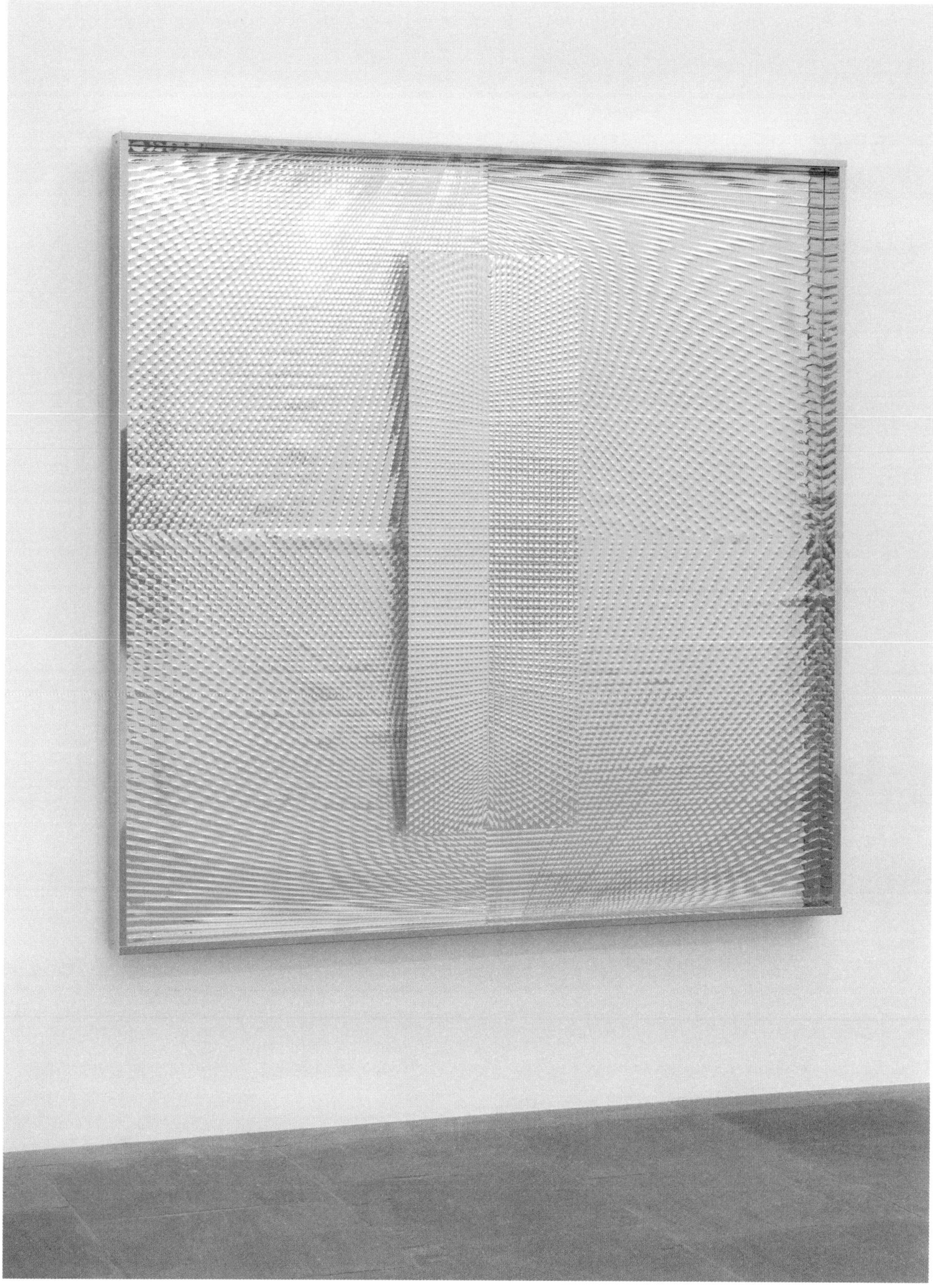

Heinz Mack, *Silberrelief*, 1965-1967, hand-embossed aluminium on wood, stainless steel, acrylic glass, 206 × 203 × 12.5 cm

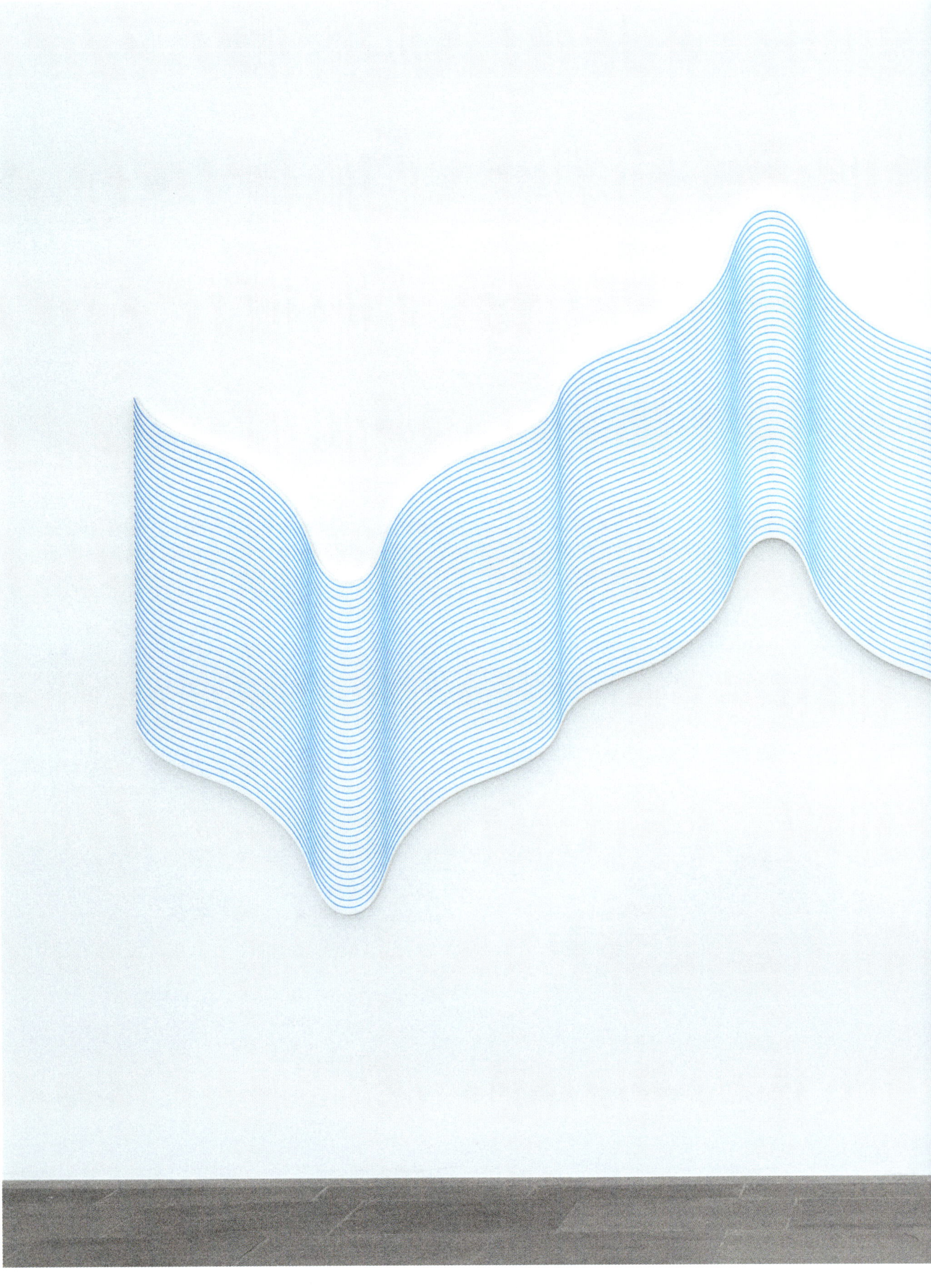

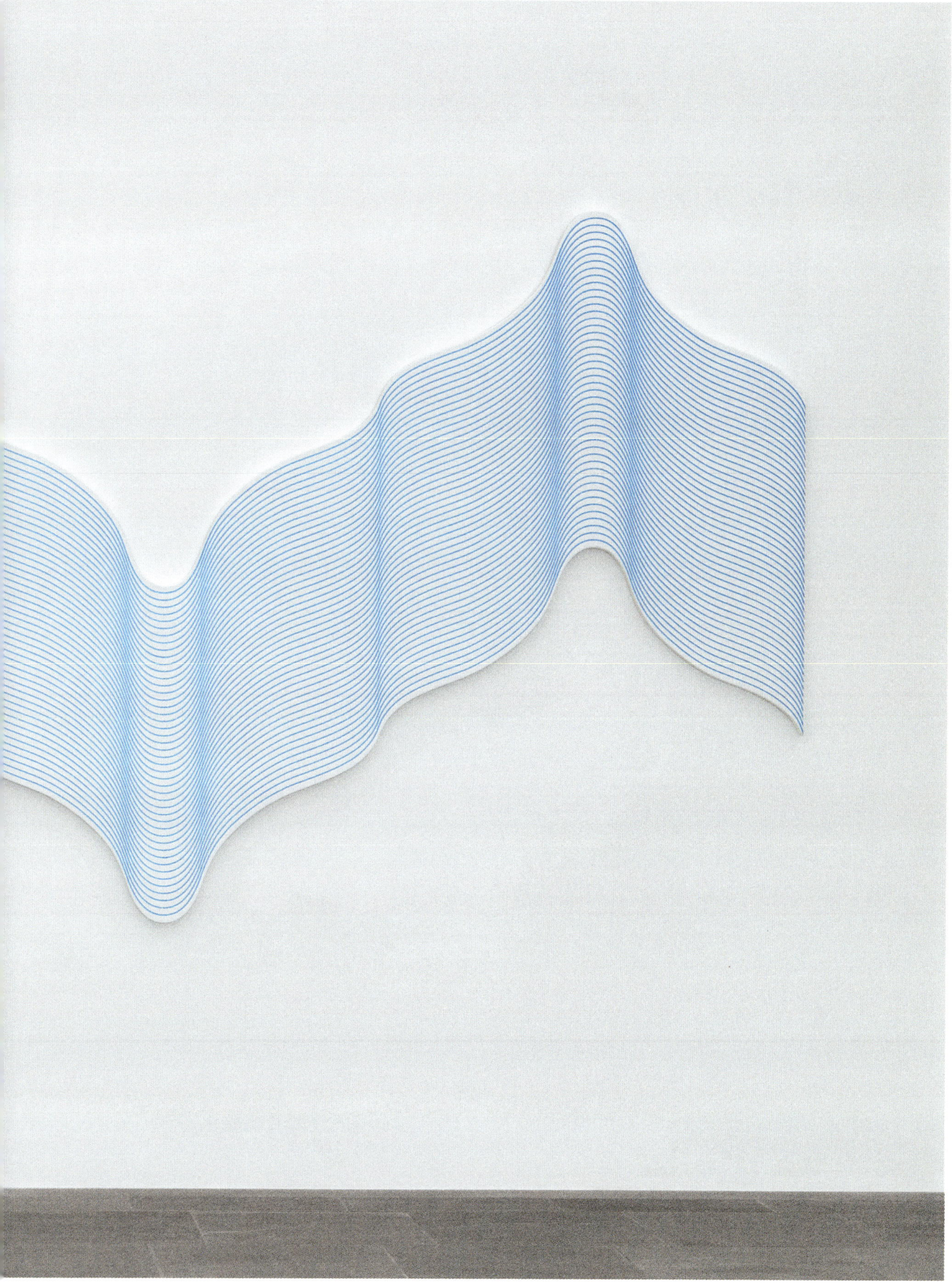

Philippe Decrauzat, *newwave*, 2025, acrylic on canvas, iridescent blue, 2 sections: 204 × 250 cm; 204 × 500 cm (overall)

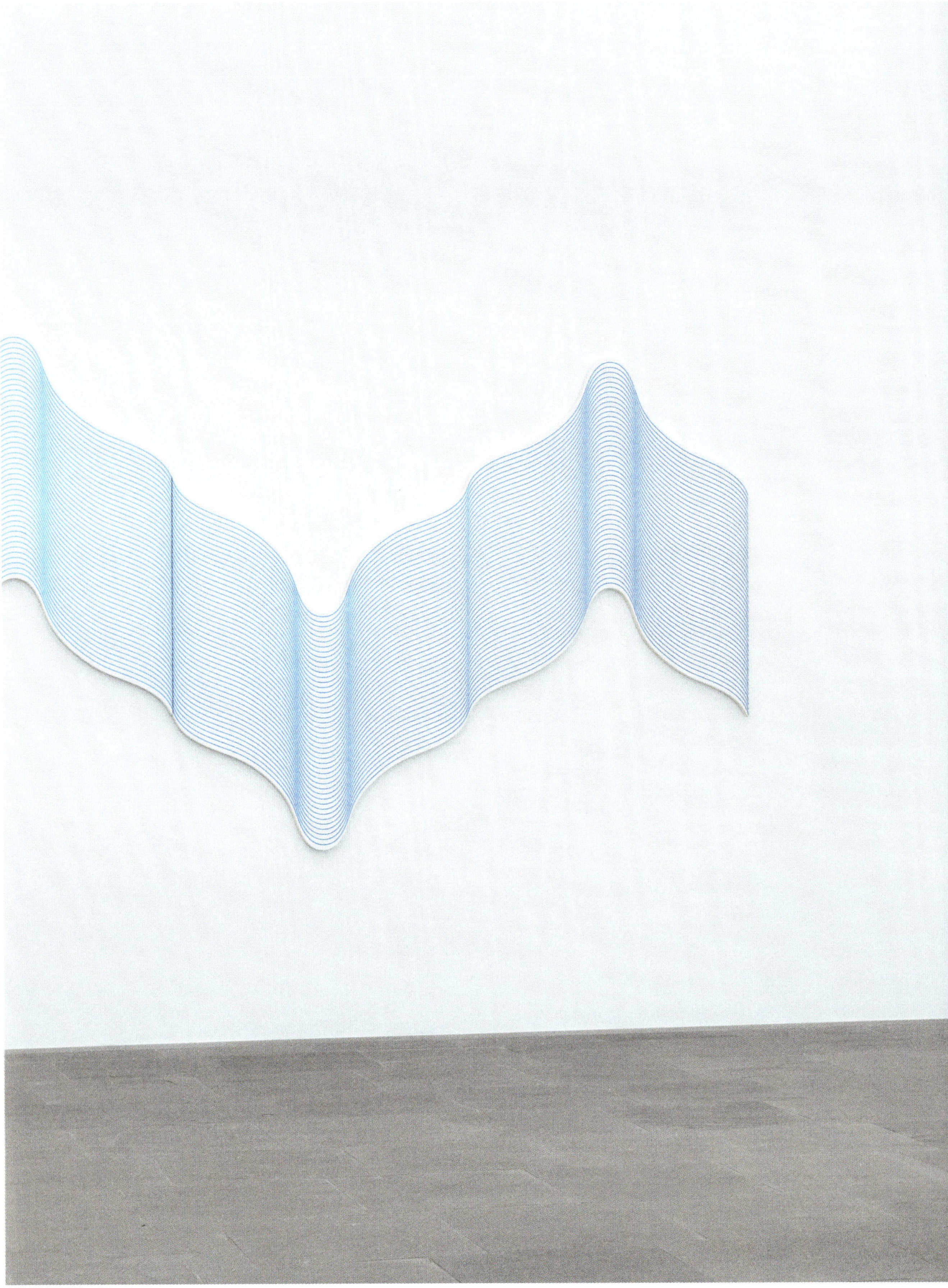

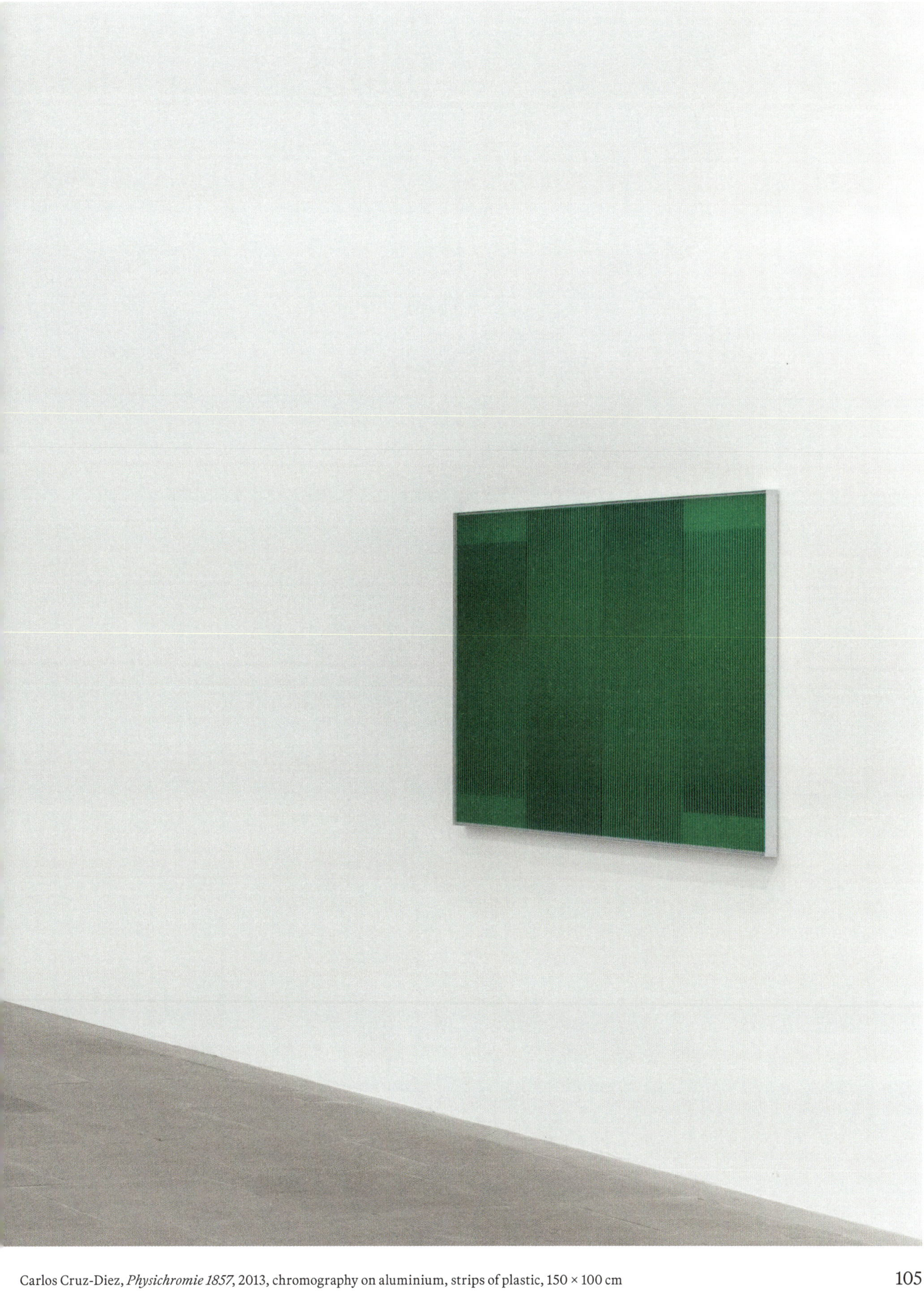

Carlos Cruz-Diez, *Physichromie 1857*, 2013, chromography on aluminium, strips of plastic, 150 × 100 cm

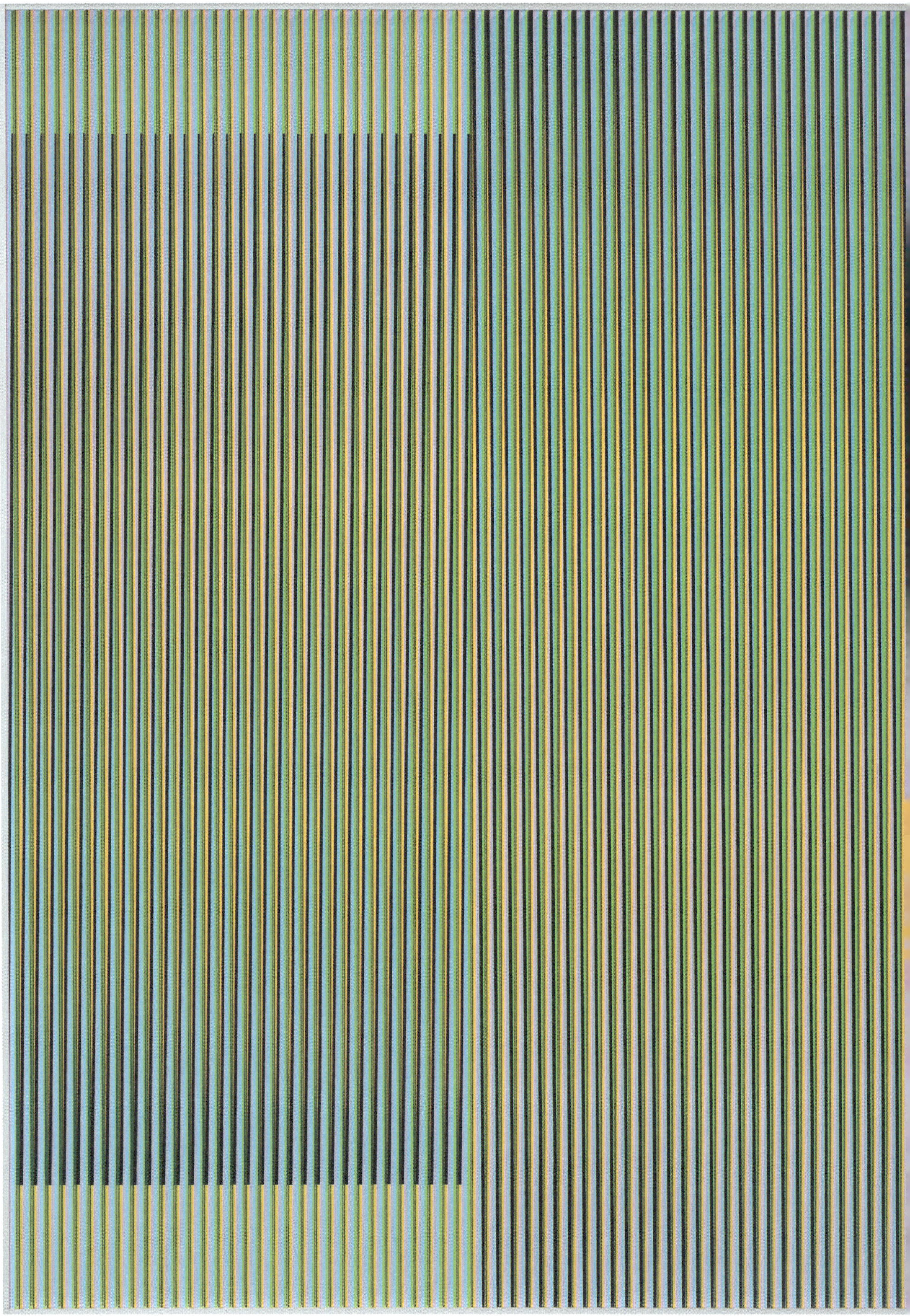

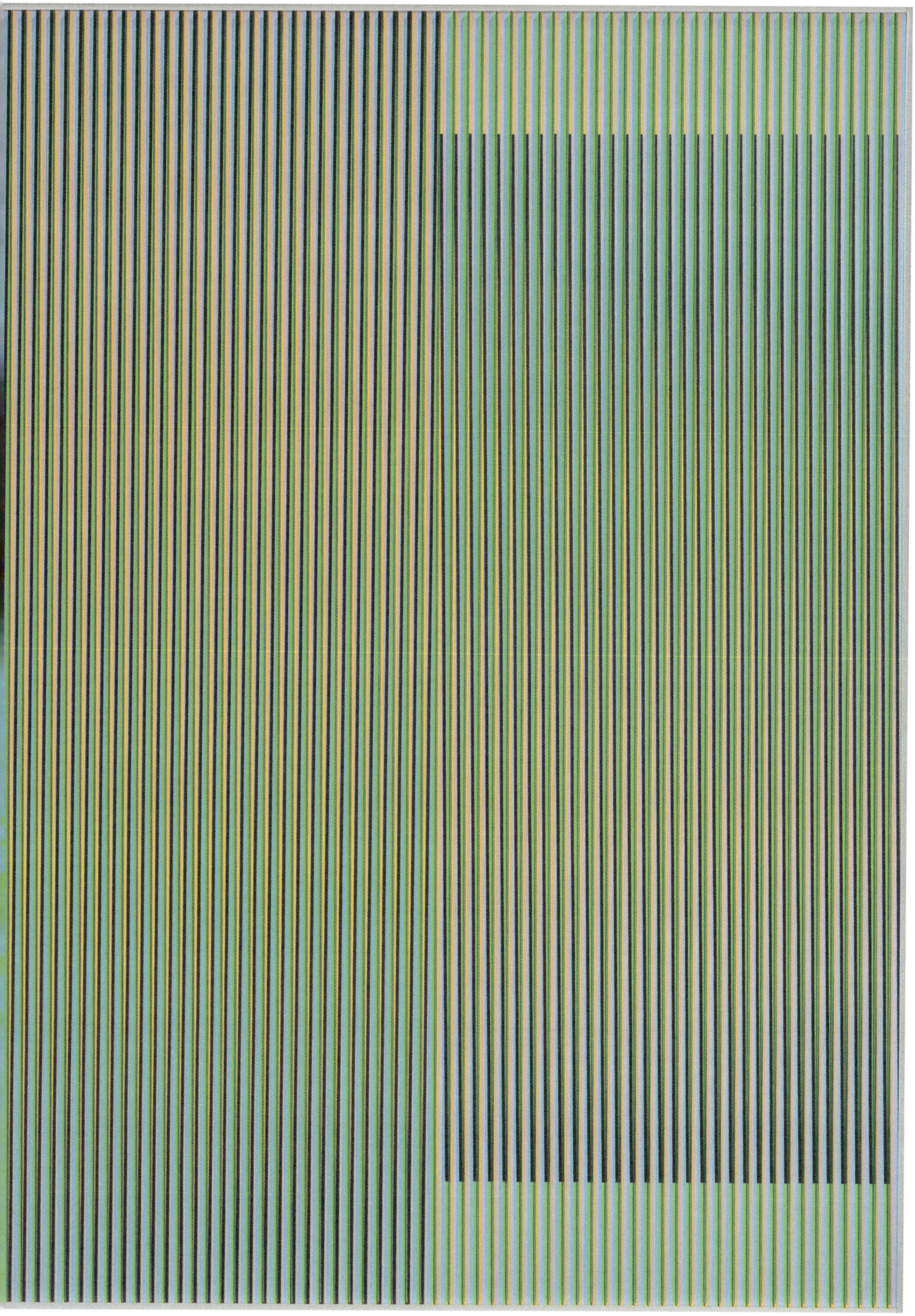

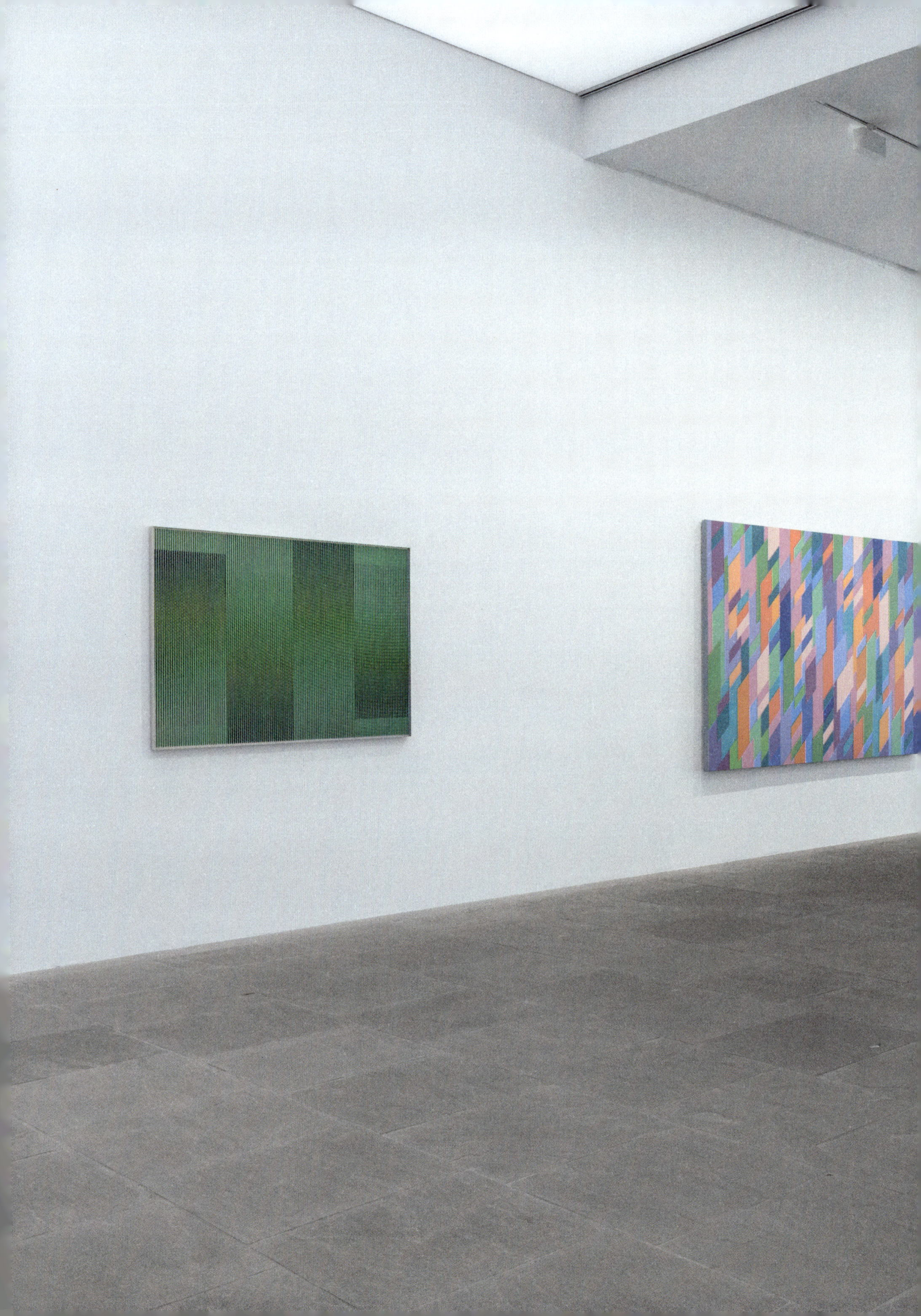

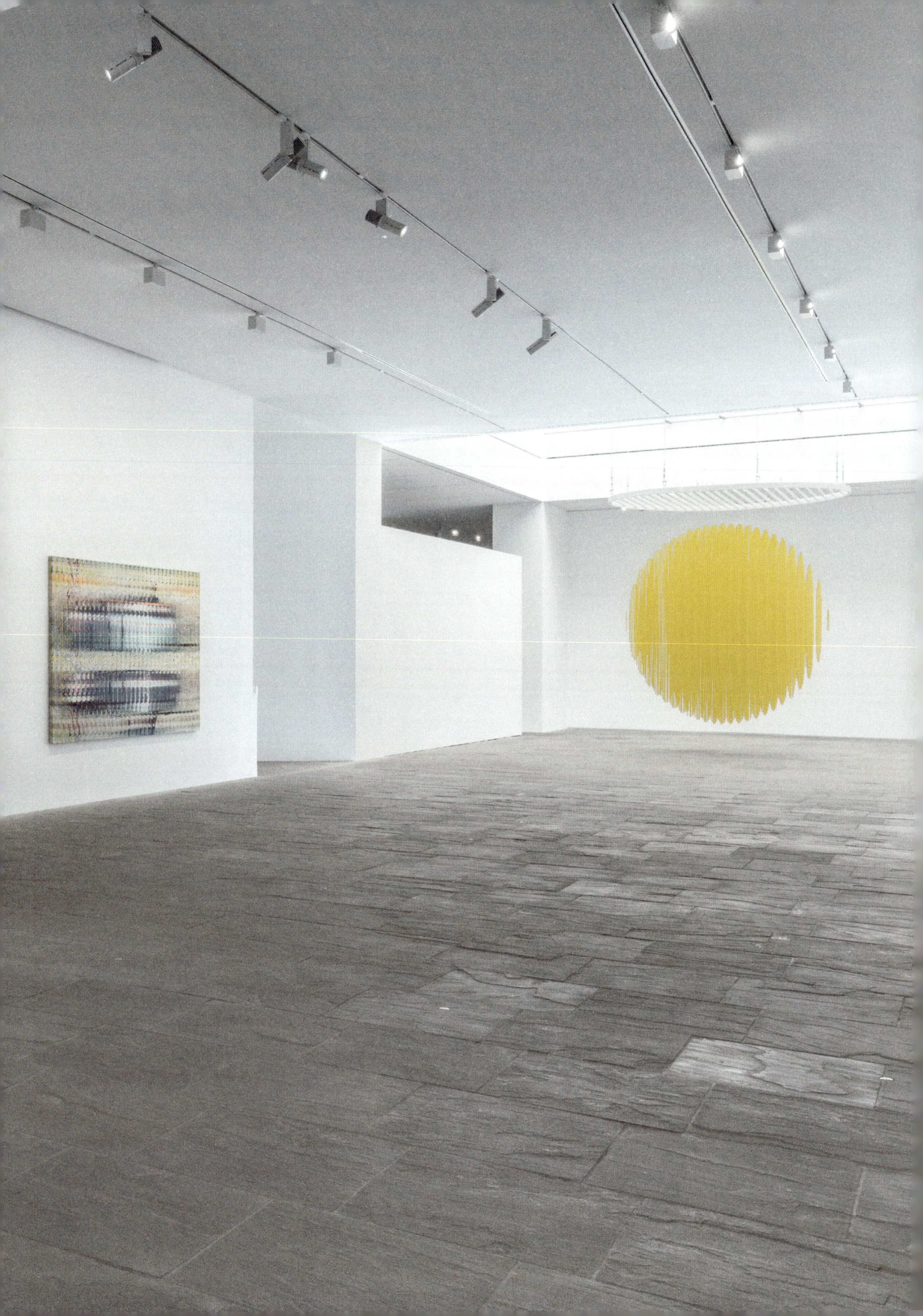

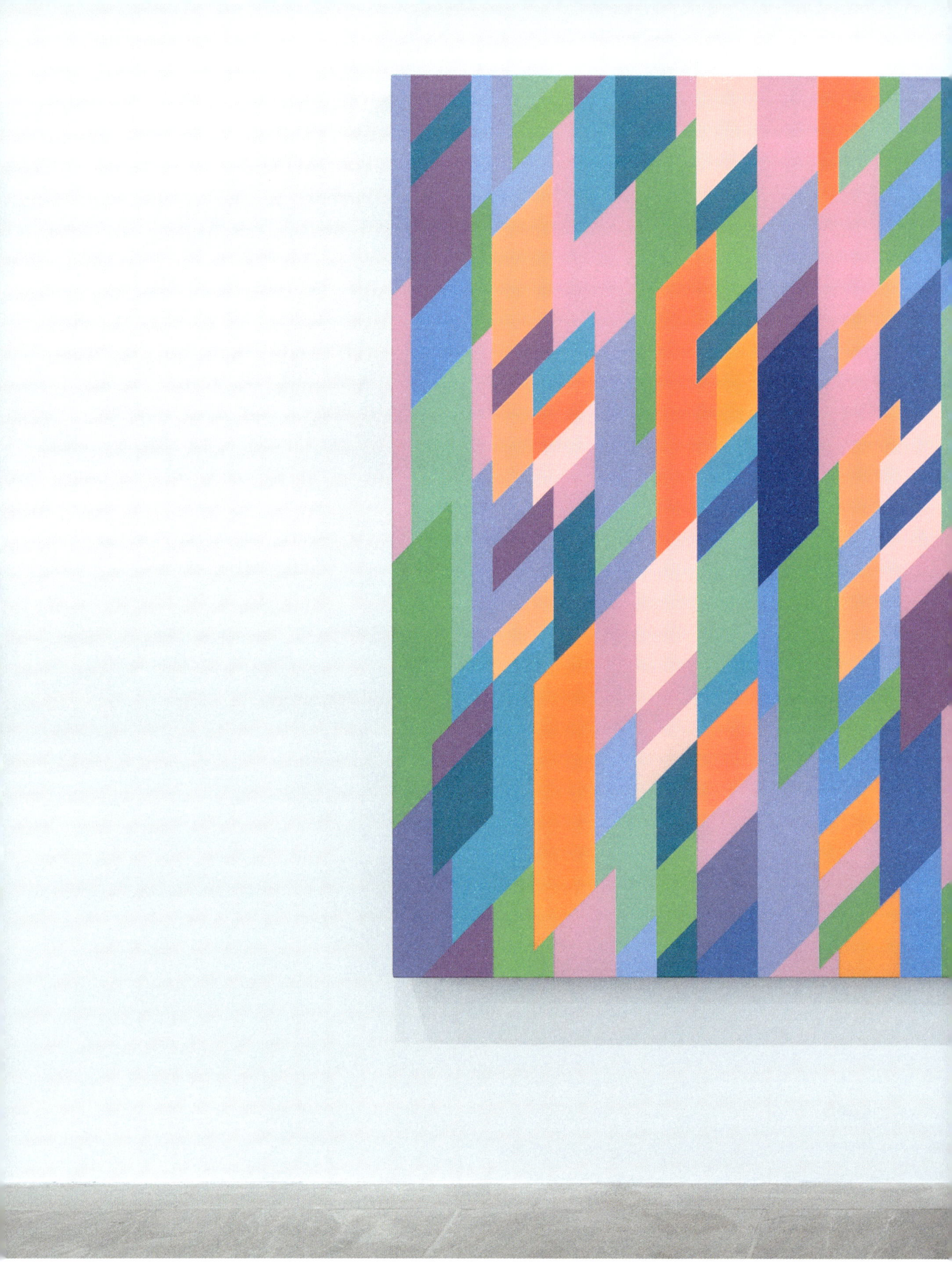

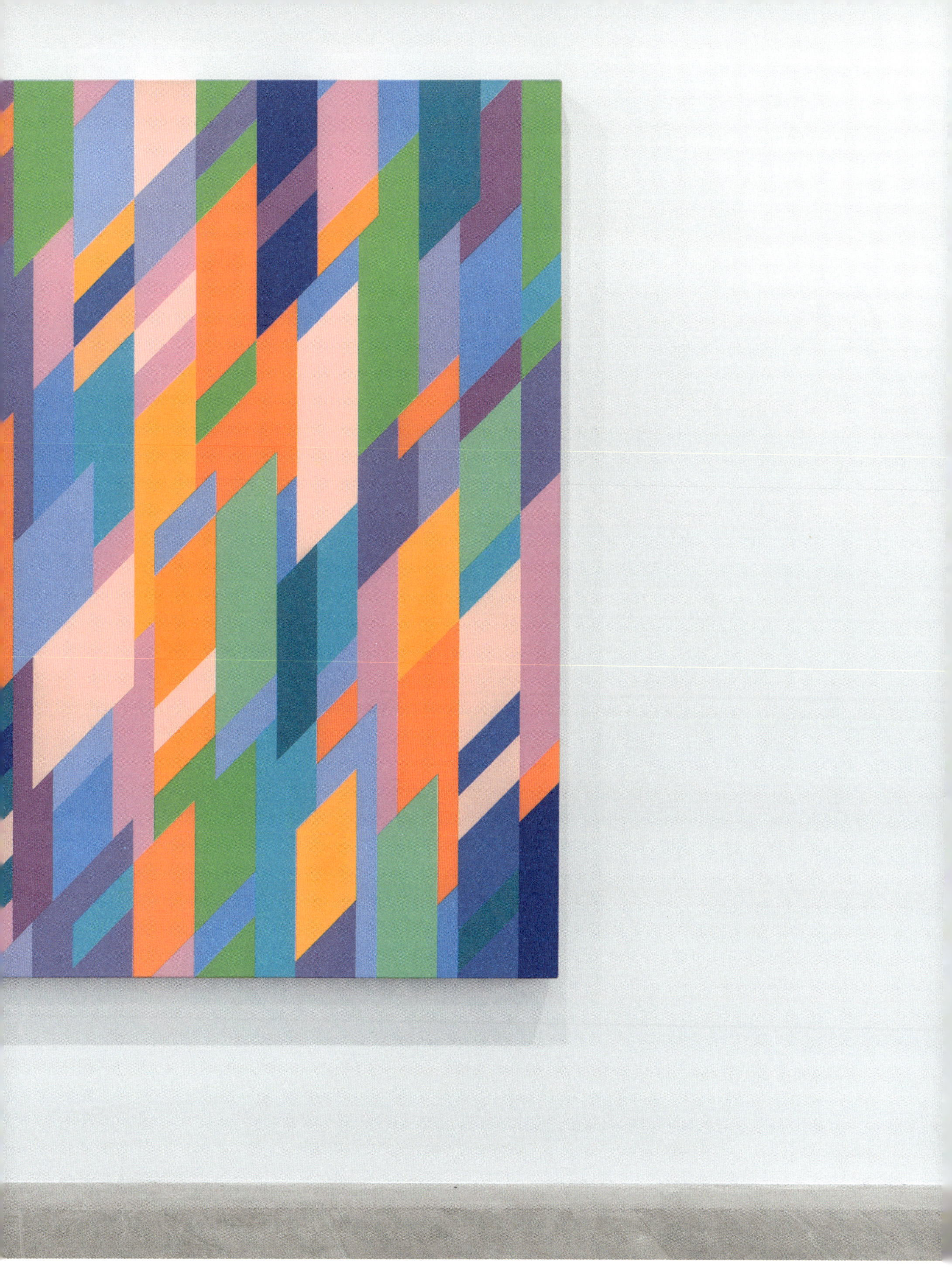

Bridget Riley, *For Genji*, 1995–1996, oil on linen canvas, 165.1 × 228.6 cm

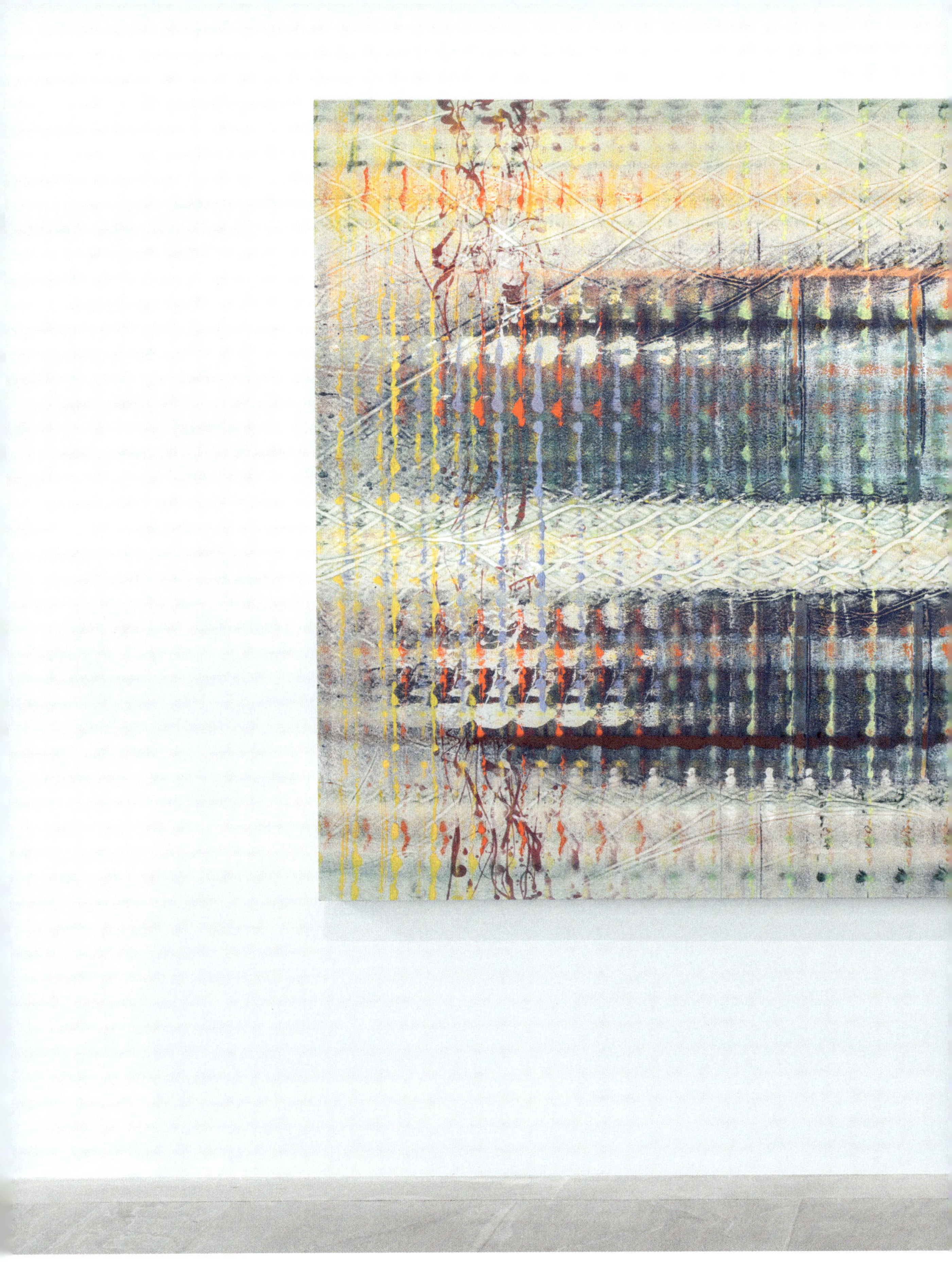

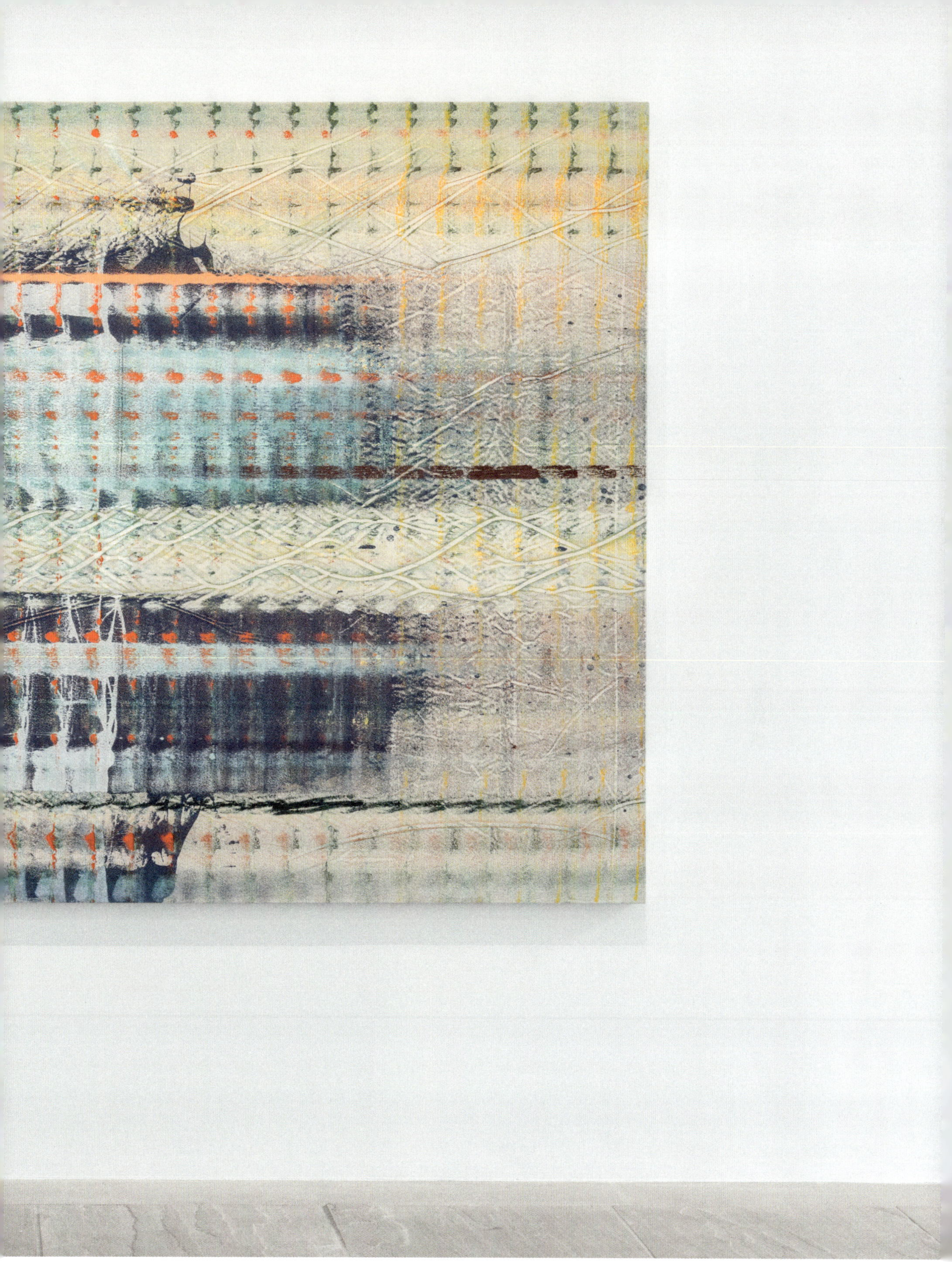

Emily Kraus, *Stochastic 1*, 2022, oil on canvas, 170 × 300 cm

EMILY KRAUS

(United States, 1995)

Stochastic 1, 2022

Oil on canvas
170 × 300 cm

Emily Kraus creates her paintings by rolling a blank canvas around four steel uprights to form a cube. She works within the cube space, adding touches of colour to the canvas and uprights to let the movements of the machine shape the composition. This gives rise to an element of chance in her work, hence the title *Stochastic 1*, a reference to the processes of random movements in mathematics.

Emily Kraus's works are a space of paradoxical encounter, bringing opposites into dialogue: the cyclical time of South-East Asian religions and Western linear time, chaos and order, humanity and nature, humanity and machines. The process creates a vibrant landscape with echoes of the rhythm of the waves or undulating music.

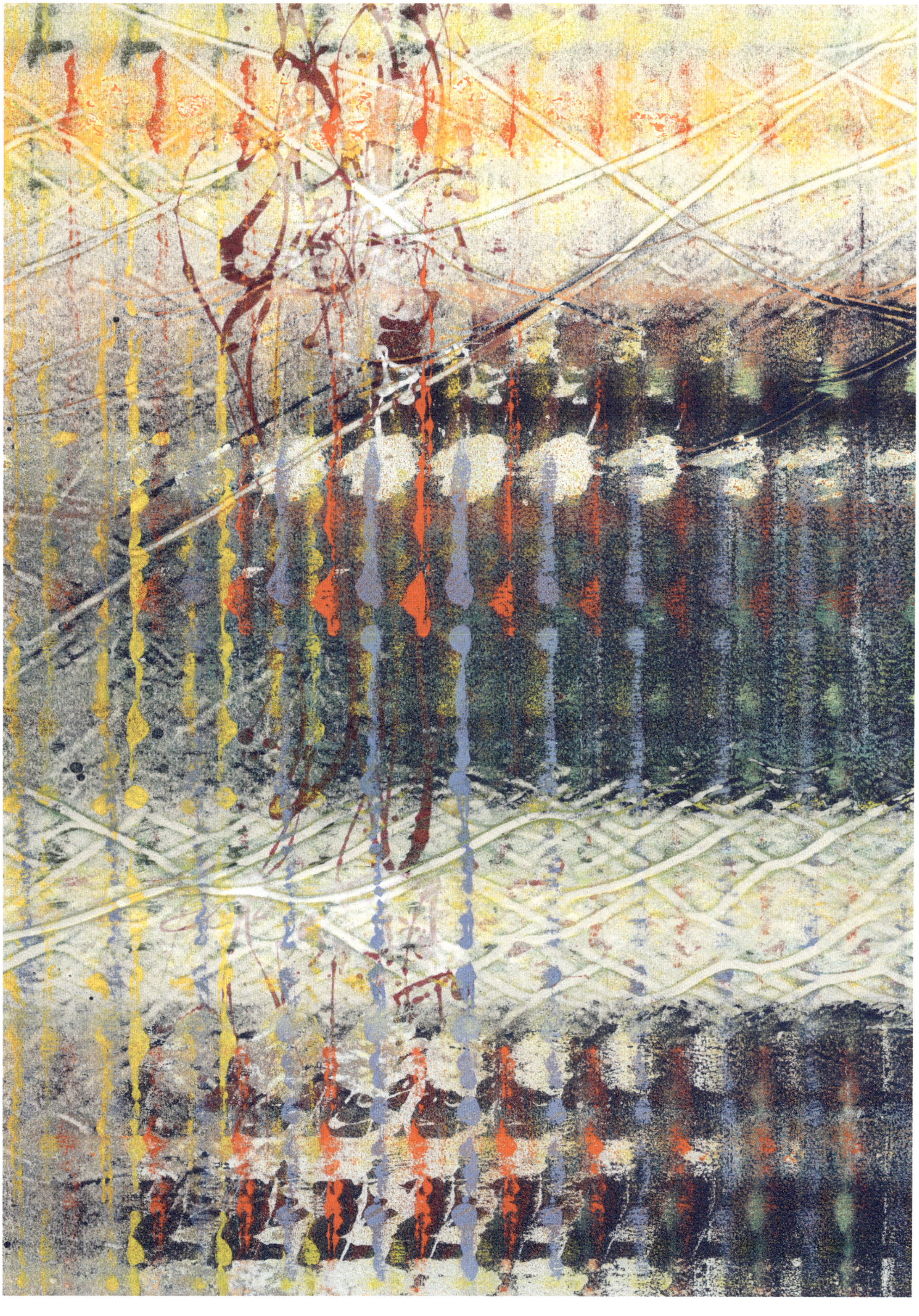

THE THRESHOLD, THE MIRAGE

AND THE ABYSS

At first sight, nothing seems to disturb the neutral tranquillity of these artworks; they do not have the images, signs or constructions you might expect to find in traditional painting. And yet, they are the vector of a singular aesthetic experience, reinforced by the same experiences that natural phenomenon can procure – all that is required is to project yourself mentally into it, immerse yourself in it, without, however, hoping to fully understand a particular object or reach a safe place. For the artists in this section, a visual phenomenon is not just the recording of a shape or an object: it may resemble the dynamic contemplation of natural phenomena, such as the ocean floor, a clear sky, the dazzling sun, a moonless night or even a heavy fog that wipes away the contours of a landscape. In an exchange with the exhibition space, they open up virtual passages or abysses of pure colour within it. The eye is carried along by the silent vibrato of light, which, like a mirage, seems to free itself from the mount. These mental pathways are given various positions, sometimes at a window and sometimes pinned to the floor or at the junction between floor and wall. Aware of the spatial potential of his monochrome screens, Yves Klein used his blue pigment to cover a canvas on a rectangular stretcher hung on the wall, or even, in this present context, spread them across the floor, without any binder except that of gravity itself, suggesting a sea of colour.

In a similar vein, Heinz Mack, a close friend of Klein's from the avant-garde group ZERO in the early 1960s, hammered an aluminium surface into a regular pattern. Like Anna-Eva Bergman's painting covered almost entirely in silver foil, Mack's relief vibrates in a silent optical *staccato*, where the light pulsates, establishing the very essence of the artwork and eclipsing the materiality of its mount. Metallic and reflective also, a second sculpture by Artur Lescher in polished brass converses with Yves Klein's *Pluie bleue*, whose blue lines, coated in pure pigment, seem suspended mid-drip.

As for Lescher's strange sculpture in the round, it seems endowed with magnetic properties: with its slender, four-metre-tall silhouette appearing almost liquid-like, it captures and directs the gaze towards its shining base, a horizontal surface where large concentric discs heighten the sense of depth.

Free of any familiar shape or composition, these surfaces allow the gaze to glide over them, or, quite the opposite, enable it to cross a threshold and become immersed in their coloured abysses. This is because these often-pure colours are presented in various states: powdery and matte in the painting and on the floor for Yves Klein's pigments, pulverised and ethereal in the wall painting of Isabelle Cornaro, as if evaporated in the painting by Gerhard Richter, and replying to the incessant sparkling of the glitter in John Armleder's work. Jef Verheyen explores another facet of this by creating a subtle gradient that tends towards a visual endpoint, where a triangular shape alternately appears then vanishes. For Isabelle Cornaro, an extremely fine, almost indistinct layer of pulverised blue pigments is applied directly on the wall itself. Hugo Schüwer Boss's artwork, a painting whose frame is in the trompe-l'oeil shape of a religious altarpiece, demarcates a wide, ambiguous expanse of blue with no subject, vaguely suggestive of the sea or sky. This game of perception reaches a particular radicality and complexity in James Turrell's work: a simple lumino-chromatic projection, in the darkness of a special room, makes one think of a shining portal, located at the point where the cyma begins, at the junction with the floor. The shape unfolds in a large rectangle that despite its virtuality, captures our gaze and directs it mentally towards a parallel universe, a world without any visual hold.

Previous page: Hugo Schüwer Boss, *Eleonor* (detail), 2024, acrylic and varnish on plywood mounted on concealed wooden frame, 160 × 120 cm
Opposite: Yves Klein, *Monochrome bleu sans titre* (IKB 68), 1961, pure pigment and synthetic resin, gravel, on gauze mounted on wood panel, 194 × 140 cm

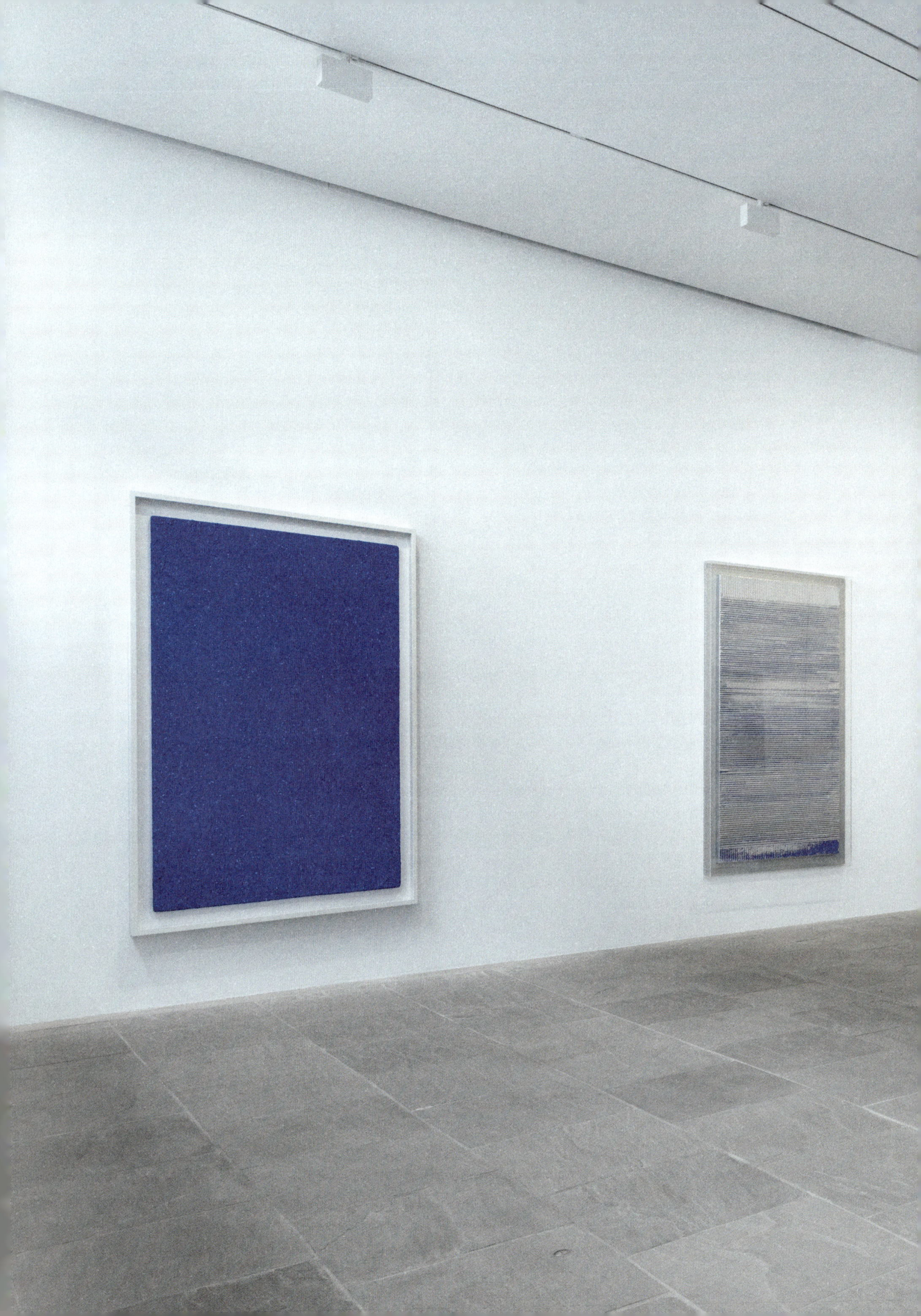

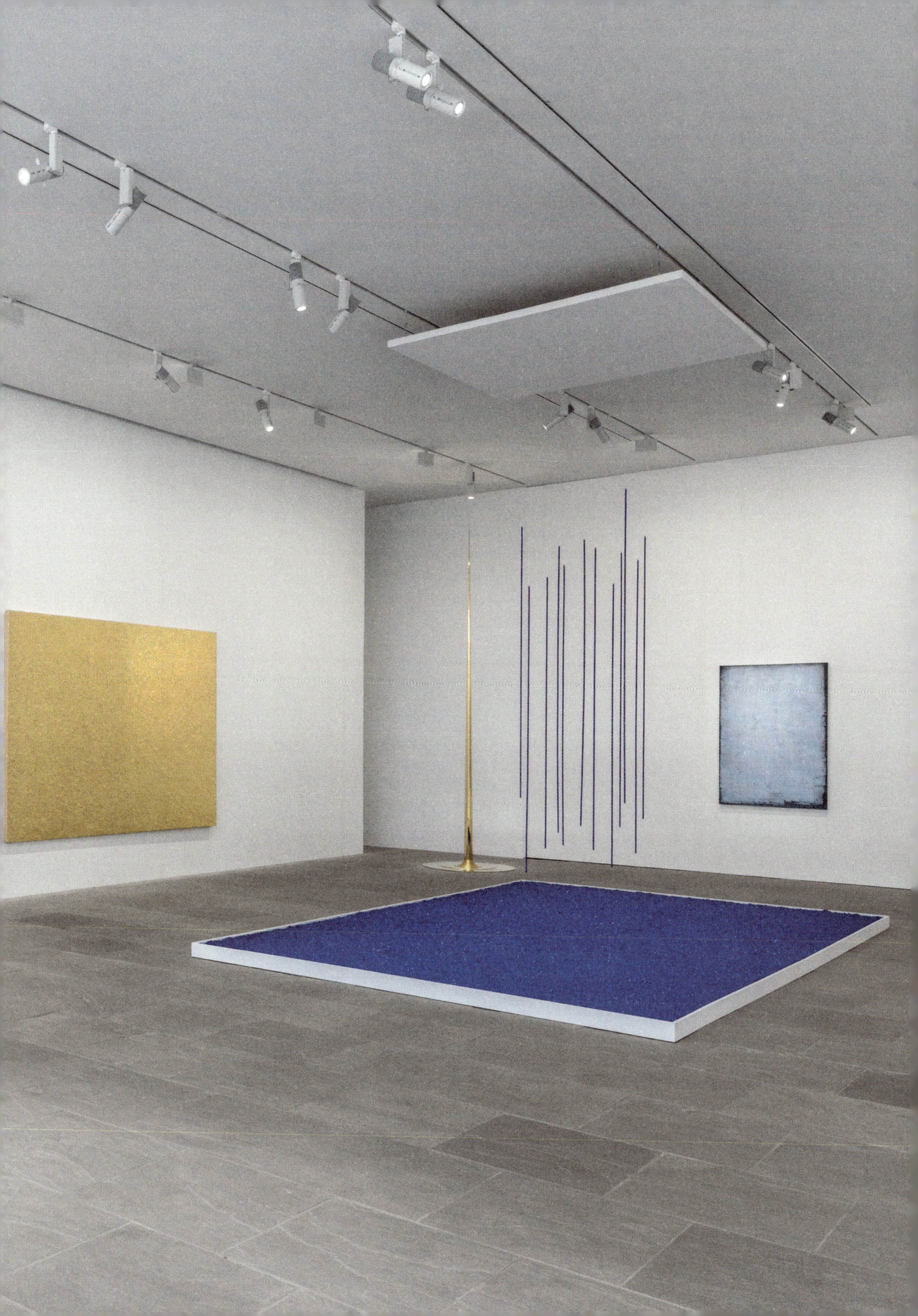

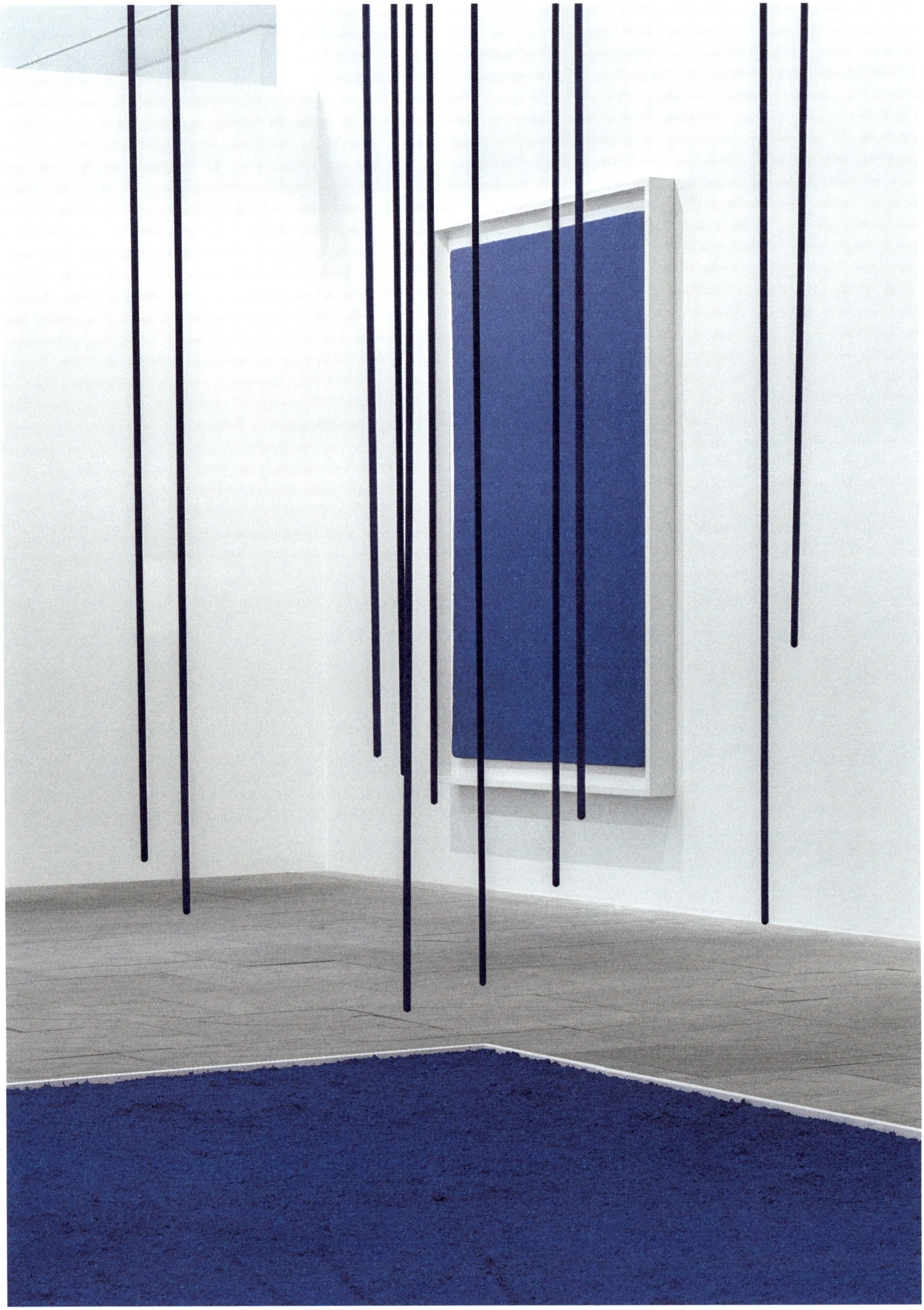

YVES KLEIN

(France, 1928-1962)

Monochrome bleu sans titre (IKB 68), 1961

Pure pigment and synthetic resin, gravel, on gauze mounted on wood panel
194 × 140 cm

Pigment pur, original artwork 1957 posthumous installation 2025

Pure pigment
300 × 500 cm

Pluie bleue (S 36), original artwork 1957 posthumous edition 2018

Pure pigment and synthetic resin on 12 wooden rods
209 × 1.1 cm

Recognisable thanks to the intensity of its "Klein blue", developed by the artist in 1956 then patented in 1960 under the name IKB (International Klein Blue), the installation of pure pigments arranged on the floor immediately catches our eye. One of the famous series of monochromes – of which a version from 1961 is exhibited here – it offers for our contemplation a surface covered entirely in evenly applied unvarying colour. The ultramarine hue "recalls more than anything else the sea, or the sky, that which is most abstract in tangible, living nature". In keeping with his desire to abandon the restrictive support of the canvas in order to spread pure colour in space, Klein, through his use of the monochrome, brought forth an invisible presence that extends beyond all material appearance and invites us to experience the void. This quest for spirituality and transcendence found expression that same year in the mobile *Pluie bleue*. This work is typical of the way Klein often sought to transcribe the natural elements and atmospheric forces around us. Consisting of twelve wooden rods covered in pigment, this suspended piece marked a new stage in the dematerialisation of the painting, a final attempt to appropriate the infinite blue of the sky.

Heinz Mack, *Das Meer I – Licht-Relief*, 1963, aluminium on bronze and silver-plated wood, 199 × 99 × 4.5 cm

John Armleder, *L.A. Gold*, 2014, sequins on wood panel, 200 × 300 cm

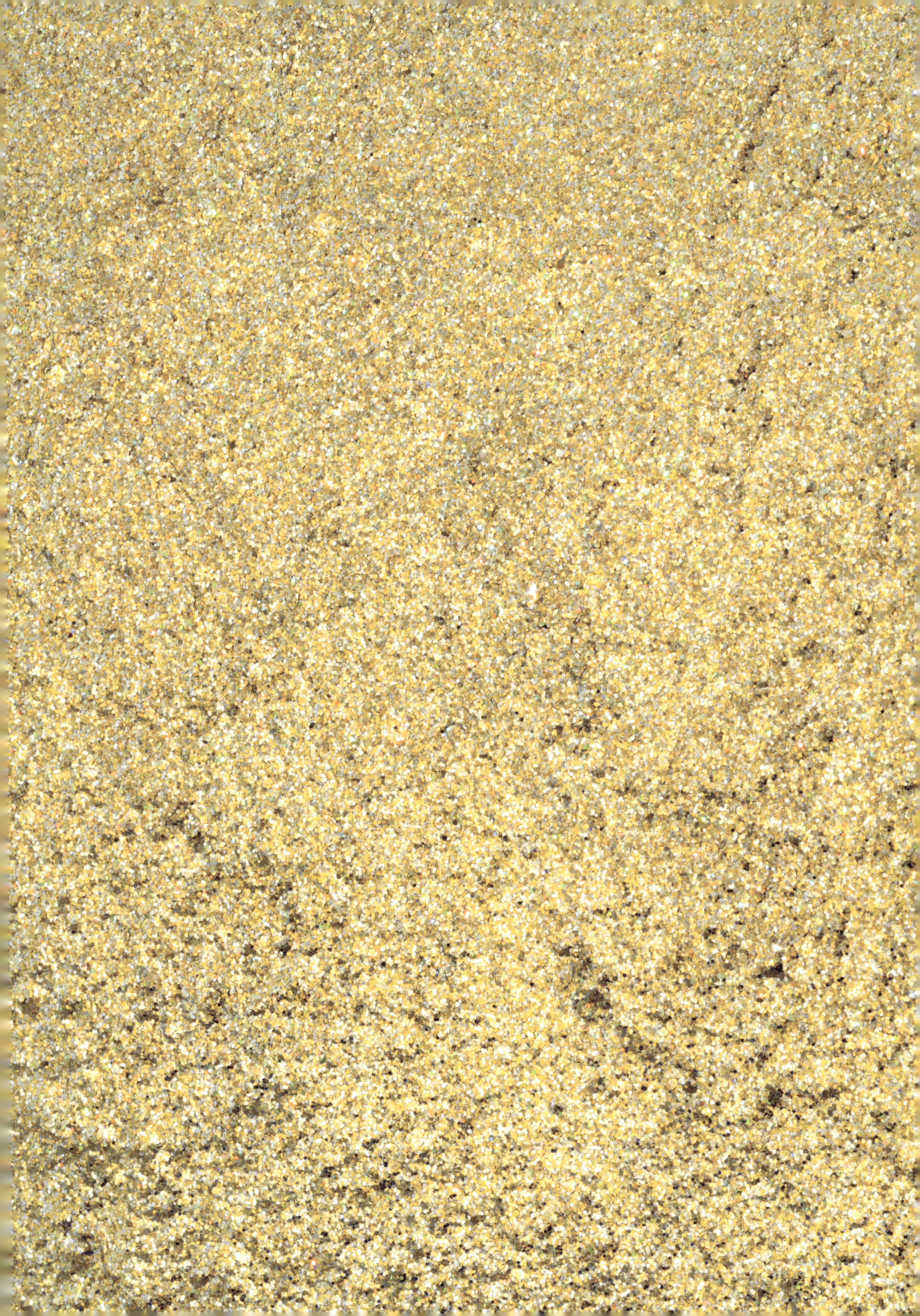

ANNA-EVA BERGMAN

(Sweden, 1909-1987)

Nº 15B-1963
Néant d'argent, 1963

Vinyl paint and silver leaves on canvas
146 × 114 cm

Anna-Eva Bergman covered her metallic painting in silver leaves – a personal technique she developed in the early 1960s. The artist adopted this reflective process, which enabled her to sculpt the reflected light, throughout her career, in a quest to dematerialise the landscapes that pervade her work. Bergman fixed the material to the canvas with varnish or tempera. Her work usually verges on the abstract, here offering a perfectly flat surface, and evokes the powerful Nordic light and twinkling stars. For this pantheistic painter steeped in Scandinavian mythology, art was an initiatory quest that led to spiritual rebirth, in which light, nature, transcendence and spirituality are closely linked.

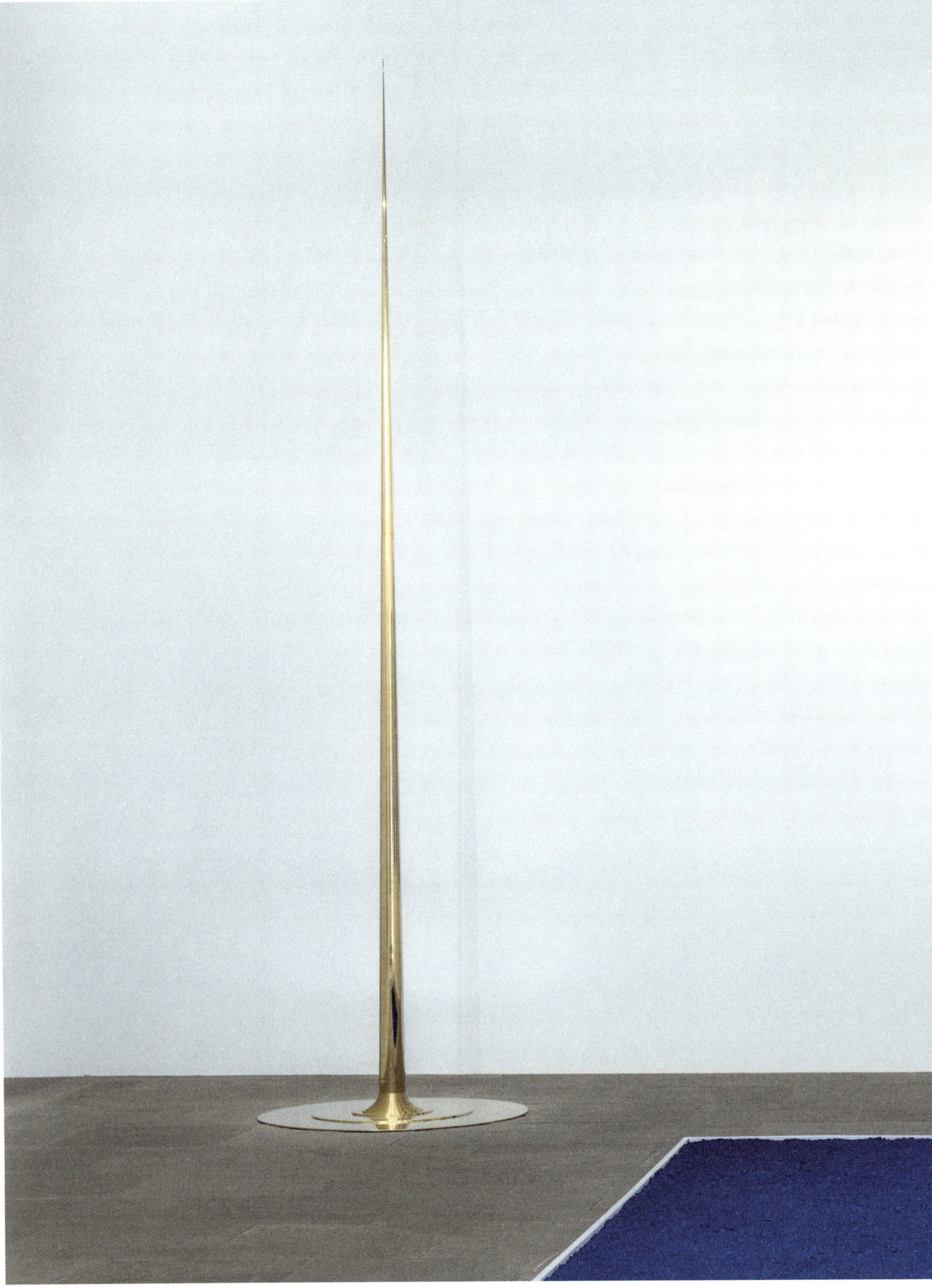

Artur Lescher, *Apolinário*, 2014, brass, 400 × 100 × 100 cm. Yves Klein, *Pluie bleue* (S 36), original artwork 1957 – posthumous edition 2018, pure pigment and synthetic resin on 12 wooden rods, 209 × 1.1 cm

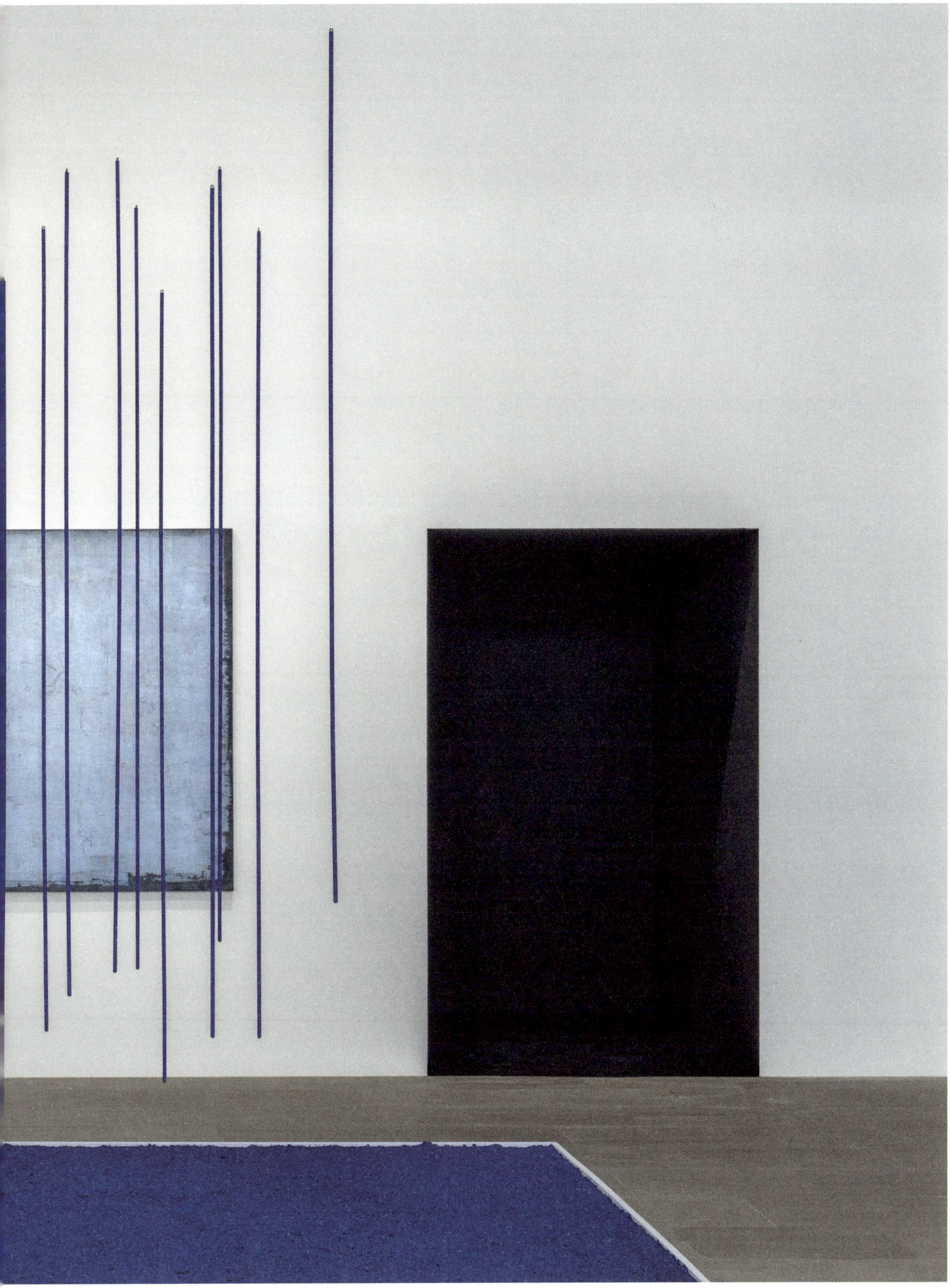

Anna-Eva Bergman, *N°15B-1963 Néant d'argent*, 1963, vinyl paint and silver leaves on canvas, 146 × 114 cm
Following pages: James Turrell, *Prado, Red*, 1968, projection, variable dimensions

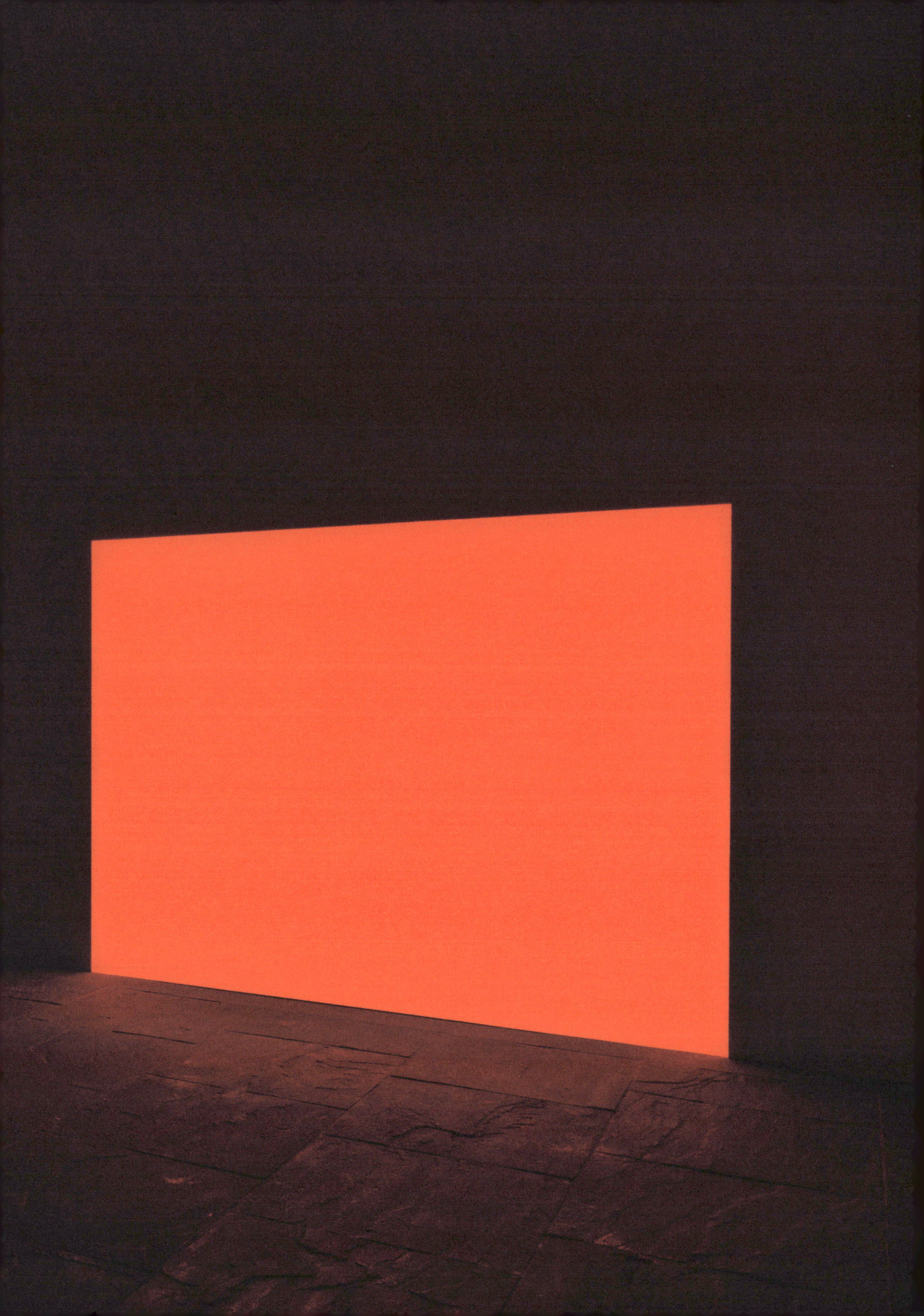

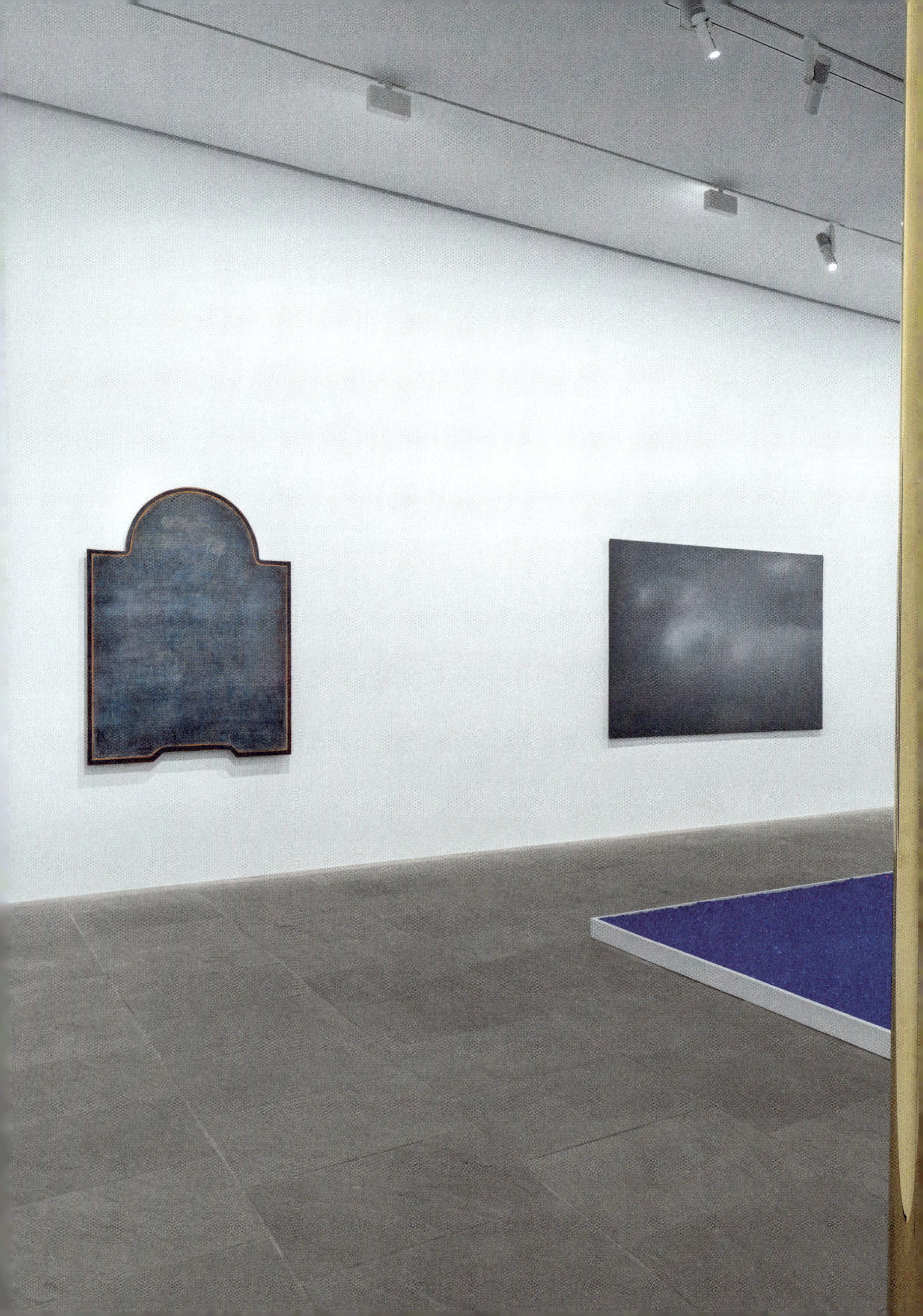

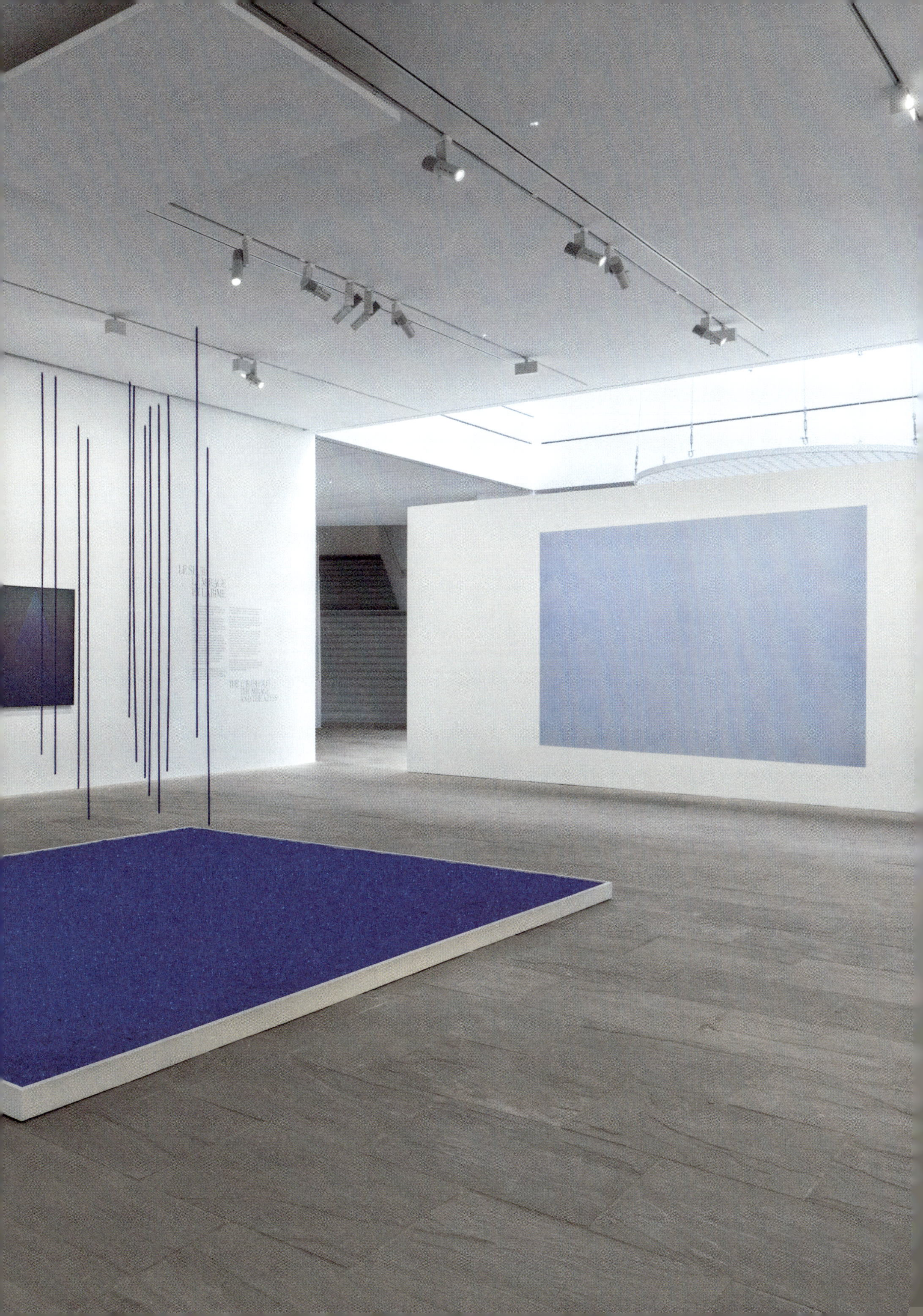

HUGO SCHÜWER BOSS

(France, 1981)

Eleonor, 2024

Acrylic and varnish on plywood mounted on concealed wooden frame
160 × 120 cm

Although the overall shape of *Eleonor* is reminiscent of religious altarpieces, Hugo Schüwer Boss does not represent a subject of any kind in his canvas. He invites us to immerse our gaze in an expanse of blue whose shades evoke the variations of a misty sky. Schüwer Boss, who has created a trompe-l'oeil reproduction of a wooden frame for this work, evokes the sacredness associated with this age-old form in order to offer a formal reinterpretation of it that is centred on the treatment of colour. Following in the footsteps of abstract painters whose work was guided by a quest for the divine, Schüwer Boss here works with the medium's asperities, eschewing any attempt at creating an entirely homogeneous surface. As a result, although the work creates the impression of having been tested by time, *Eleonor* allows the ineffable to reveal itself, acting as an invitation to enter the immaterial.

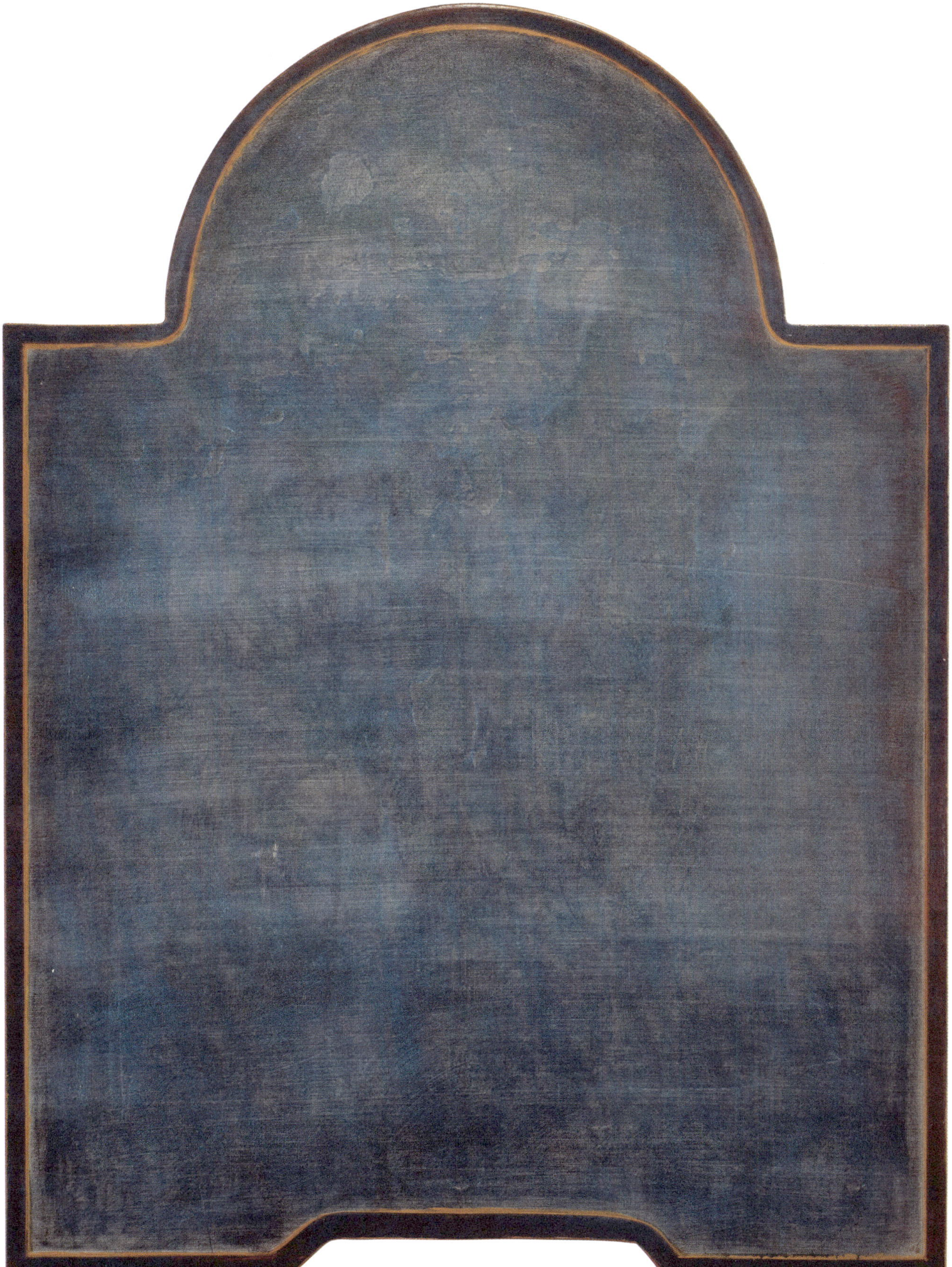

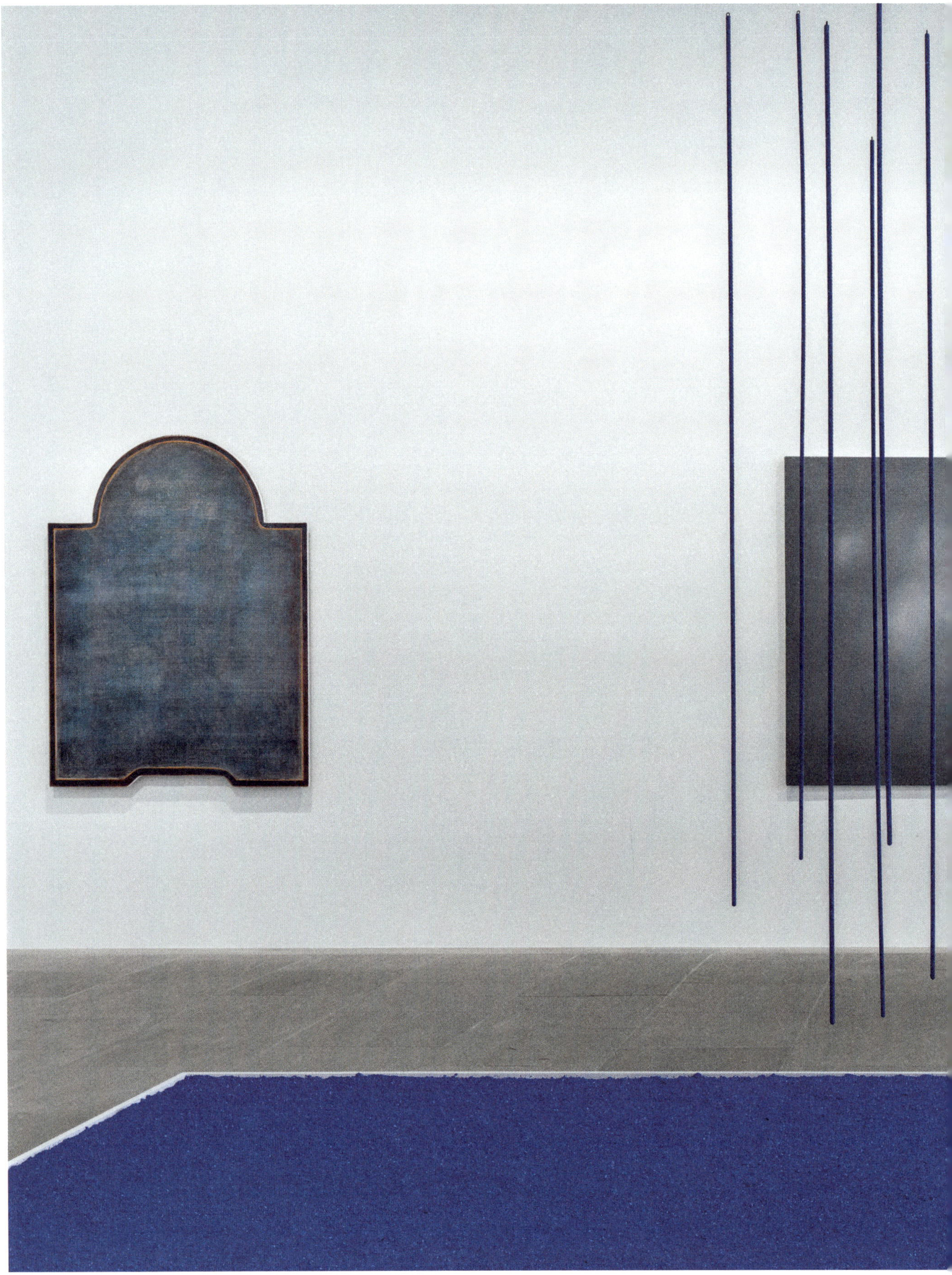

Hugo Schüwer Boss, *Eleonor*, 2024, acrylic and varnish on plywood mounted on concealed wooden frame, 160 × 120 cm
Gerhard Richter, *Wolken (Grau)*, 1969, oil on canvas, 150.2 × 200 cm

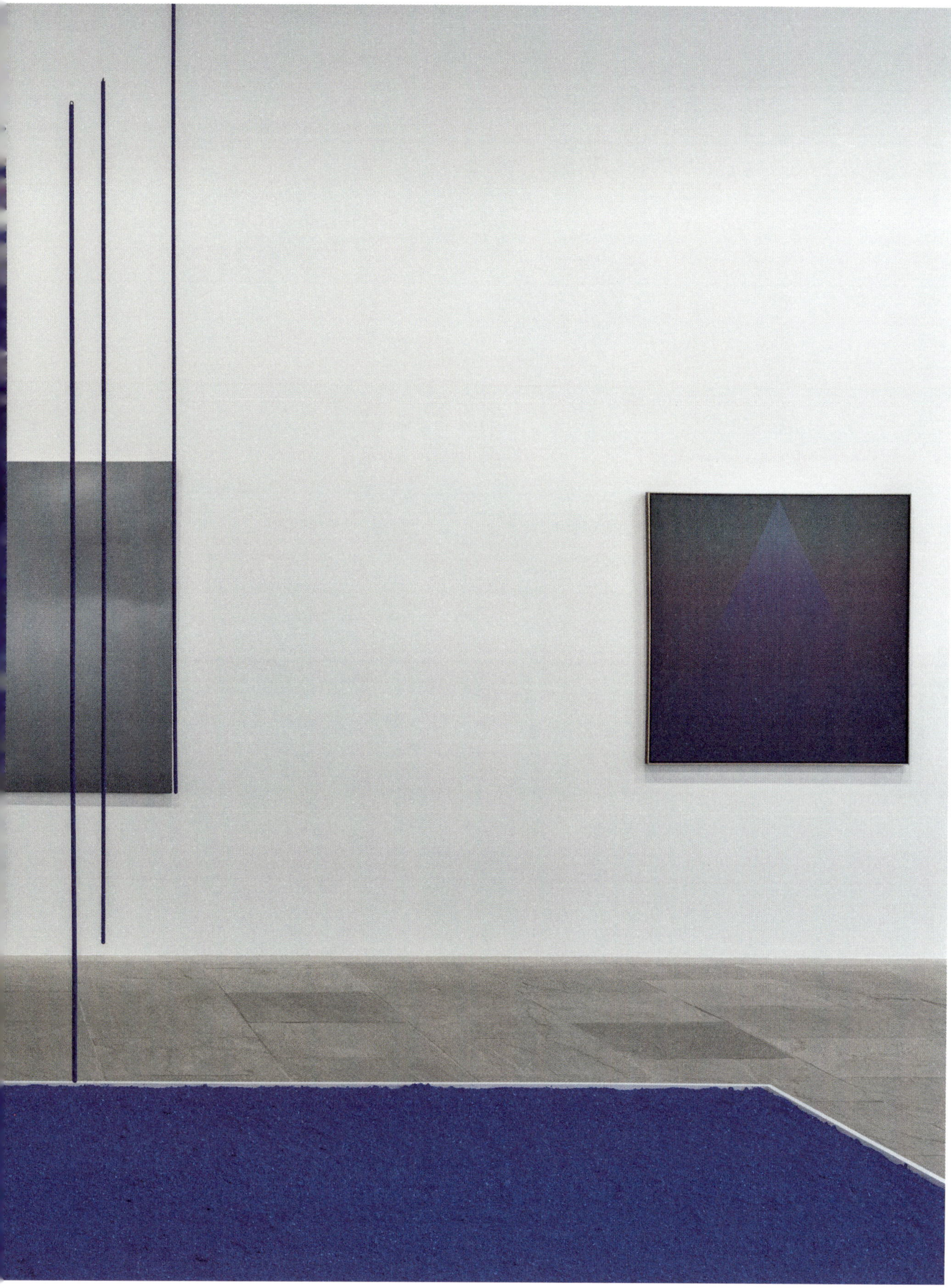

Jef Verheyen, *Natte zielen*, 1979, matte lacquer on canvas, 120 × 120 cm

LE SEUIL,
LE MIRAGE
ET L'ABÎME
THE THRESHOLD,
THE MIRAGE
AND THE ABYSS

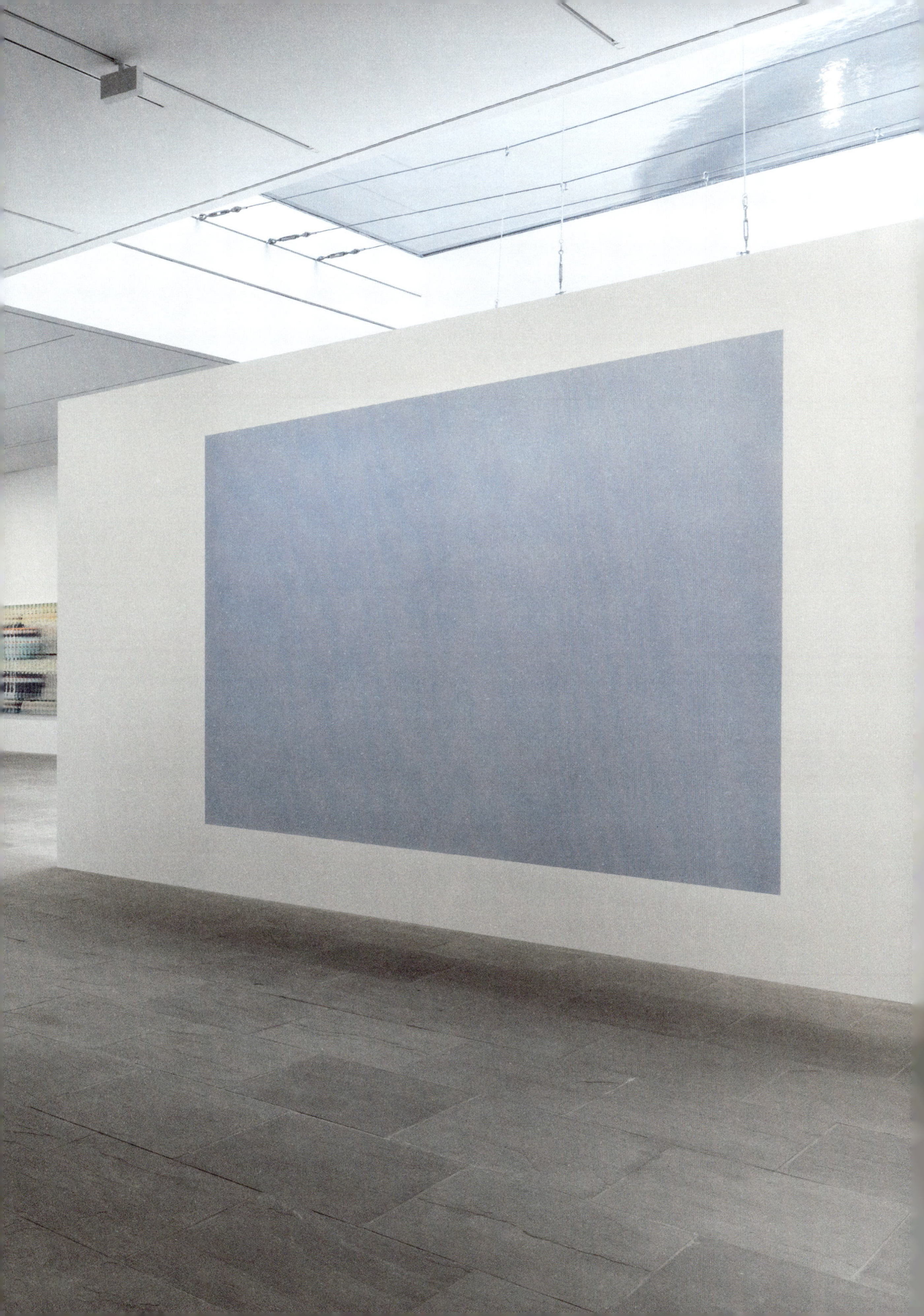

Jef Verheyen, *Natte zielen*, 1979, matte lacquer on canvas, 120 × 120 cm

Isabelle Cornaro, *Reproductions I (#4)*, 2010, acrylic spray paint, 250 × 332.5 cm
Following page: Olafur Eliasson, *Colour experiment no. 118 (Blue Lagoon)* (detail), 2023, acrylic on canvas, diam. 160 cm

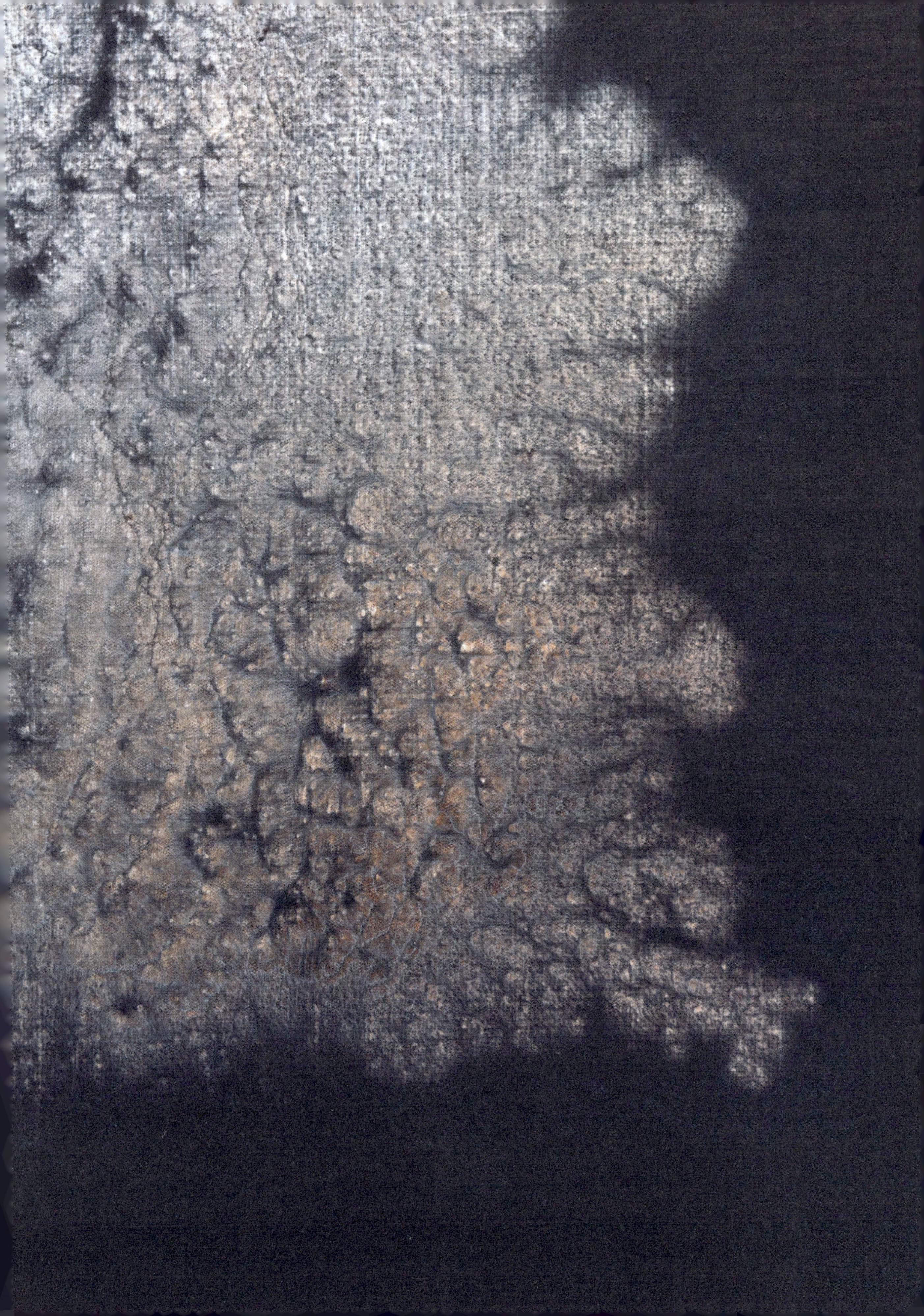

TELLURIC VISIONS

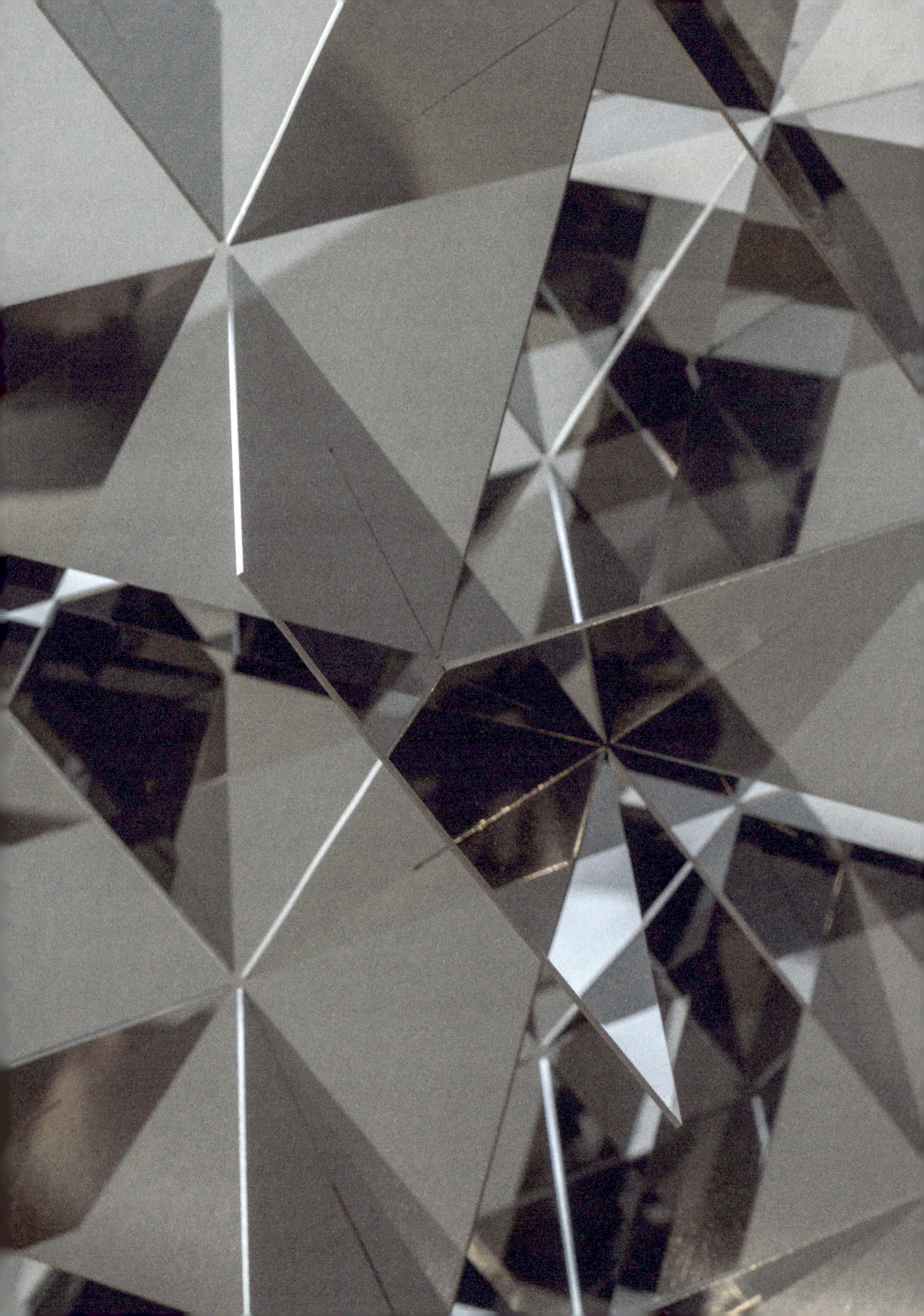

This section explores the register of telluric forces – geological or volcanic – that have been incubating under the Earth's crust since its creation. The artworks seem to result from an alchemical transformation performed by the artist, who controls, manages or accompanies various physical forces and energies. Their creations, even though most of them are hung on the wall, serve as a crucible, where a mineral substance evolves into an optical and atmospheric phenomenon. Although the artworks repudiate figuration, we shall approach them with a collective imagination that has been forged through contact with natural landscapes. In a continuation of our ascension to the second floor, Lynn Chadwick's immaculate and spiral *Mobile* floats at the whim of the passage of air and, through its movements, seems to encourage dynamic mutations to the mineral substance that characterises this chapter: vortices, plumes of smoke, gestural tornadoes and various auroras. Like a chemist, or even an alchemist, each artist makes use of gestures, gravity, sound waves, temperature or even the melting of glaciers to control, manage or accompany the physical energy of the gesture or that of gravity. It is above all a question of transforming an inert mineral substance into an optical and atmospheric phenomenon.

Hephaestus, the Greek god of fire, comes especially to mind in the work of Raphael Hefti, who effects a kind of chromatic genesis by creating singular paintings without brushes, pigments, binders or canvas-stretcher. He begins by using the chemical properties of bismuth, a metal that when cast (here in a rectangular mould in the shape of a painting) changes in appearance and colour, depending on the delicate interplay of temperature and handling. The result of this managed random process suggests the optical phenomenon of phosphenes, those blurry and scintillating colourful shapes that appear when your retina is overworked or when you press on your closed eyes with your fingers. Olafur Eliasson's kaleidoscope gives a filtered, unstable and augmented view of the Villa's surroundings, like some dizzying alchemical mutation where the physical matter of the landscape is transformed into an immaterial optical phenomenon. His *tondo*, a circular table, is painted in chromatic shades from a photograph the artist took in Iceland. The ordered redistribution of these colours onto the canvas is achieved through a unique gradation of colour in rays, which, like a wheel or helix, draw the gaze into a movement that is both concentric and eccentric. Above the centre floats a yellow shape, which is itself circular. It calls to mind a sun, but one partially hidden by haloes of thick black smoke. The fluctuating shapes of the marks do not issue from a pictorial gesture but from fragments of glacier applied by the artist onto the canvas, which, as they melted, gradually released the bright minerals they contained. The ensemble somewhat resembles a macular stain on the surface of the eye when the fovea (the area of the retina responsible for sharp vision) is partly filled in.

Previous pages: Lynn Chadwick, *Mobile (Version II White)*, 1952, steel rods and shapes, 105 × 133 × 133 × 122 cm
Opposite: Francisco Sobrino, *Structure permutationnelle* (detail), 1963-2014, polished stainless steel mirror, 150 × 60 × 60 cm

Natural phenomena and the evocation of mountain and lakeside scenery are prevalent in the painting by Bernard Frize, which results from a process combining rigour and chance: with a large brush, the artist paints horizontal strips in a mixture of acrylic paint, ink, mother-of-pearl and resin. The still-wet canvas is then tilted, bringing gravity into play and resulting in somewhat unpredictable combinations and drips from one pictorial strata to another. Before the completed painting, the viewpoint lifts into the air and our gaze follows, from one horizontal register to another, the ascending and descending sinusoids of a silent score. The eye is projected and floats endlessly in a wholly mental immensity of jagged peaks. In Pier Stockholm's painting, we feel a similar spatial sensation, the same sense of vertigo before what we perceive as an immensity: the viewpoint again seems to rise above these teeming and fluctuating shapes, making us see, as if from the sky, a unique landscape in this ethereal pulverisation of navy-blue paint with its vague contours. A similar atmospheric disruption can be found in Chu Teh-Chun's painting of a nebulous and complex polychromatic landscape, in which the successive brushstrokes and the gaseous substance is reminiscent of the *sfumato* of Leonardo da Vinci, but also of Hans Hartung and Mark Rothko, Chu Teh-Chun's contemporaries. Véronique Joumard's translucent screen, made of assembled Fresnel lenses, filters, modulates, distorts and reverses the image of both the surrounding landscape and the viewers, immersed in a swirling vortex.

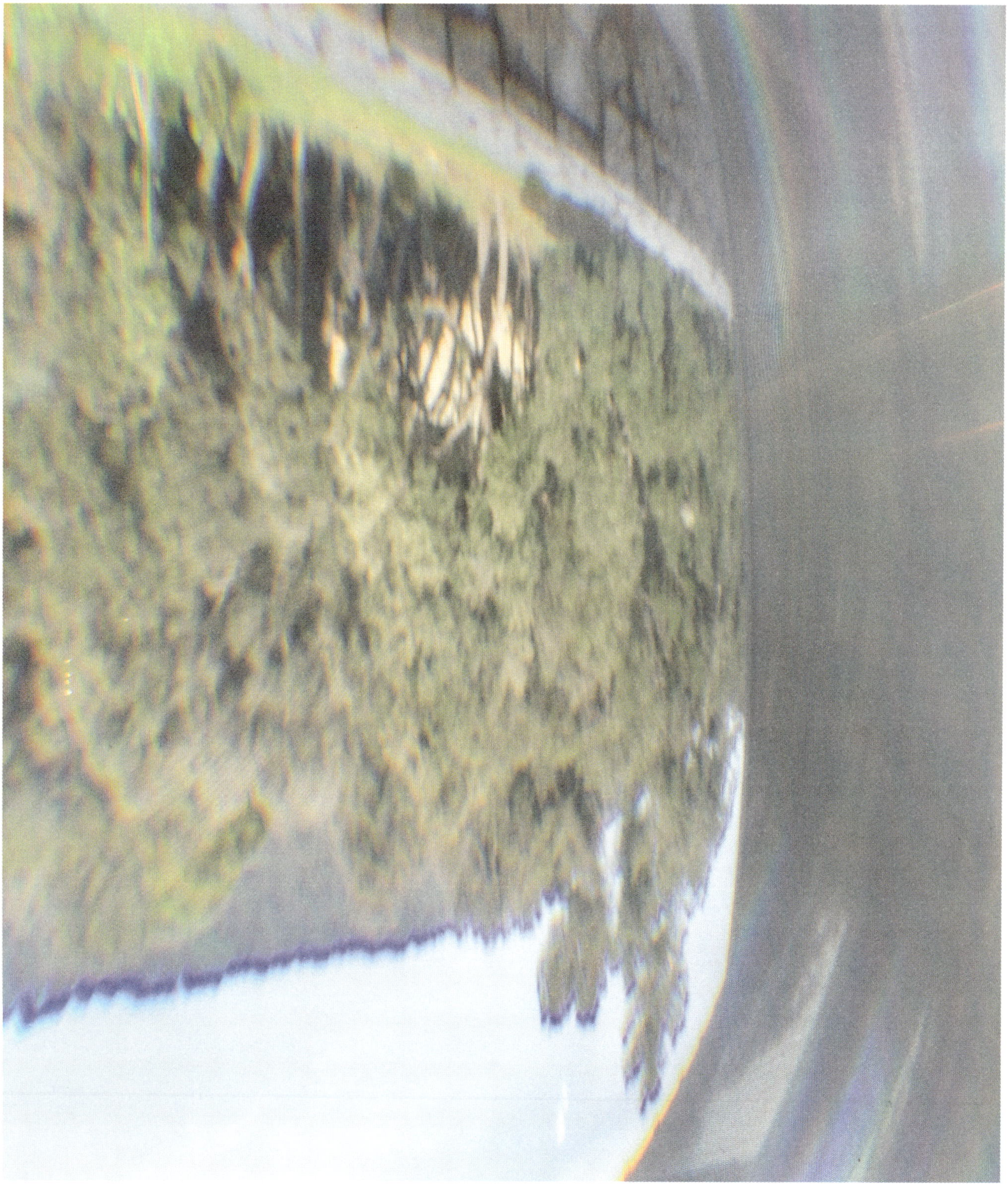

Véronique Joumard, *Paravent* (detail), 2018, steel and Fresnel lens, plexiglas, 180 × 60 × 2 cm

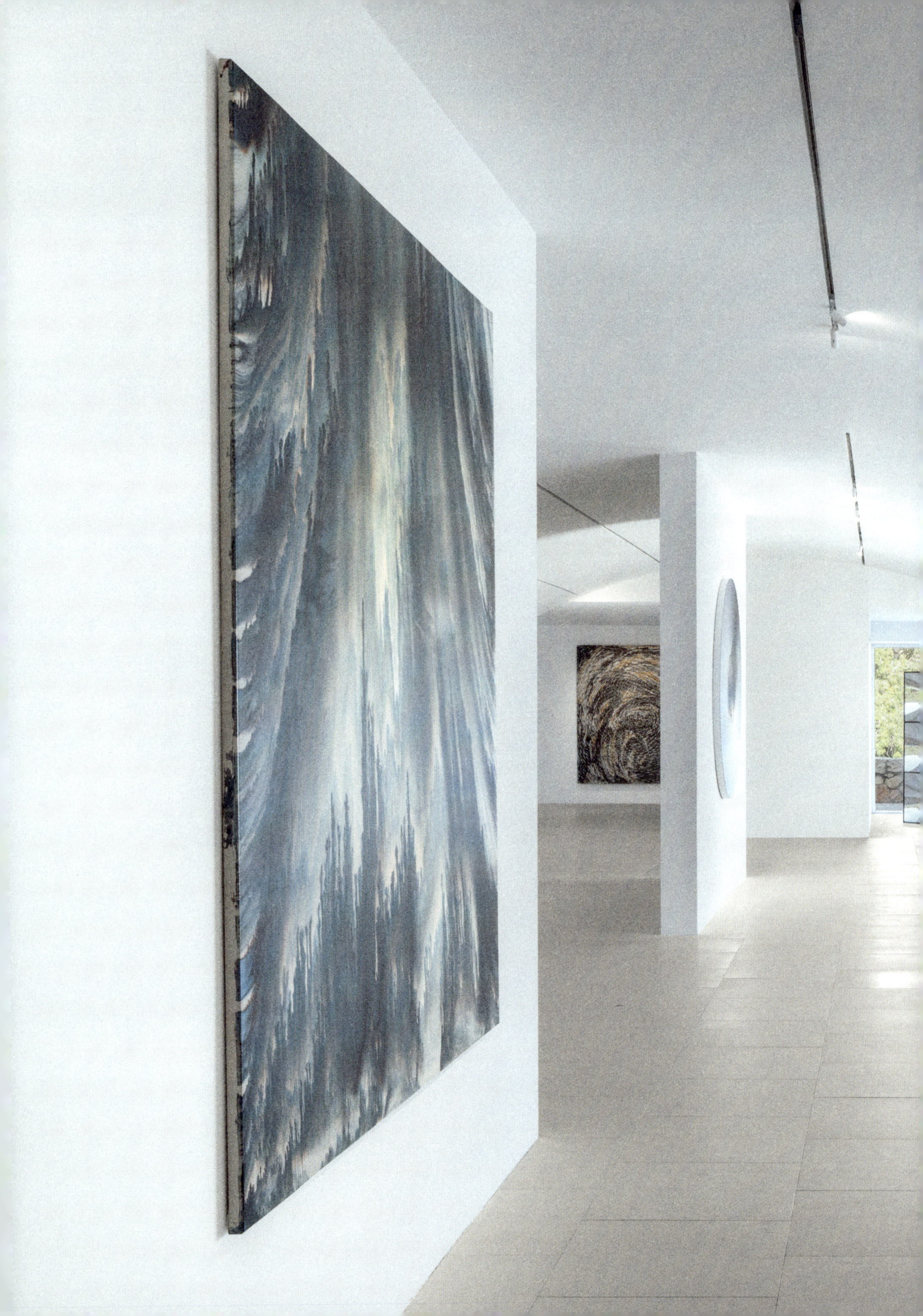

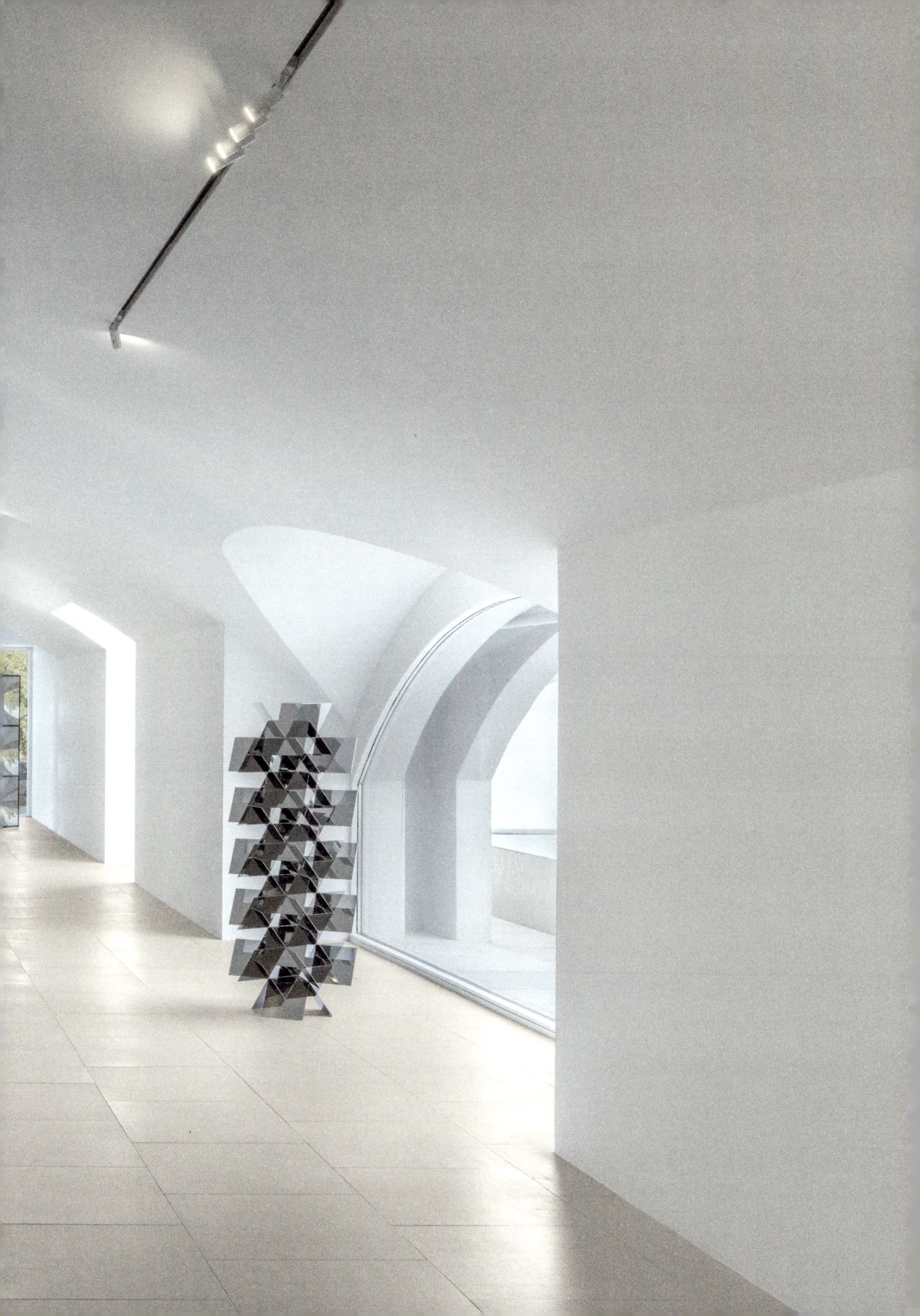

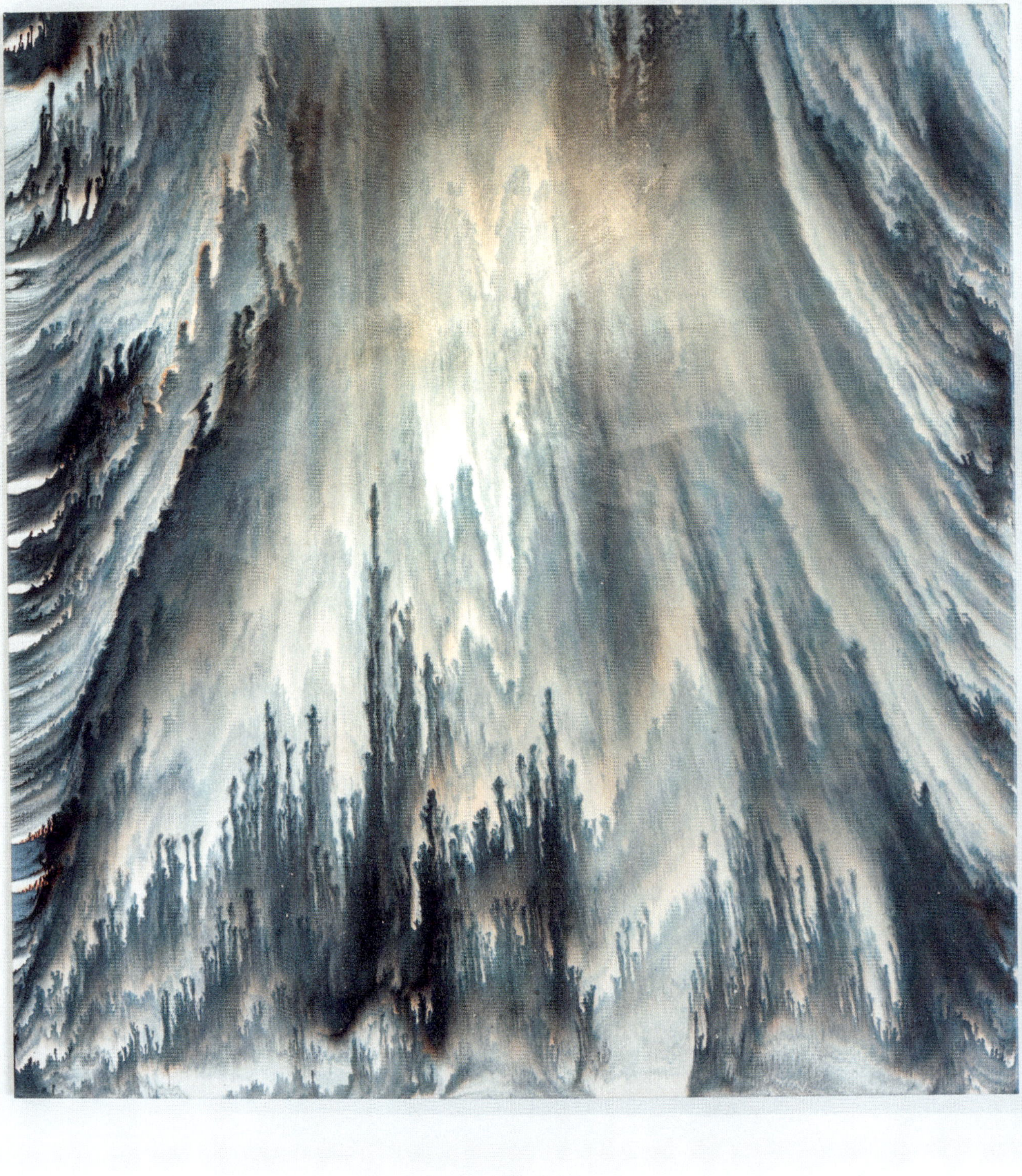

Bernard Frize, *RAMI*, 1993, acrylic, ink, mother-of-pearl and resin on canvas, 205 × 194 cm

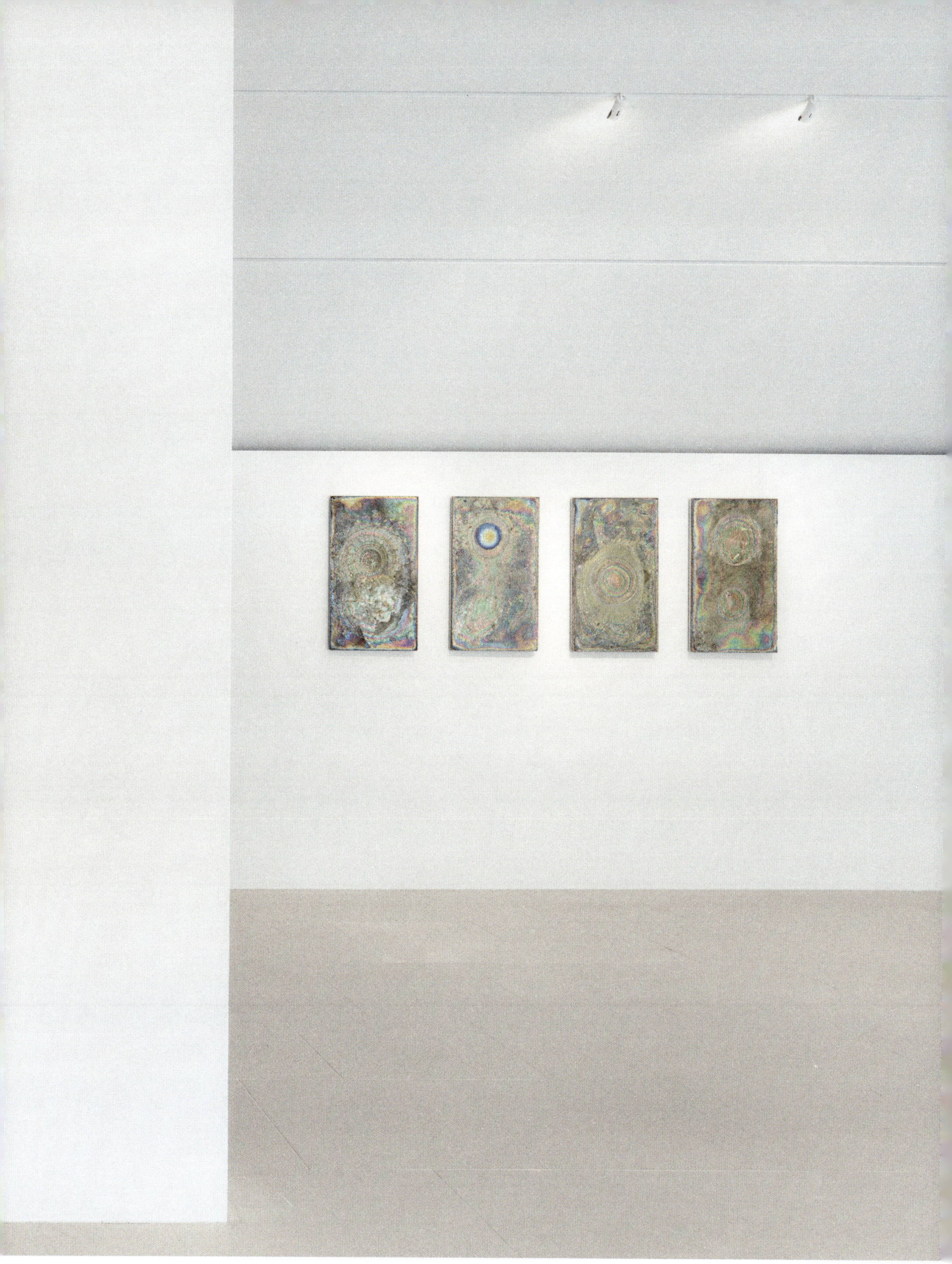

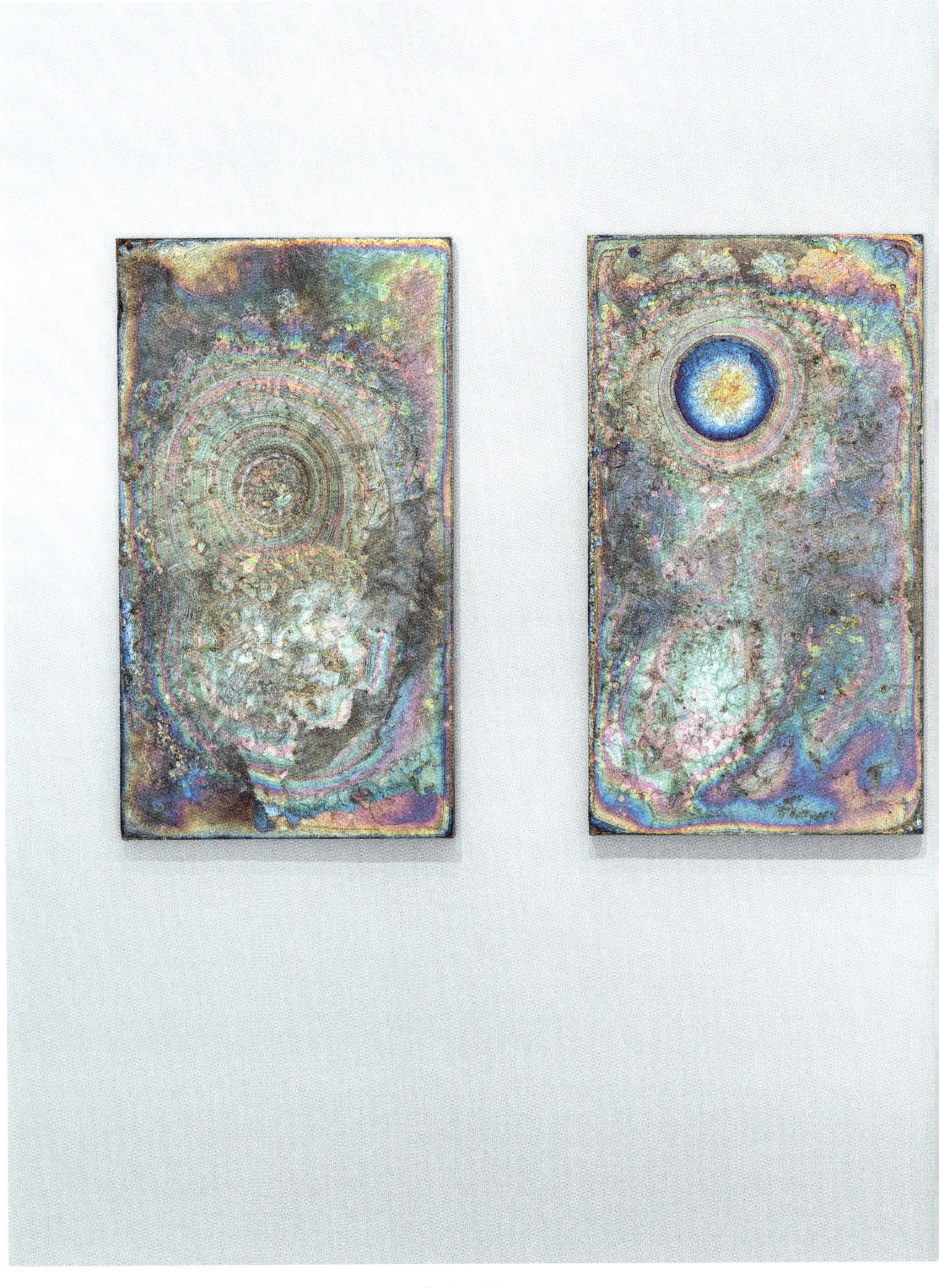

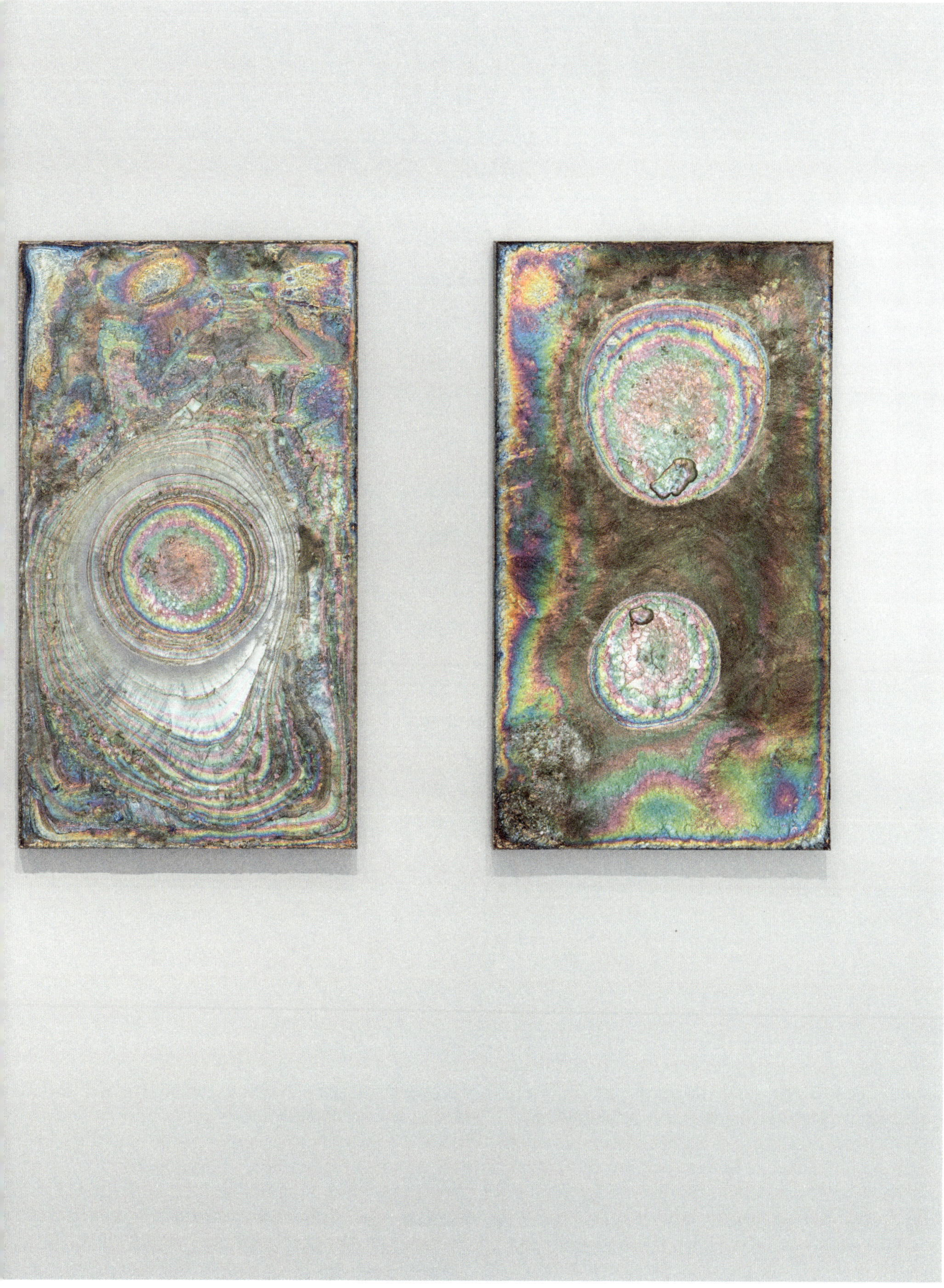

Raphael Hefti, *Exit, pursued by a bear*, 2025, bismuth, 70 × 40 cm each

RAPHAEL HEFTI

(Switzerland, 1978)

Exit, pursued by a bear, 2025

Bismuth
70 × 40 cm each

Raphael Hefti's work could be compared to a failed scientific experiment. It is an exploration of the properties of earthly materials whose uncertain result cannot be said to fulfil any expectation other perhaps than the search for an idea of the sublime. Like an alchemist transforming elements, here he confronts matter in the form of bismuth – a co-product of lead and tungsten metallurgy – melting it and subjecting it to various temperatures in order to create iridescent paintings. Hefti's quasi-industrial oeuvre is also an ode to nature, an exercise aimed at revealing the wonderful. Positioned opposite the Villa's arched window, facing the water ceiling and the garden, the triptych changes according to variations in light, which cause colours to dance across its surface.

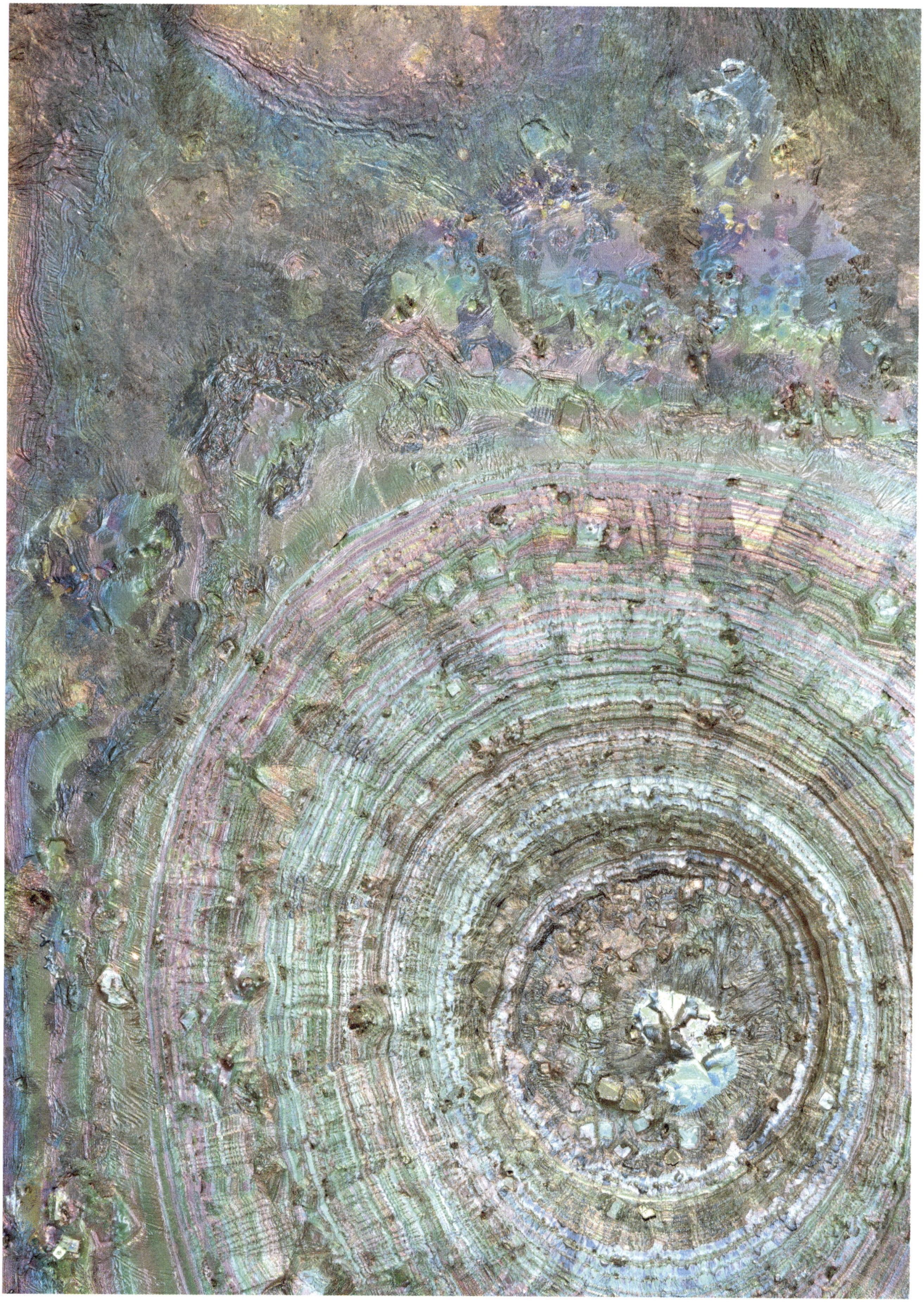

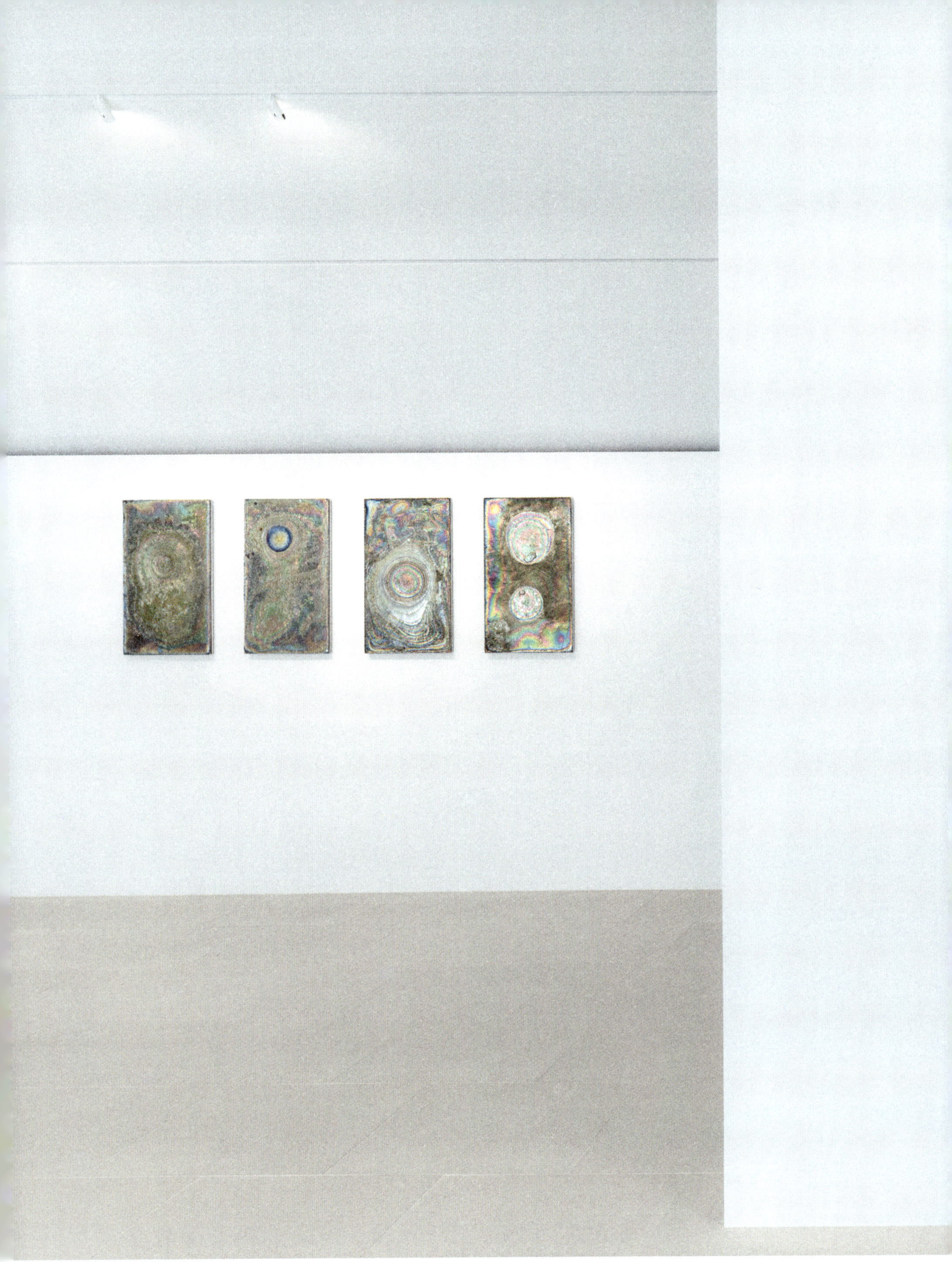

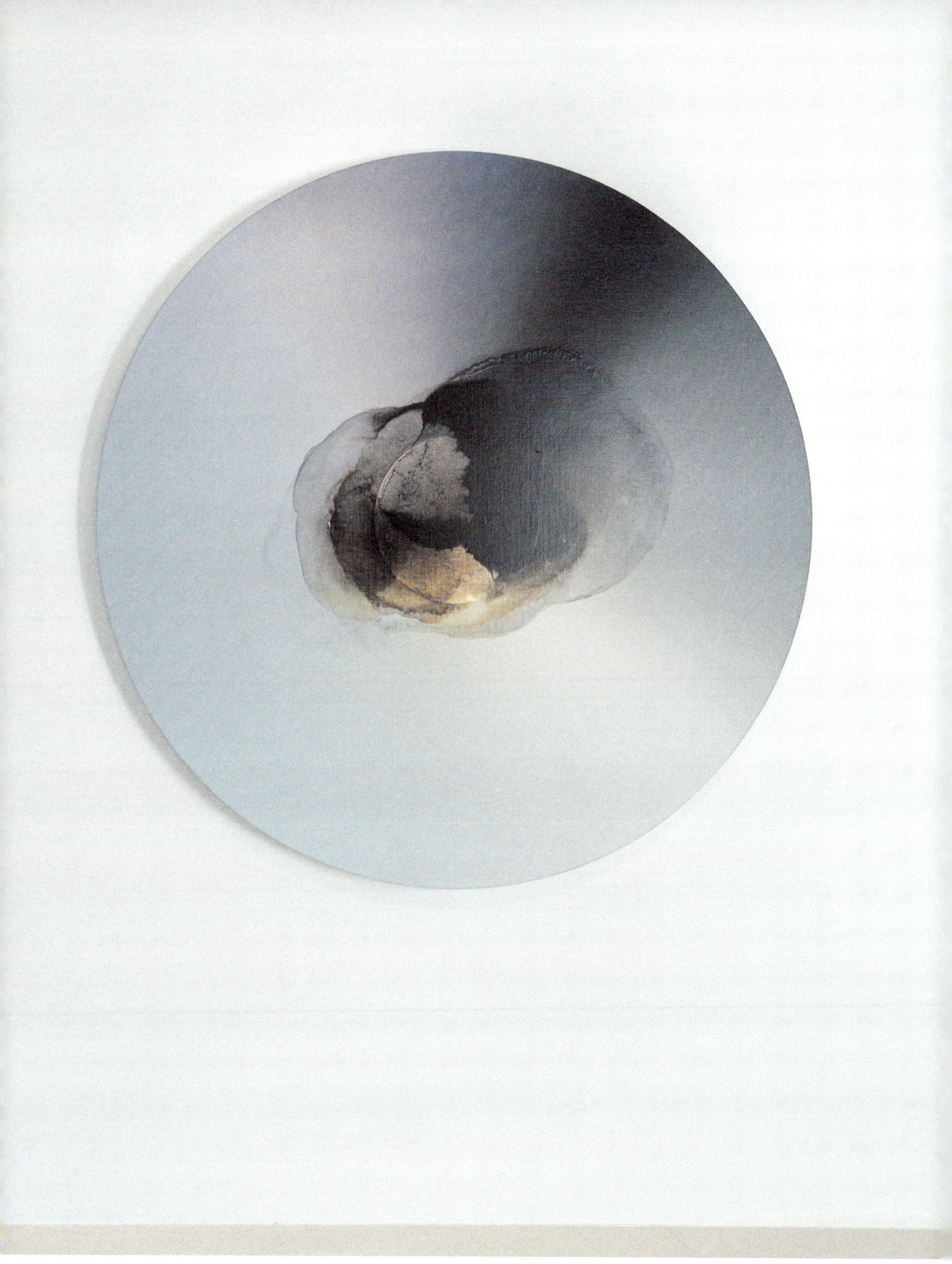

Olafur Eliasson, *Colour experiment no. 118 (Blue Lagoon)*, 2023, acrylic on canvas, diam. 160 cm

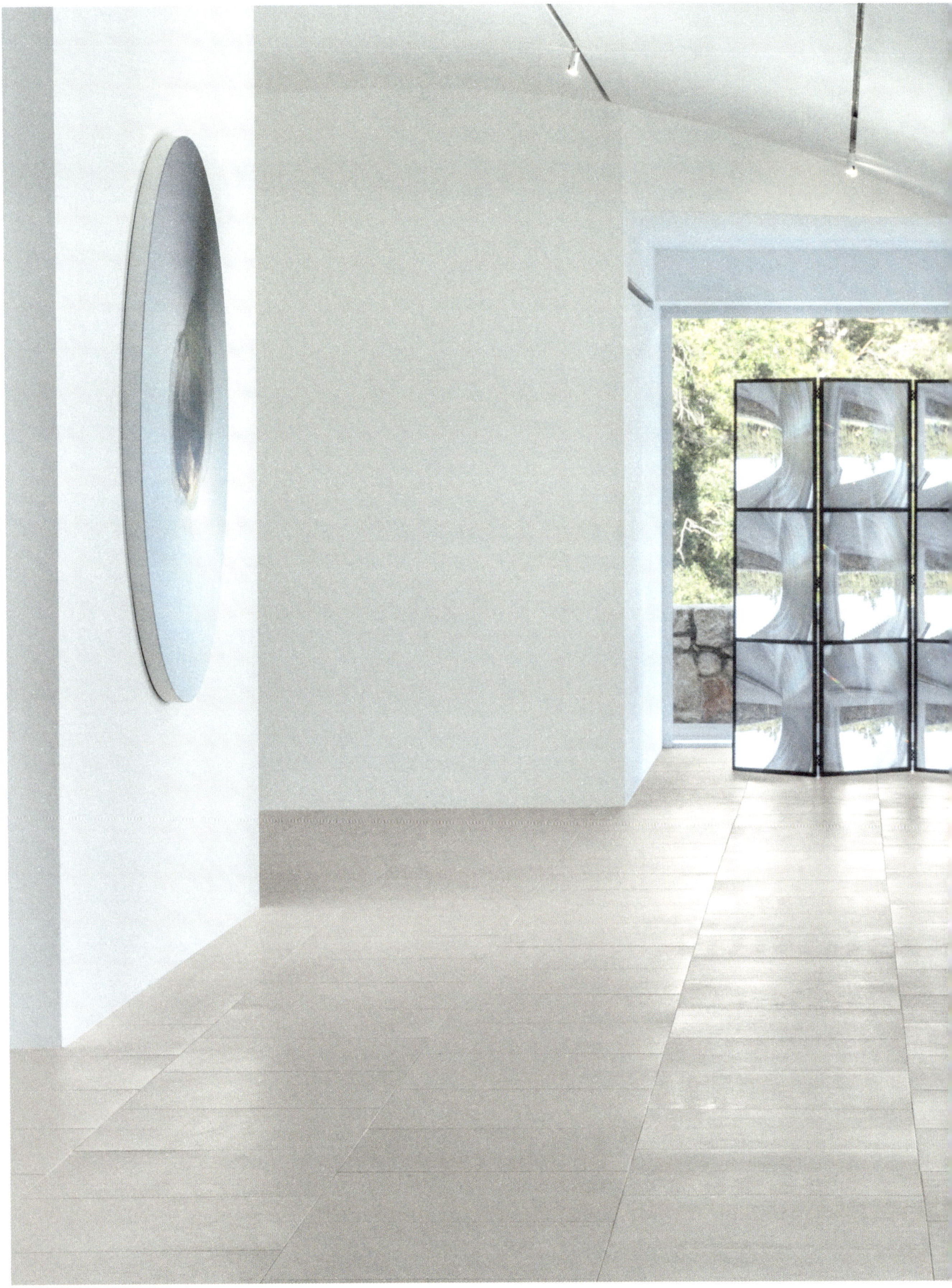

Olafur Eliasson, *Colour experiment no. 118 (Blue Lagoon)*, 2023, acrylic on canvas, diam. 160 cm
Véronique Joumard, *Paravent*, 2018, steel and Fresnel lens, plexiglas, 180 × 60 × 2 cm

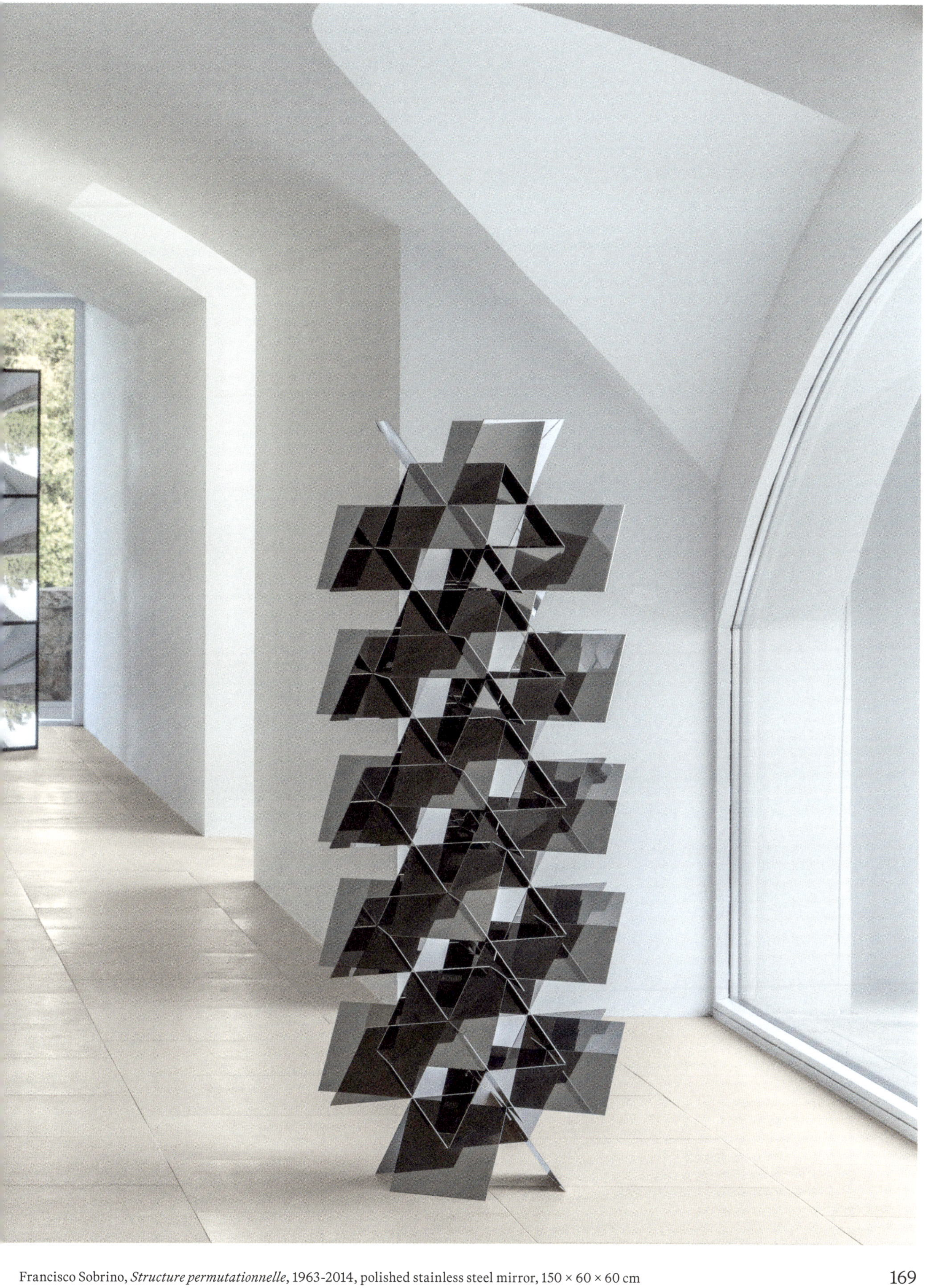

Francisco Sobrino, *Structure permutationnelle*, 1963-2014, polished stainless steel mirror, 150 × 60 × 60 cm

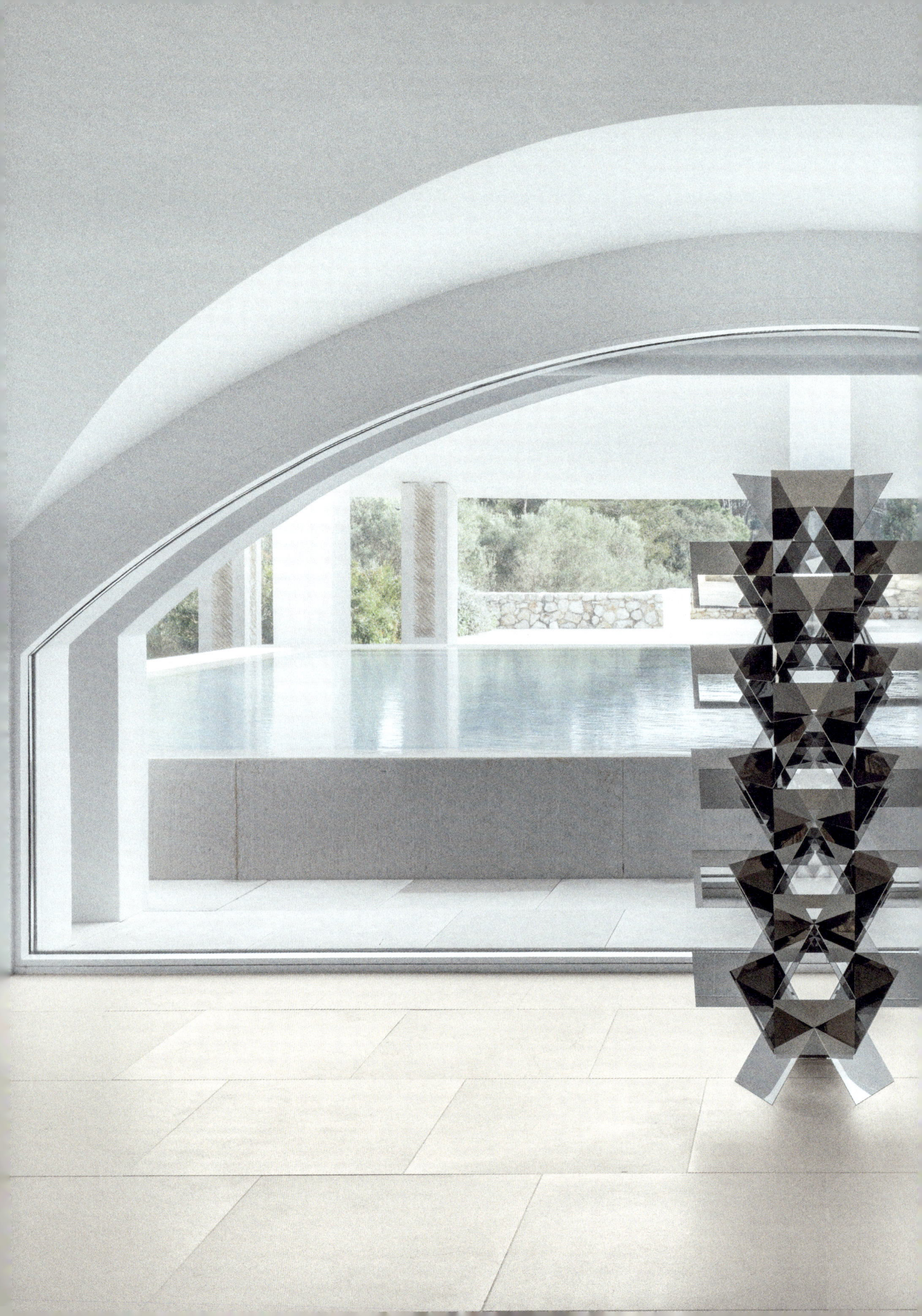

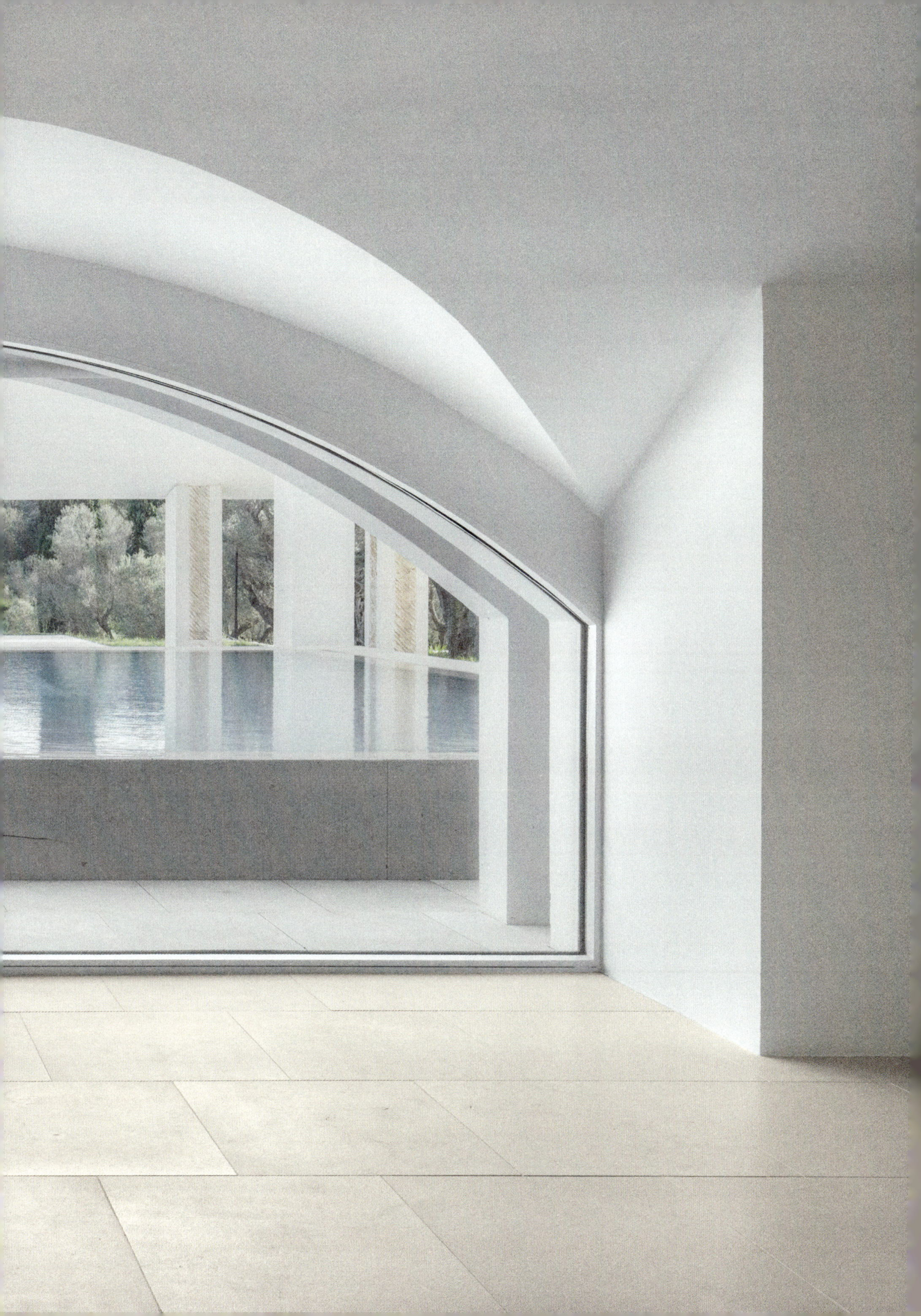

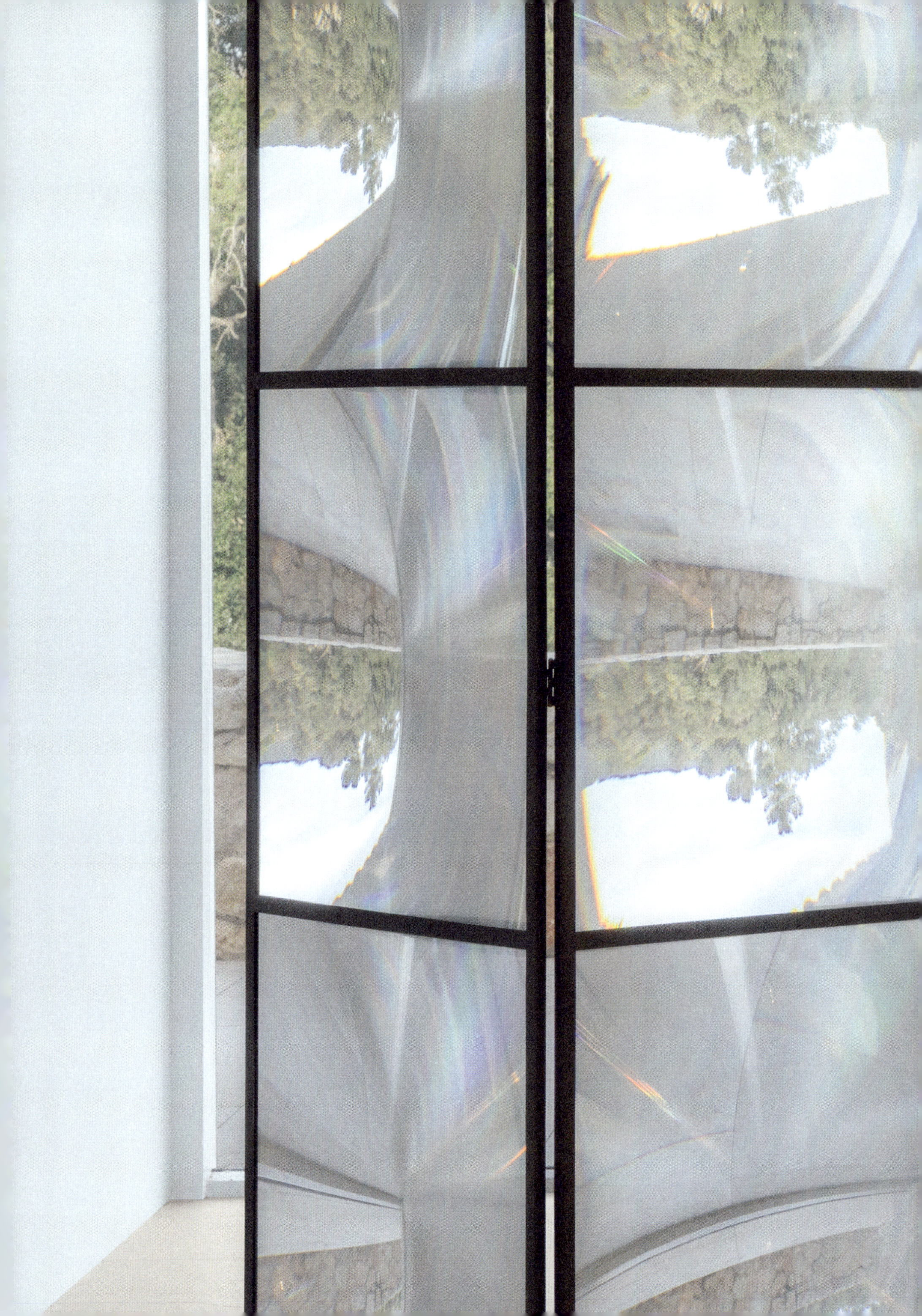

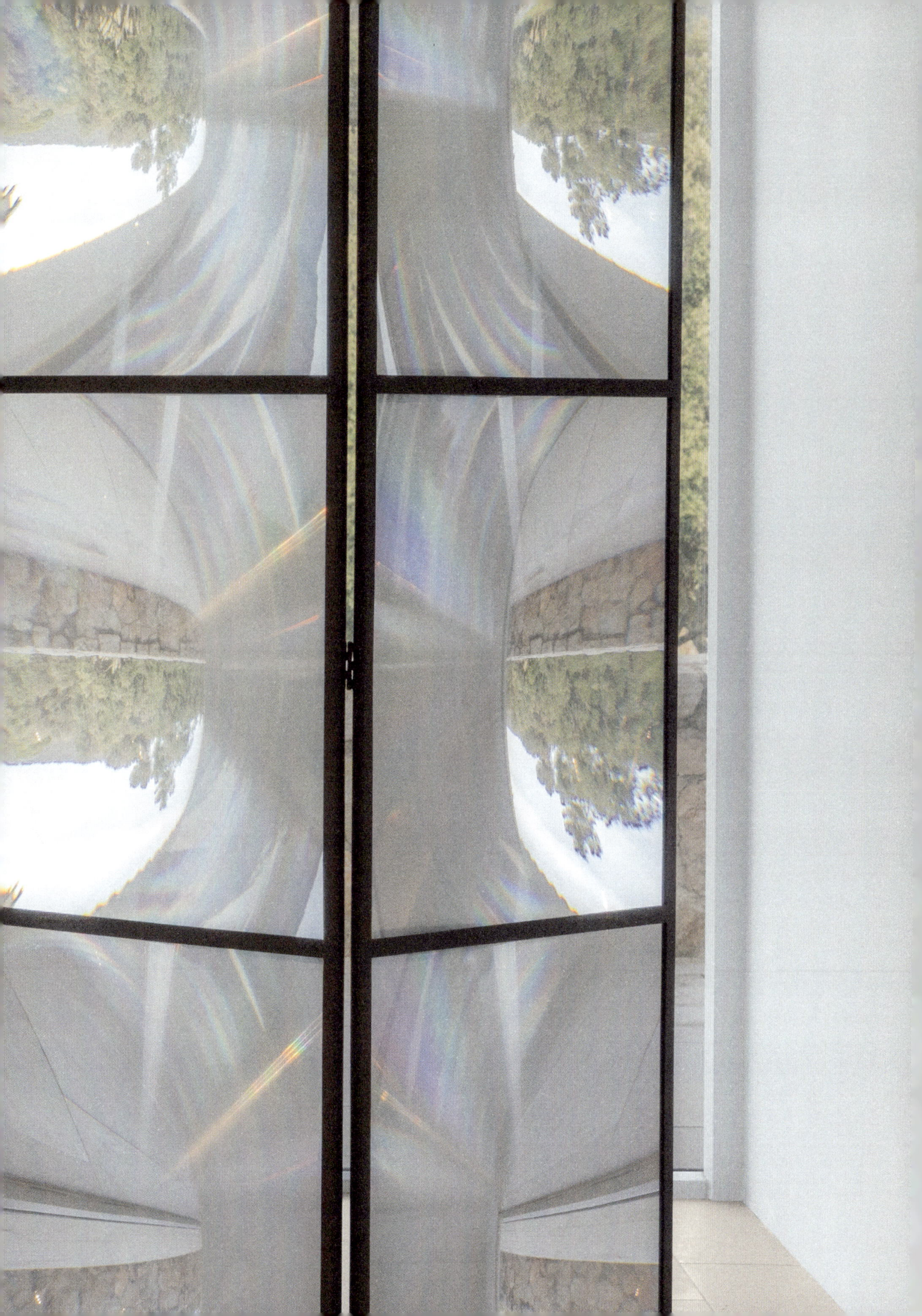

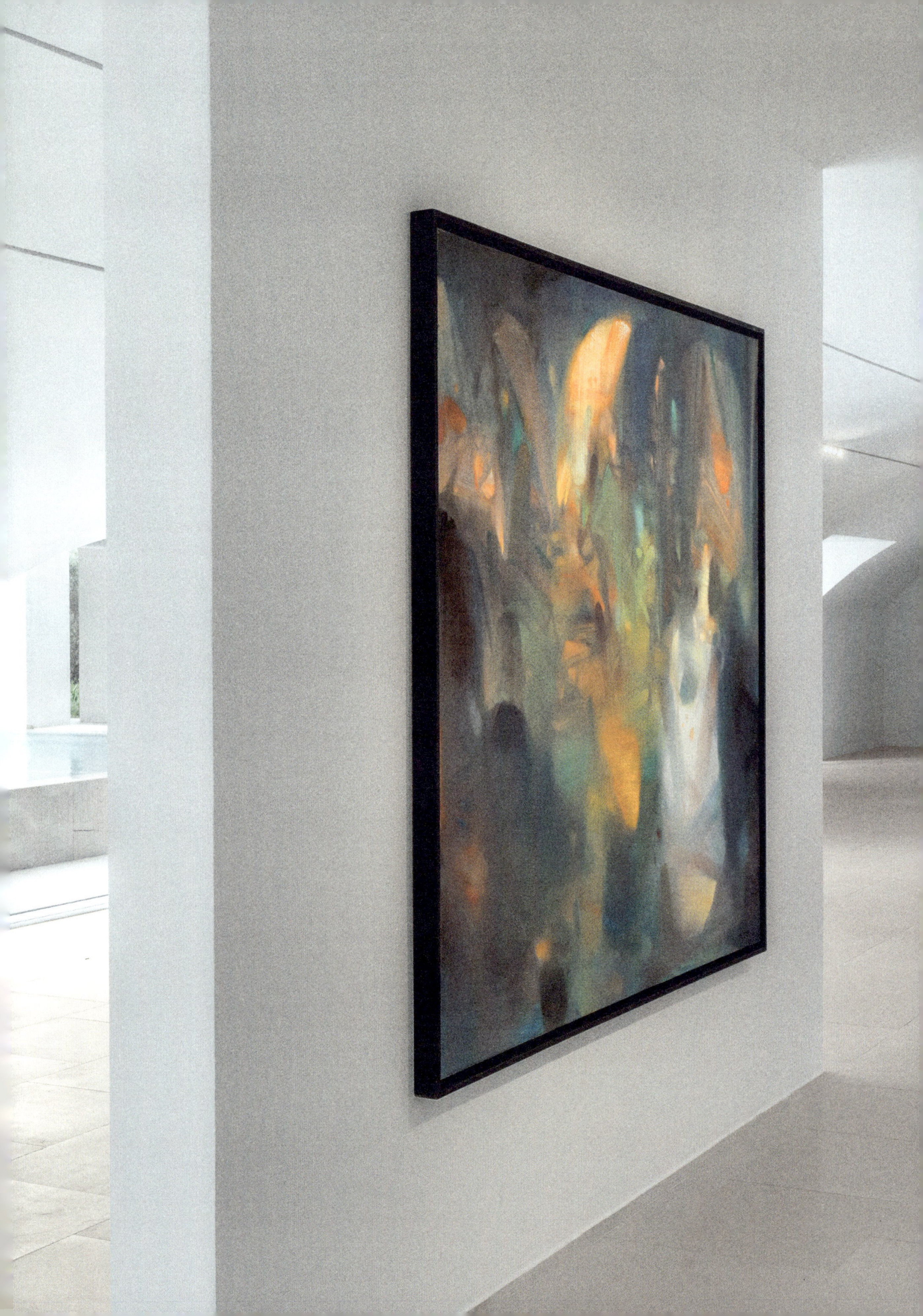

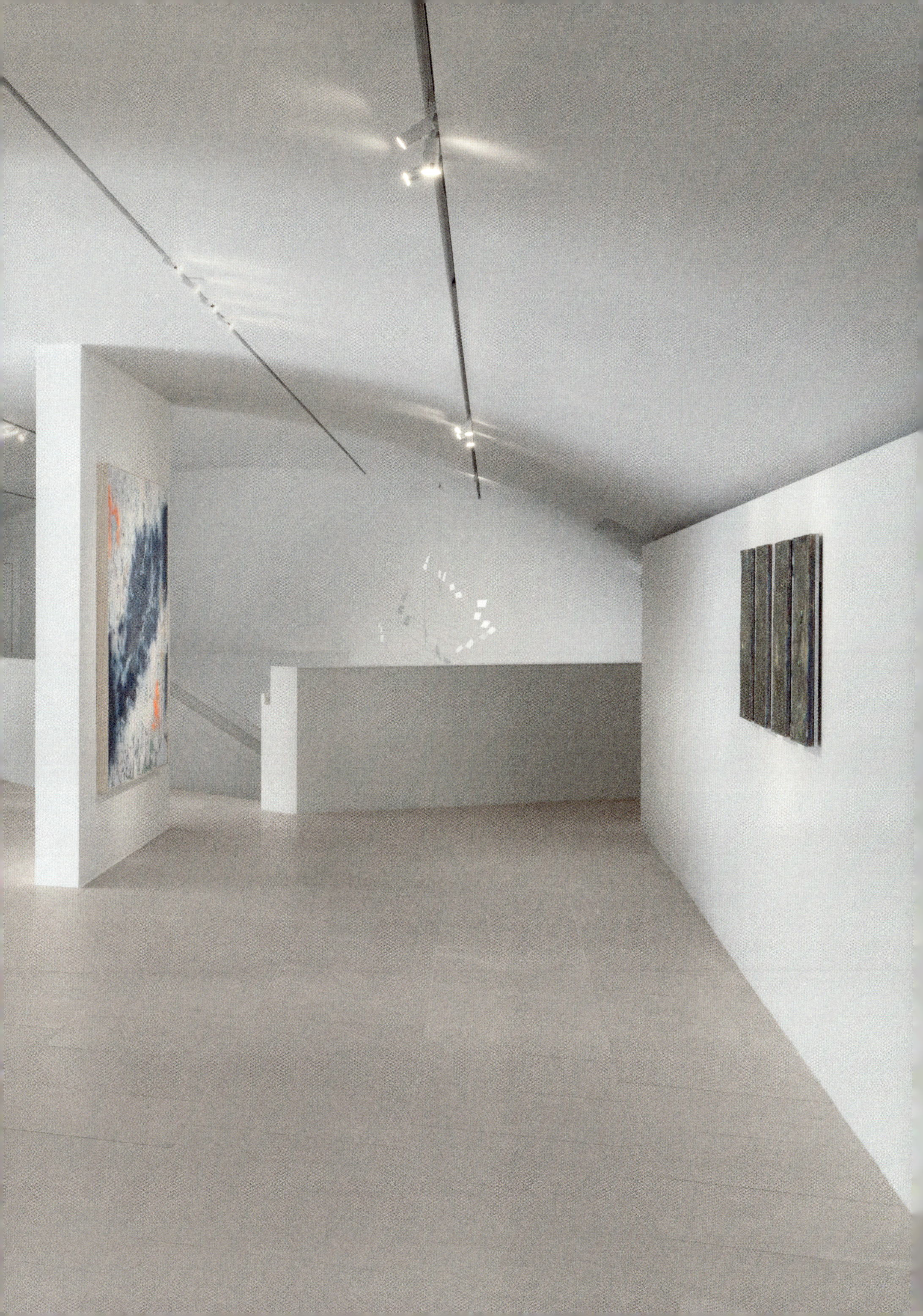

Chu Teh-Chun, *Mémoire du regard*, 1989, oil on canvas, 180 × 200 cm

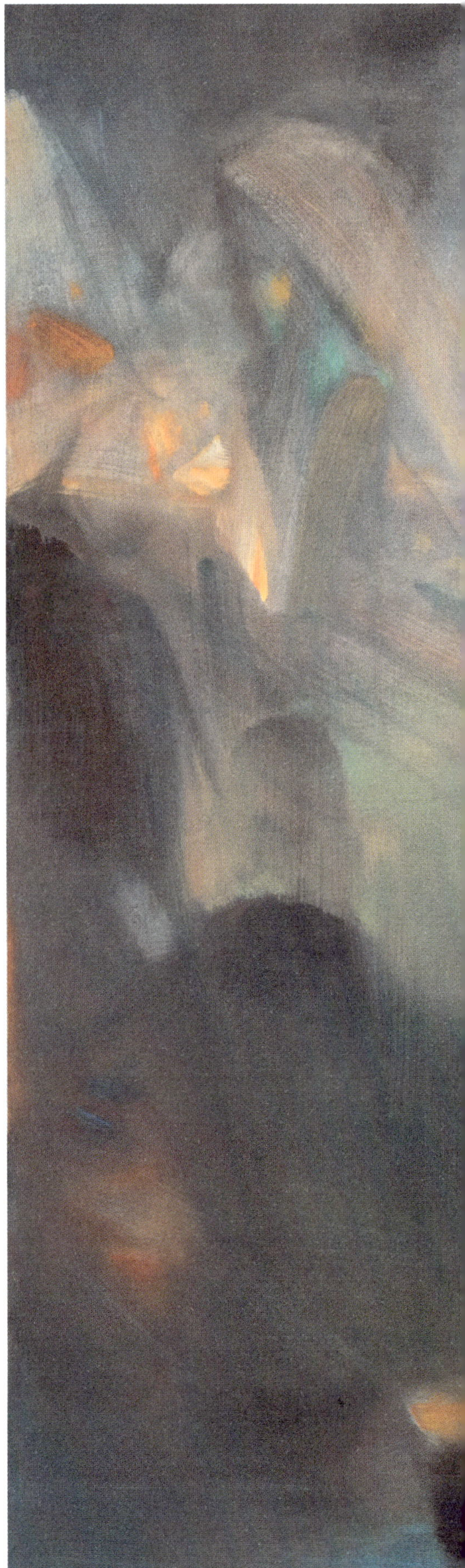

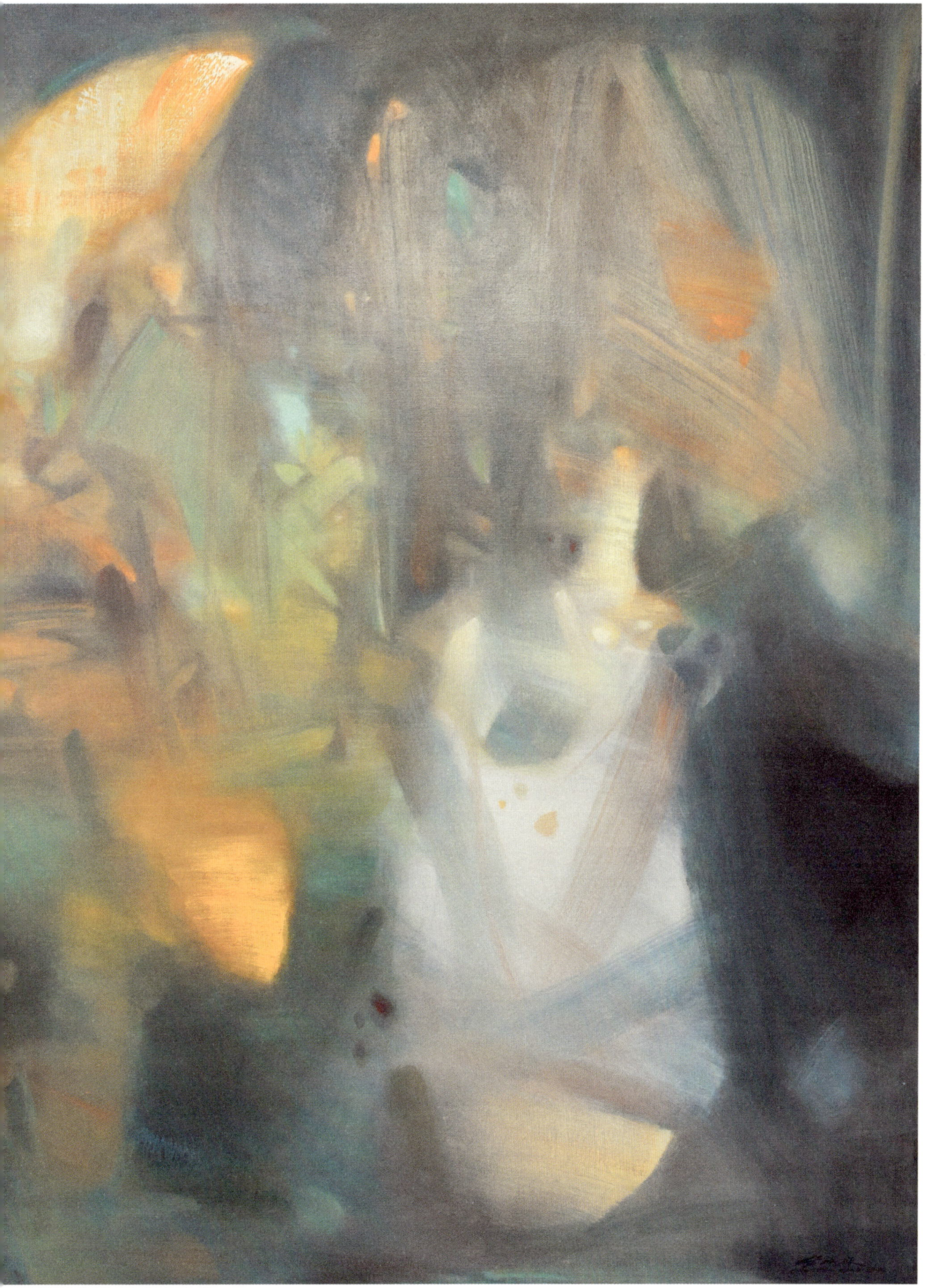

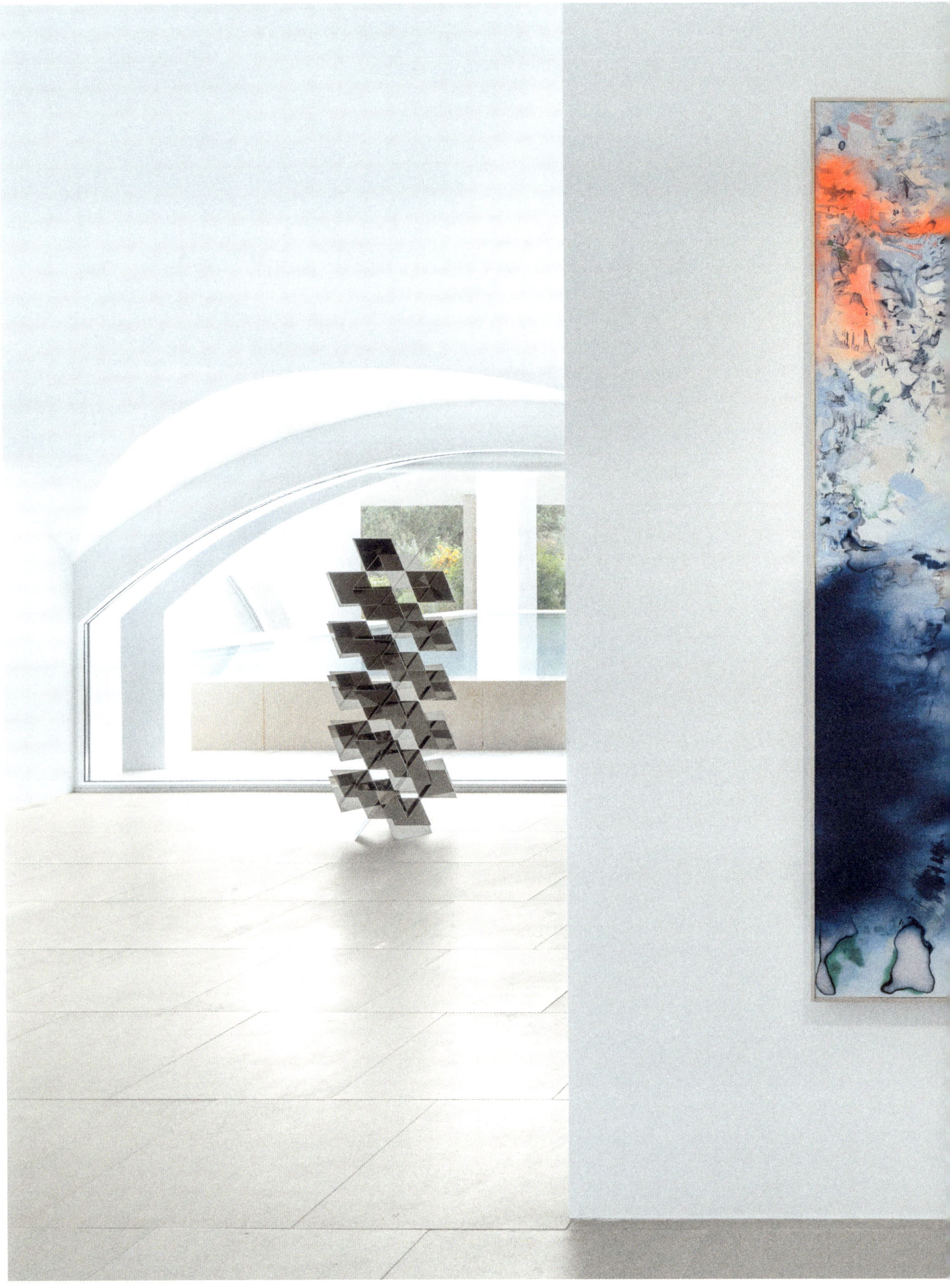

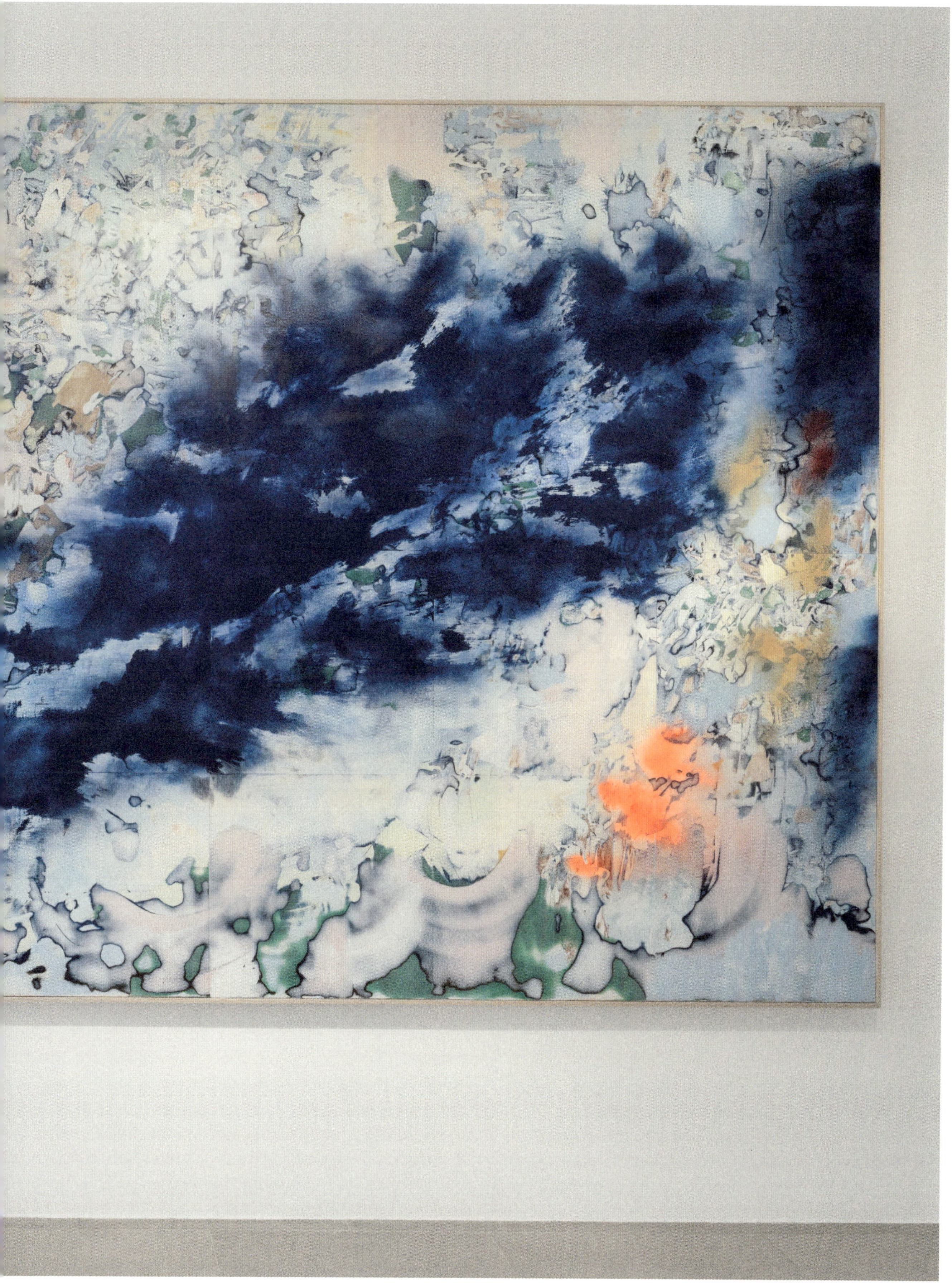

Pier Stockholm, *Ygor XLI*, 2025, ink, polyester putty for cars, paint and plywood, 190 × 240 cm

PIER STOCKHOLM

(Peru, 1977)

Ygor XLI, 2025

Ink, polyester putty for cars, paint and plywood
190 × 240 cm

Created especially for the exhibition, Pier Stockholm's painting seems to be inviting us to plunge into a vertiginous abyss that ruptures the surface of his work. We are positioned above the action, levitating, a witness to what resembles a geological movement: rocks undergoing transformation, a landscape being created. Particularly interested in gestures and materials, the artist conveys an impression of chaos through vigorous movements, sprayed paint and sanded wood, while structuring his composition by means of rigorous lines that outline the forms. His work often expresses the duality that brings to life singular landscapes and endows them with a cathartic force.

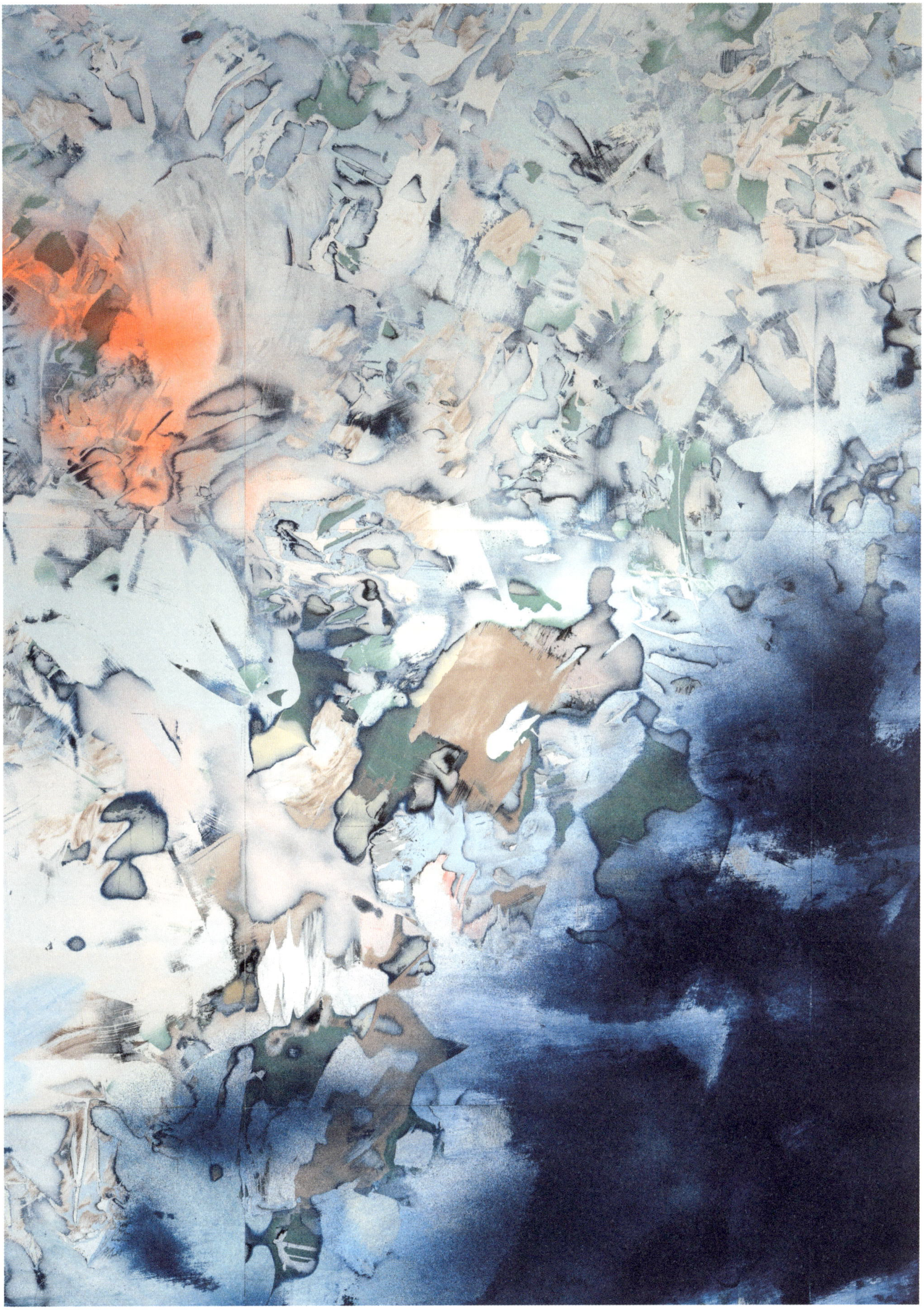

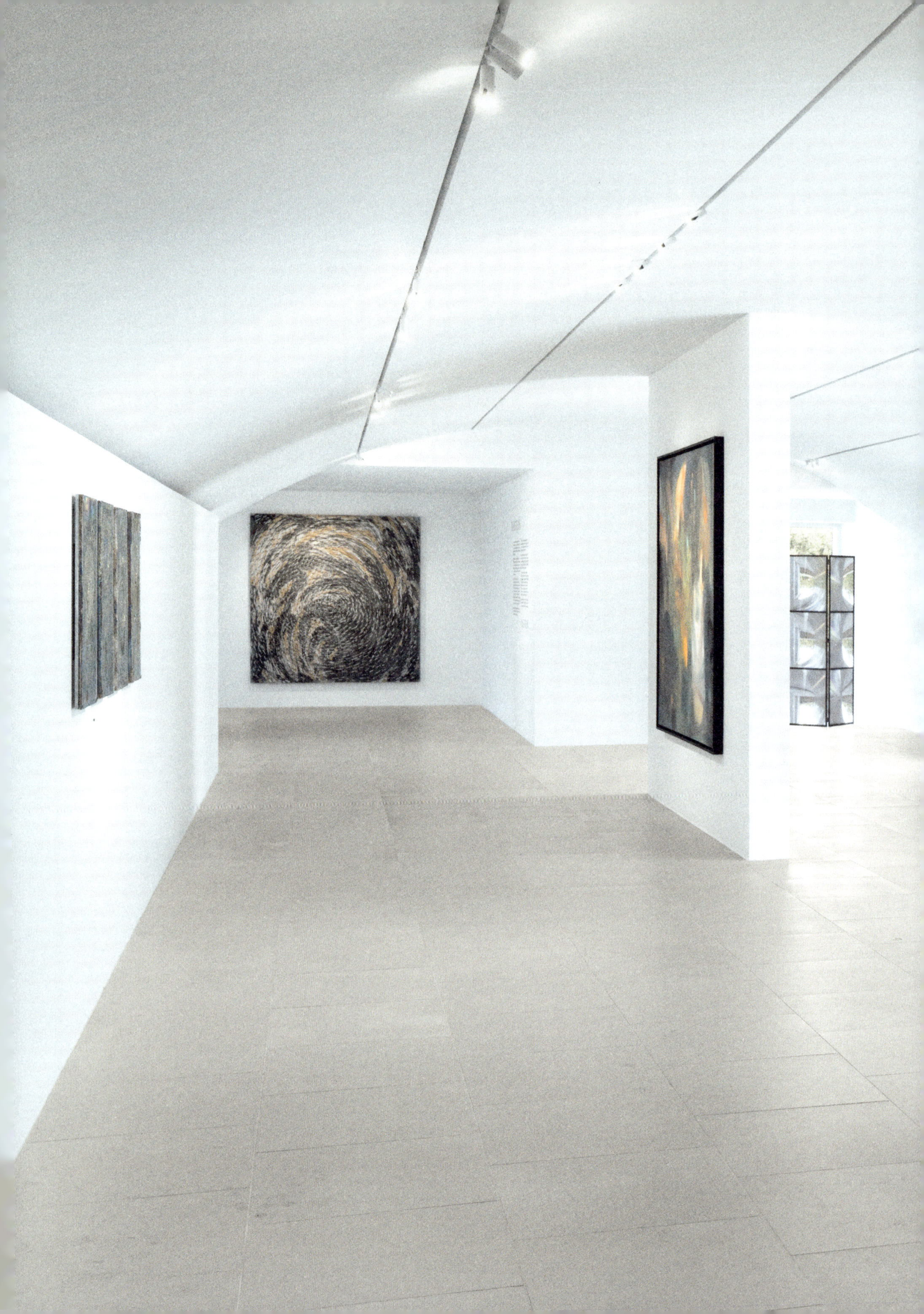

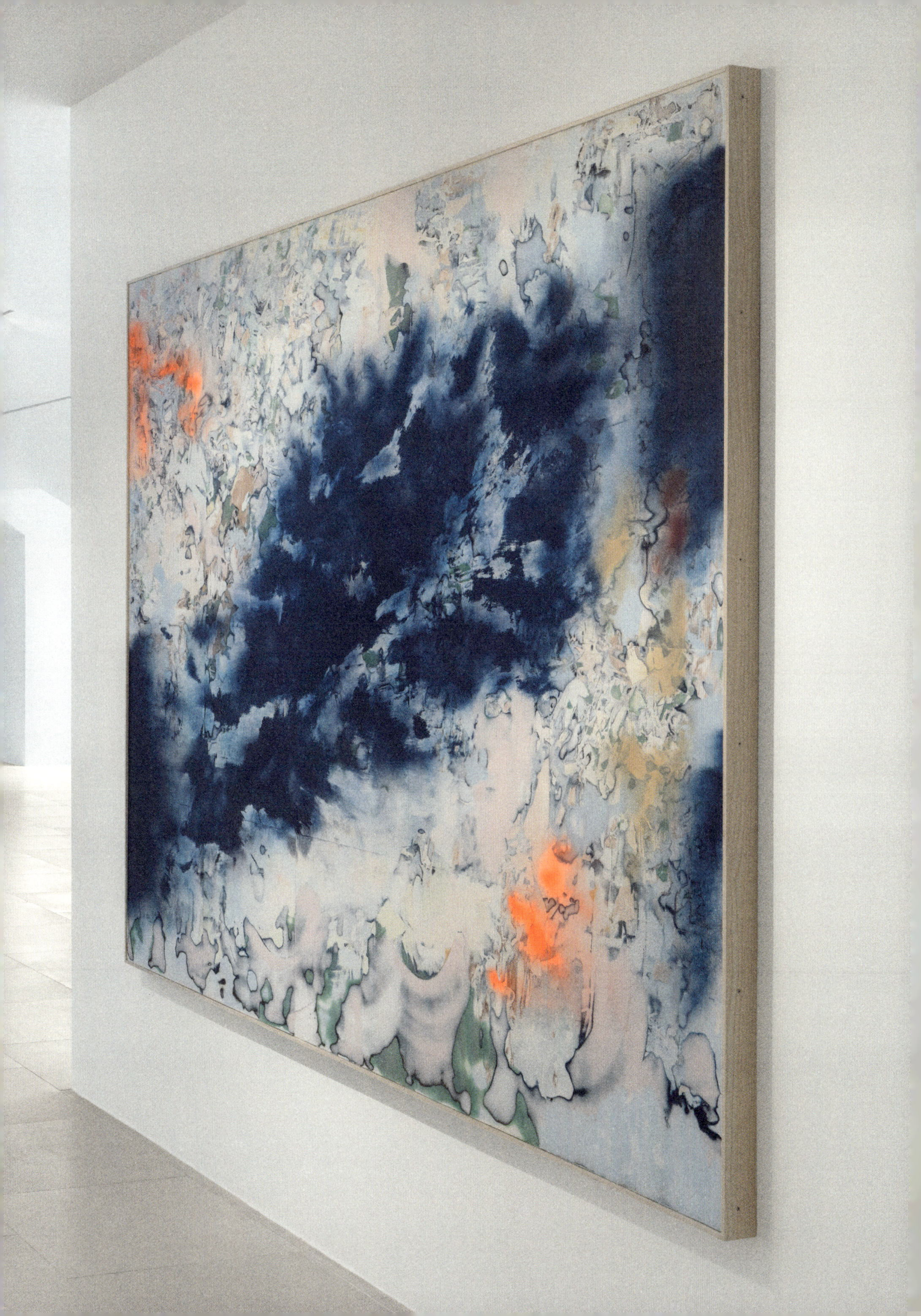

MAELSTROMS

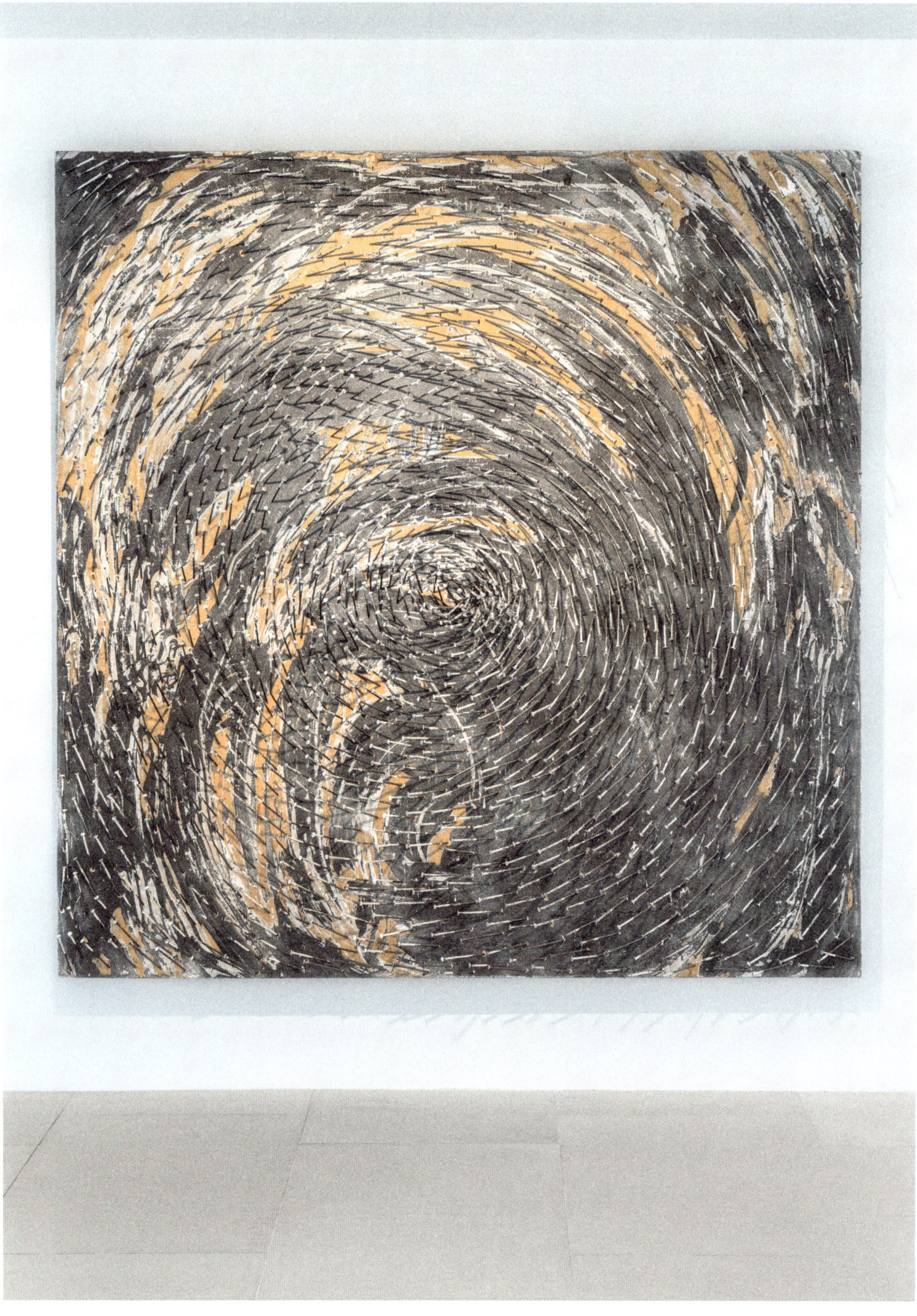

To capture the gaze and draw it into the very depths of the artwork, some artists dynamically channel and express matter in the moving forms of vortices, maelstroms or auroras through the intercession of pictorial gestures or even sound waves. By using sound waves to shift pigments, Oliver Beer creates concentric patterns that sometimes evoke tornadoes seen from the sky and at other times a hypnotic gaze. Fabienne Verdier unites the two panels of a vertical diptych through a spiral drawn with a large brush in a sweeping gesture. This dynamic movement is reinforced by the sole use of blue and green pigments that are both deeply coloured and luminous, with intense optical contrast. Günther Uecker catches the eye with an optical vortex, this time made with a little paint and many nails, positioned in diagonal lines or in a spiral, as if blown flat by a powerful wind. In her painting, Thu-Van Tran presents drips and colourful clouds in a polychromatic symphony. Unusual pigments, combined with lime, seem to evaporate and, in an interplay of transparency and opacity, create a dense, almost suffocating atmosphere that is established through successive screens and several overlaid layers. These artists are actually laying traps, drawing our eye into a substance animated by continual formal and chromatic mutation. Although the form of the painting remains, it is only a frame, the perimeter around a complex maelstrom, where the eye, lost in a kind of telluric limbo, is consumed in the raging substance.

The artworks in this section, exhibited in the final gallery of the Villa, bring this visit to a close, interspersed with optical experiments, where the gaze has been tossed around and set off balance, blinded by light, gone astray among the clouds or projected to the heart of different phenomena. Which is exactly how two artworks converse with the natural spaces around them. The sculpture in the round by Francisco Sobrino, made of interlocking squares of polished steel, forms a faceted and reflective tower that, like a kaleidoscope, picks up, breaks up and reflects its human, architectural and landscaped environment. Another artwork by Olafur Eliasson, which is made up of colourful spheres, follows the laws of dioptrics, which deal with light refraction. These multiple spheres are placed on the wall opposite the windows. Their surfaces reflect, diffract and, most importantly, alter the Villa's architectural and exterior landscape. Although the artworks twist our own image as they send it back to us, they also and especially disrupt real space and time (depending on our changing perspective): viewers, buildings, the sea, earth, sky, clouds and heavenly bodies thus directly contribute to the variable and phenomenon-based existence of the artwork.

Previous page: Oliver Beer, *Resonance Painting (Lovesong)* (detail), 2024, pigments on canvas, 200 × 150 cm
Günther Uecker, *Spirale I*, 2002, paint, latex, graphite and nails on wood panel, 200 × 200 × 16 cm

For these artists, the artwork must echo a vertiginous contemplation of nature and its phenomena. This awareness developed very early on for Heinz Mack, notably after an experience he had in 1950: aged nineteen, he went to Bordeaux for the first time to visit his father's grave, a German soldier who had died during the war. Immediately afterwards, he decided to go to the ocean, which he had never before seen with his own eyes. Once on the coast, he noticed a strange phenomenon: the vibrating reflection of the sun's rays on the moving surface of the ocean seemed to detach from its liquid foundation and float in the air like a mirage. This event, which was both a visual and natural occurrence, struck him as an epiphany, and it formed the aesthetic cornerstone of his many luminous reliefs (such as those exhibited here, in the sections "Atmospheric Turbulence" and "The Threshold, the Mirage and the Abyss") and of much of his career. It was also a key moment in perceptual art. On the modest paper artwork presented in *Vertigo*, we can see two horizontal and overlaid grids, drawn in pencil. One is made up of straight lines and the other of serrated lines. The visual interference, between them and against the white background, generates a subtle optical vibration and an ambiguity that increases the gradual attenuation of the stroke in the upper part. Made in 1950, it is the oldest piece in this exhibition. It concludes our path through the Villa, while the extensive wall painting by Flora Moscovici, the most recent piece in the exhibition, one made for the occasion, welcomed us at the very beginning. All that now remains is to retrace our steps, or discover the final section, "Fields of Vision", in the grounds of the Fondation.

Fabienne Verdier, *Ti ricorda il primo amor*, 2020, acrylic and mixed techniques on canvas, 212 × 137 cm

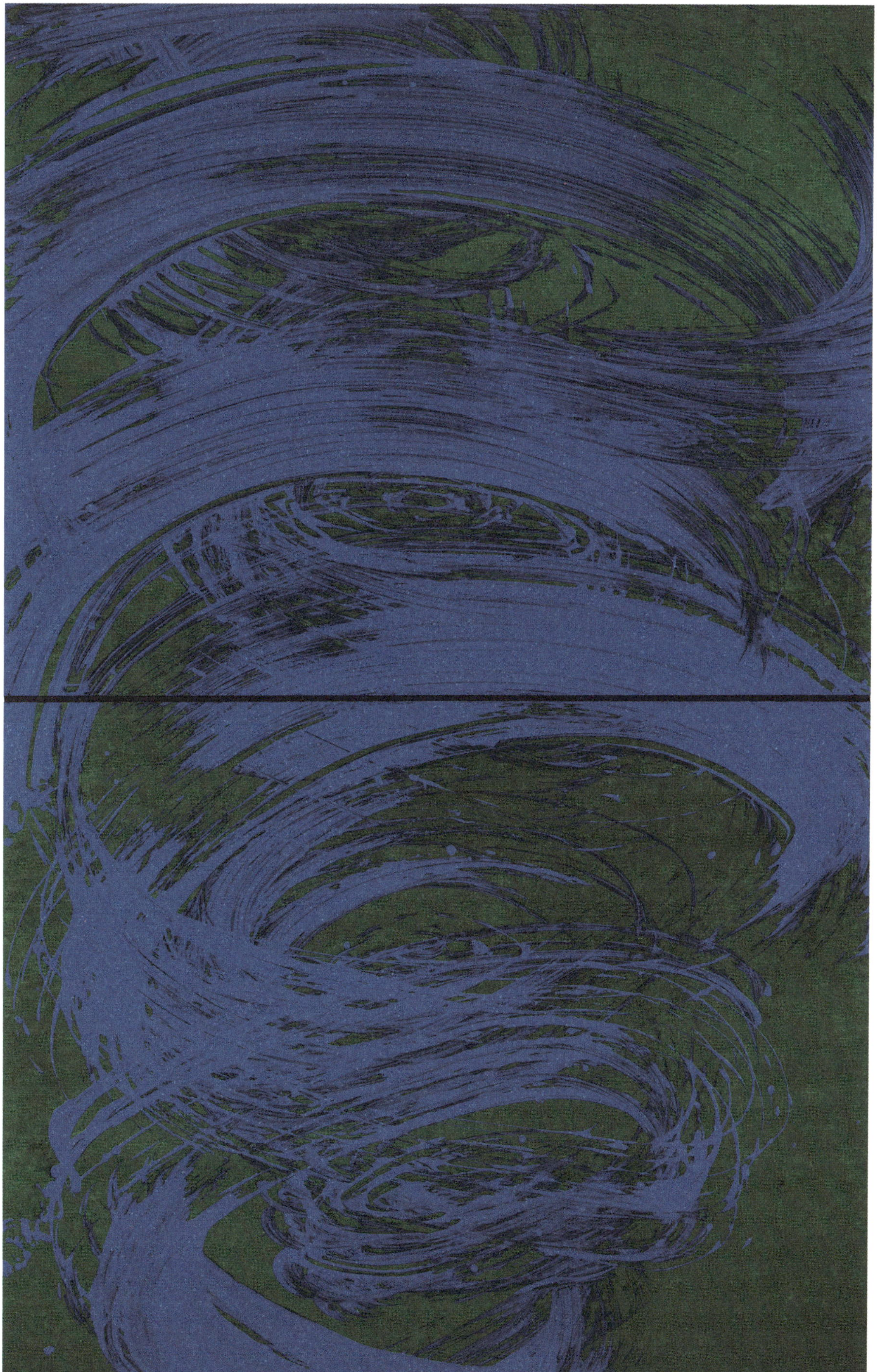

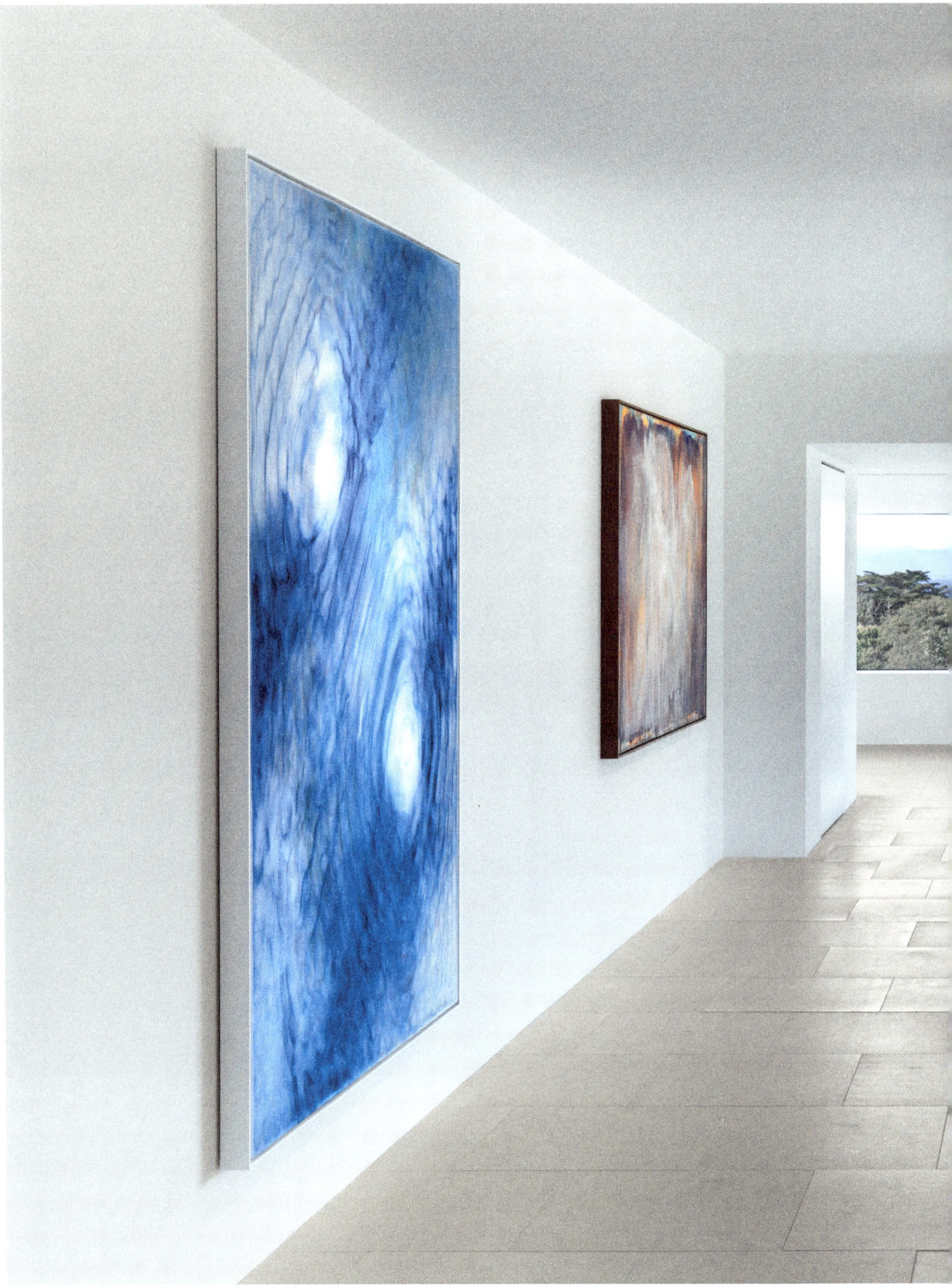

Oliver Beer, *Resonance Painting (Lovesong)*, 2024, pigments on canvas, 200 × 150 cm
Thu-Van Tran, *Les Couleurs du gris*, 2025, whitewash and pigments on linen canvas, 130 × 195 cm

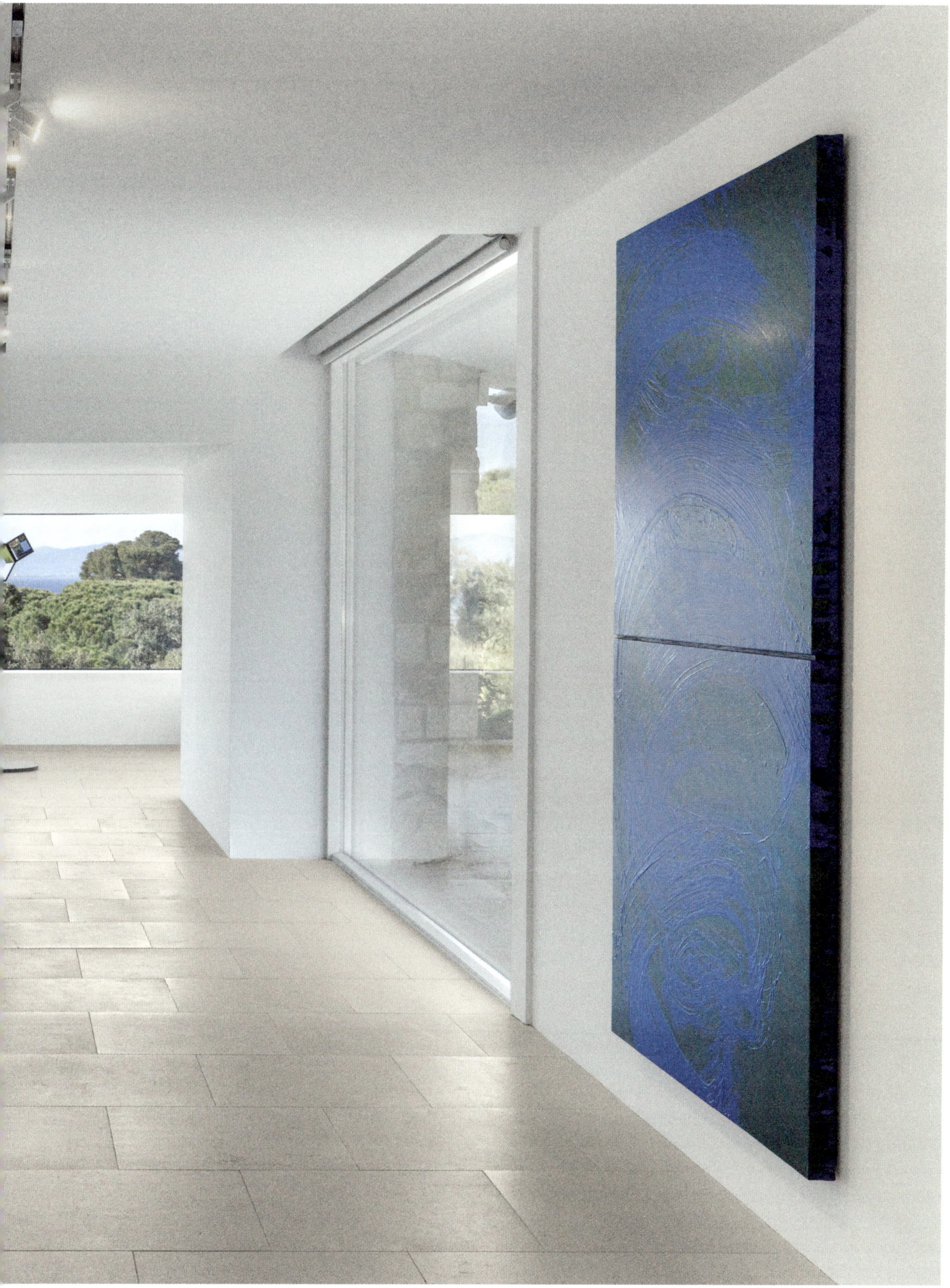

Olafur Eliasson, *Your vanishing*, 2011, bronze, filtered glass with a coloured effect (blue, pink, cyan, yellow), mirror, stainless steel, paint (black), 181 × 70 × 70 cm. Fabienne Verdier, *Ti ricorda il primo amor*, 2020, acrylic and mixed techniques on canvas, 212 × 137 cm

OLIVER BEER

(United Kingdom, 1985)

Resonance Painting (Lovesong), 2024

Pigments on canvas
200 × 150 cm

At first sight the work seems to resemble the rippling surface of an expanse of water, with concentric circles spreading across the canvas.
In reality, the artist invites us to discover a landscape with motifs composed by sound. The works in the *Resonance Painting* series were produced by means of acoustic resonances, with a loudspeaker being placed beneath the horizontal canvas, creating vibrations that give shape to the work. The sound moves the air, which causes the pigment to move: "the sound becomes the brush", revealing undulating blue forms on the surface of the canvas. Inspired by Claude Monet and the way that atmosphere changes light, Oliver Beer toys with our perception by transforming what we see by what we hear. Imagine a landscape that is formed not only of colours and atmosphere, but also of sound, made up of waves and vibrations, with each note possessing its own geometric signature.

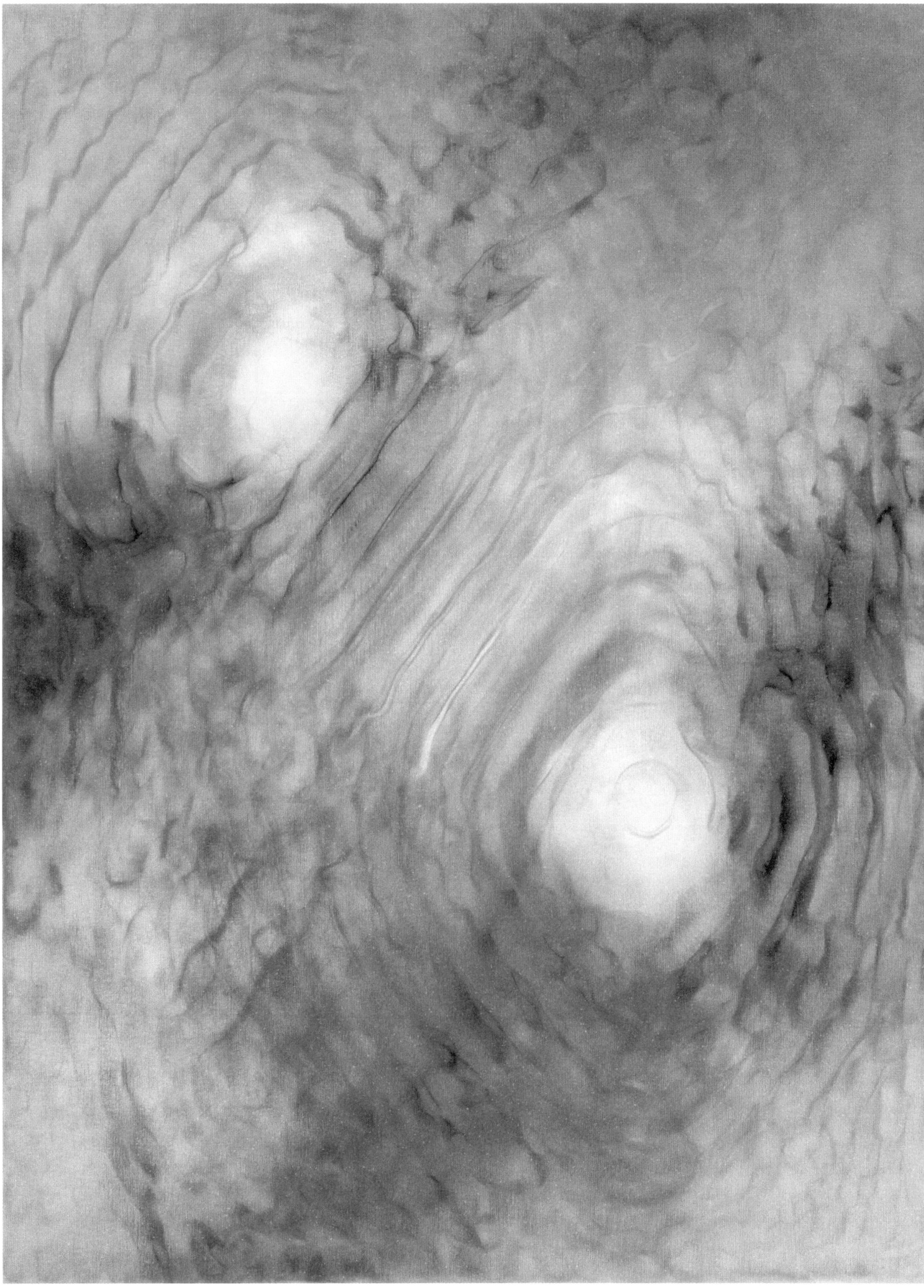

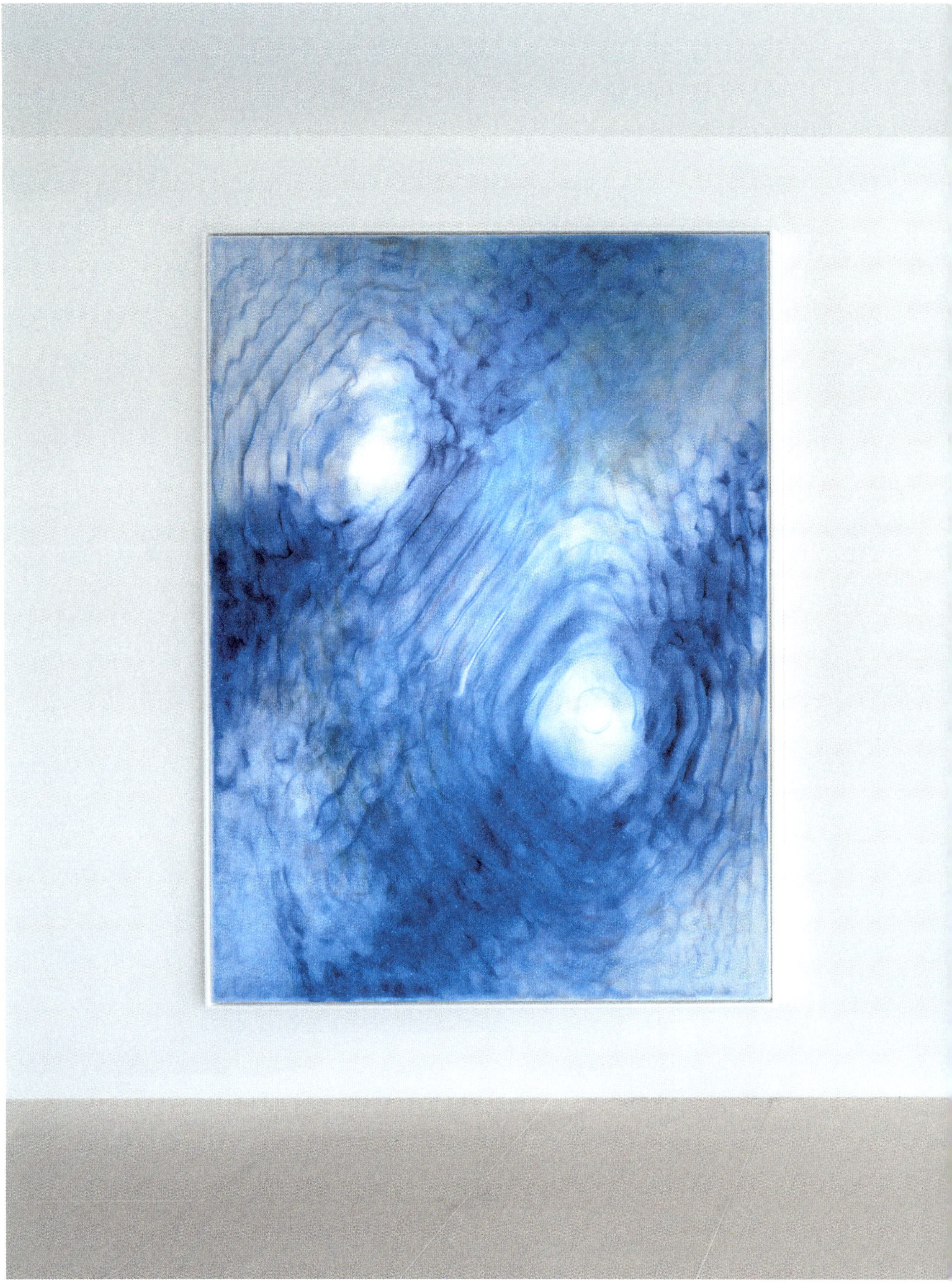

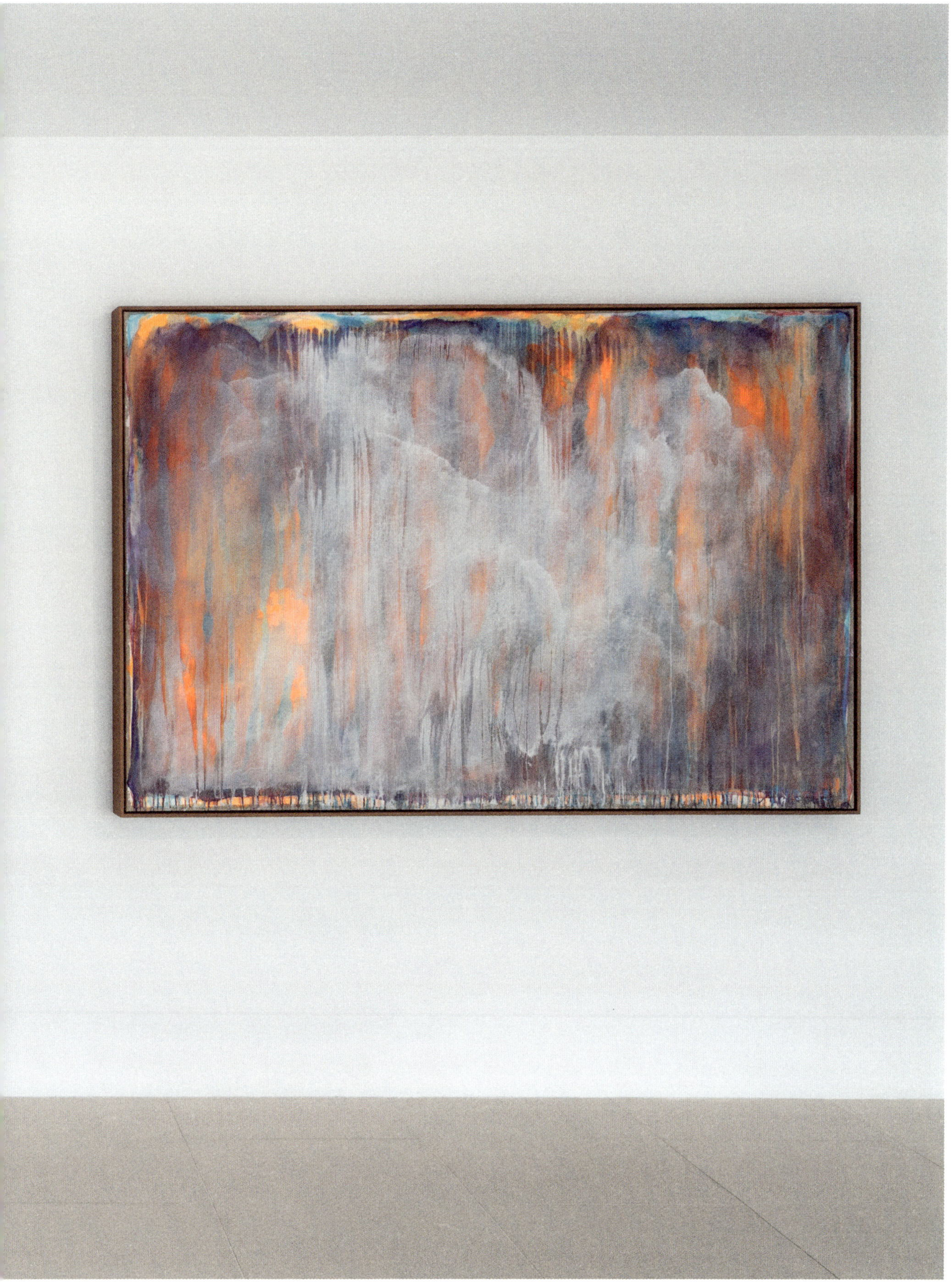

Thu-Van Tran, *Les Couleurs du gris*, 2025, whitewash and pigments on linen canvas, 130 × 195 cm

THU-VAN TRAN

(Vietnam, 1979)

Les Couleurs du gris, 2025

Whitewash and pigments on linen canvas
130 × 195 cm

Thu-Van Tran's canvas, created for this exhibition, invites the viewer to contemplate a chromatic landscape that seems to vanish behind a thick curtain of fog. The artist works around the foggy grey that gradually appears as the six layers of paint – white, pink, blue, purple, green and orange – are applied in order of varying opacities, cancelling out their own chromatic properties. The colours are those of the dioxins and herbicides used by the American military in their attacks on Vietnam and South-East Asia in the 1960s and 1970s. Thu-Van Tran's series *Les Couleurs du gris* makes the erasure of colours on the canvas a metaphor for "a telluric force that counterbalances the oxides" and "tames them".

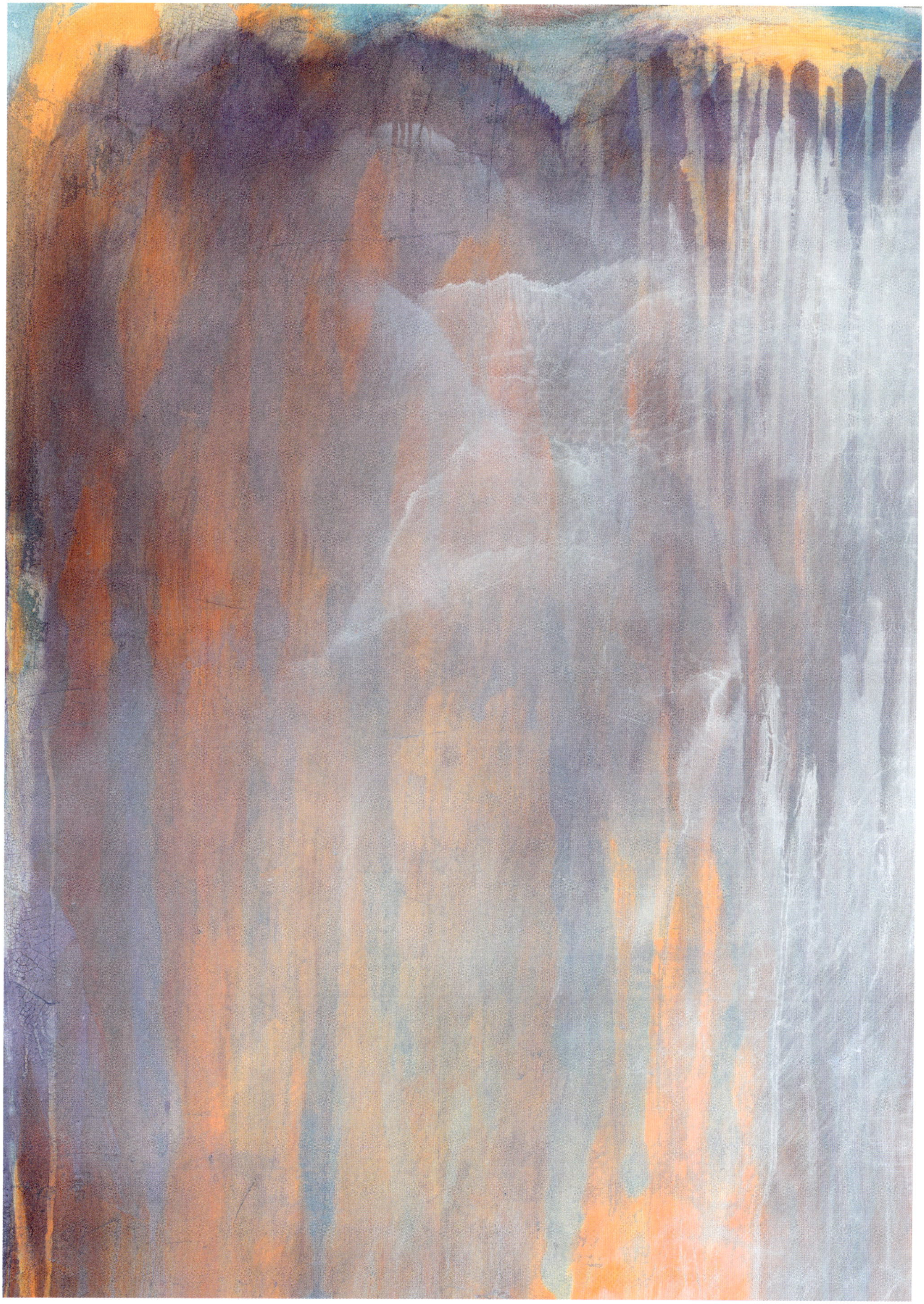

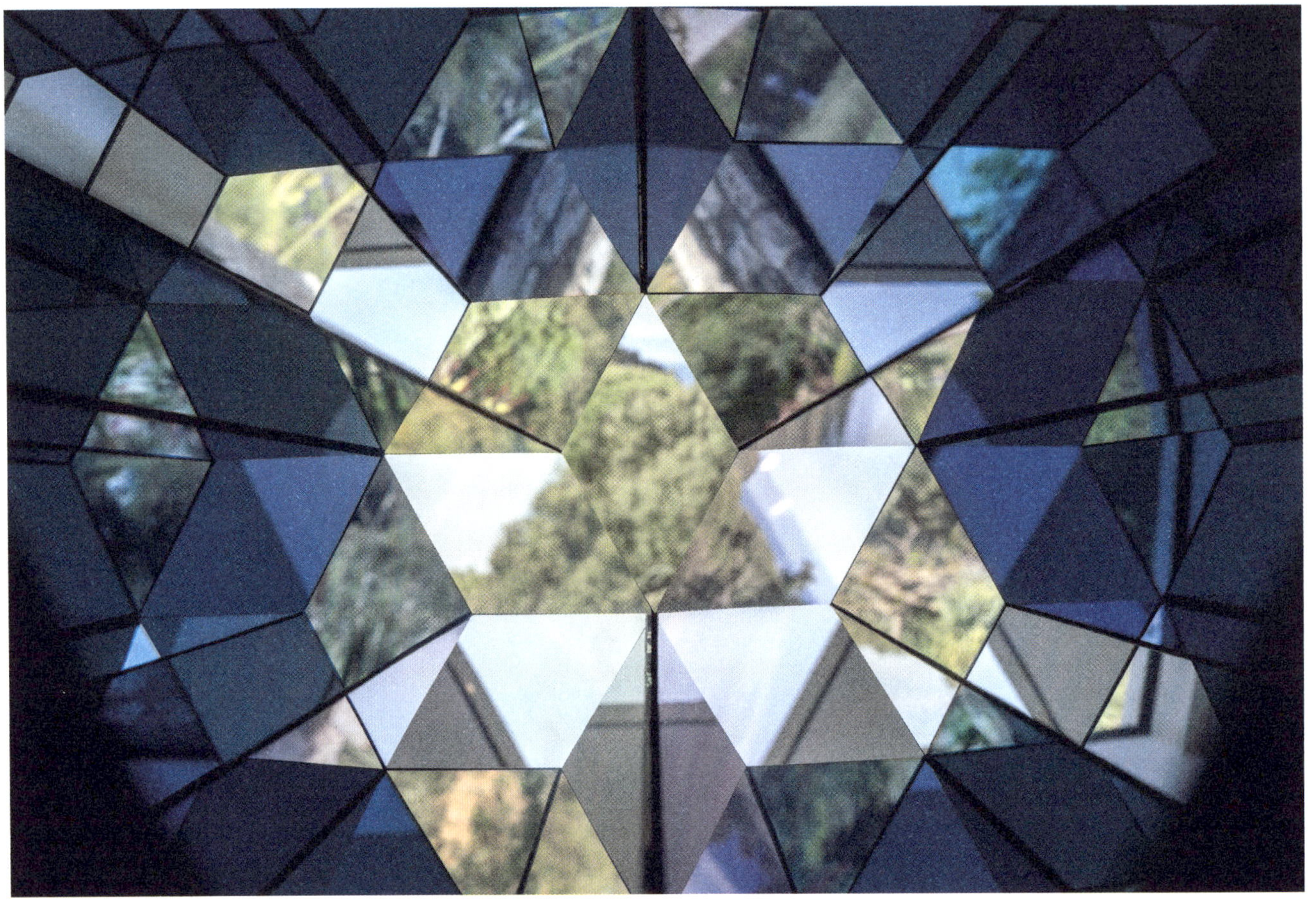

Olafur Eliasson, *Your vanishing*, 2011, bronze, filtered glass with a coloured effect (blue, pink, cyan, yellow), mirror, stainless steel, paint (black), 181 × 70 × 70 cm

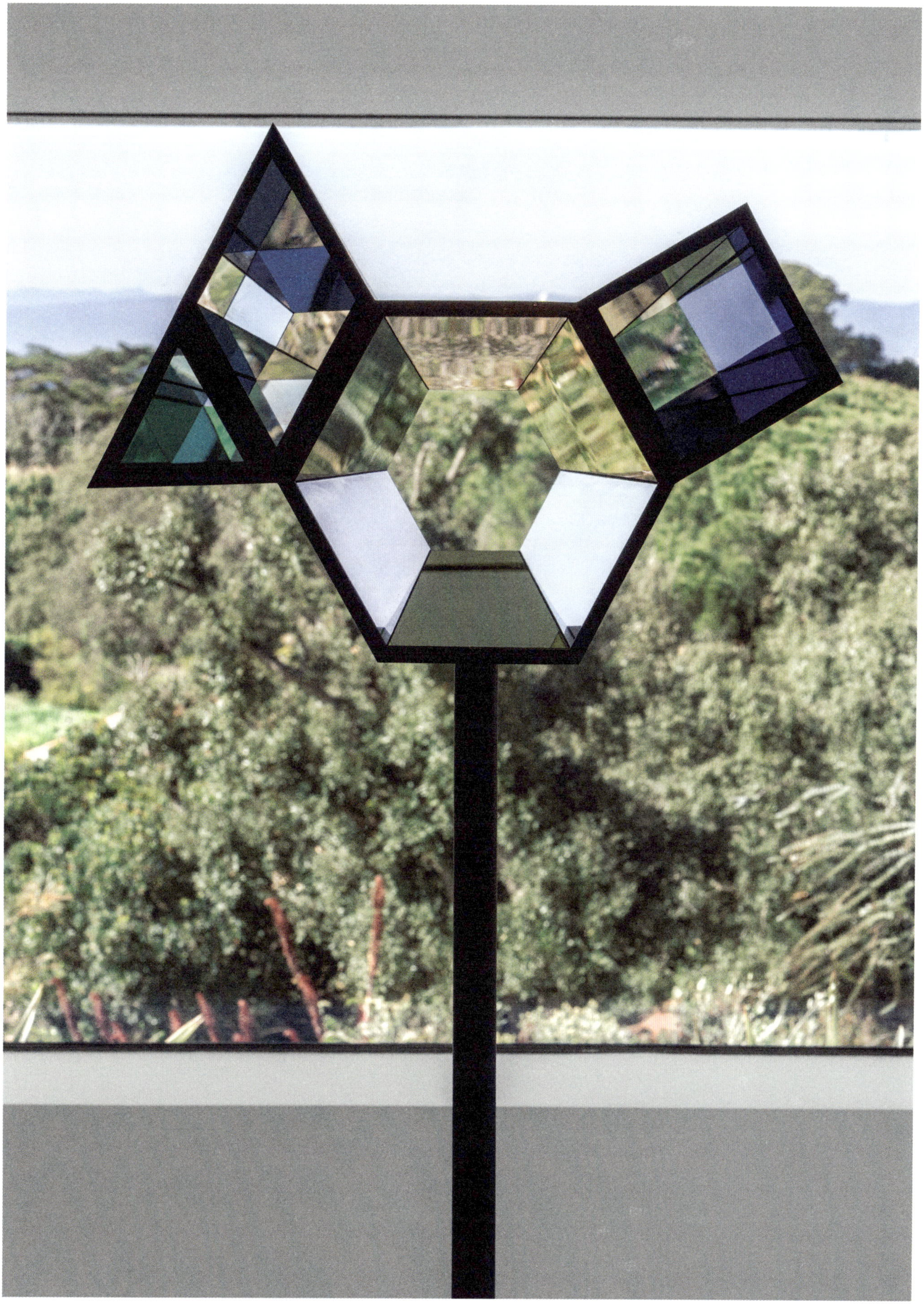

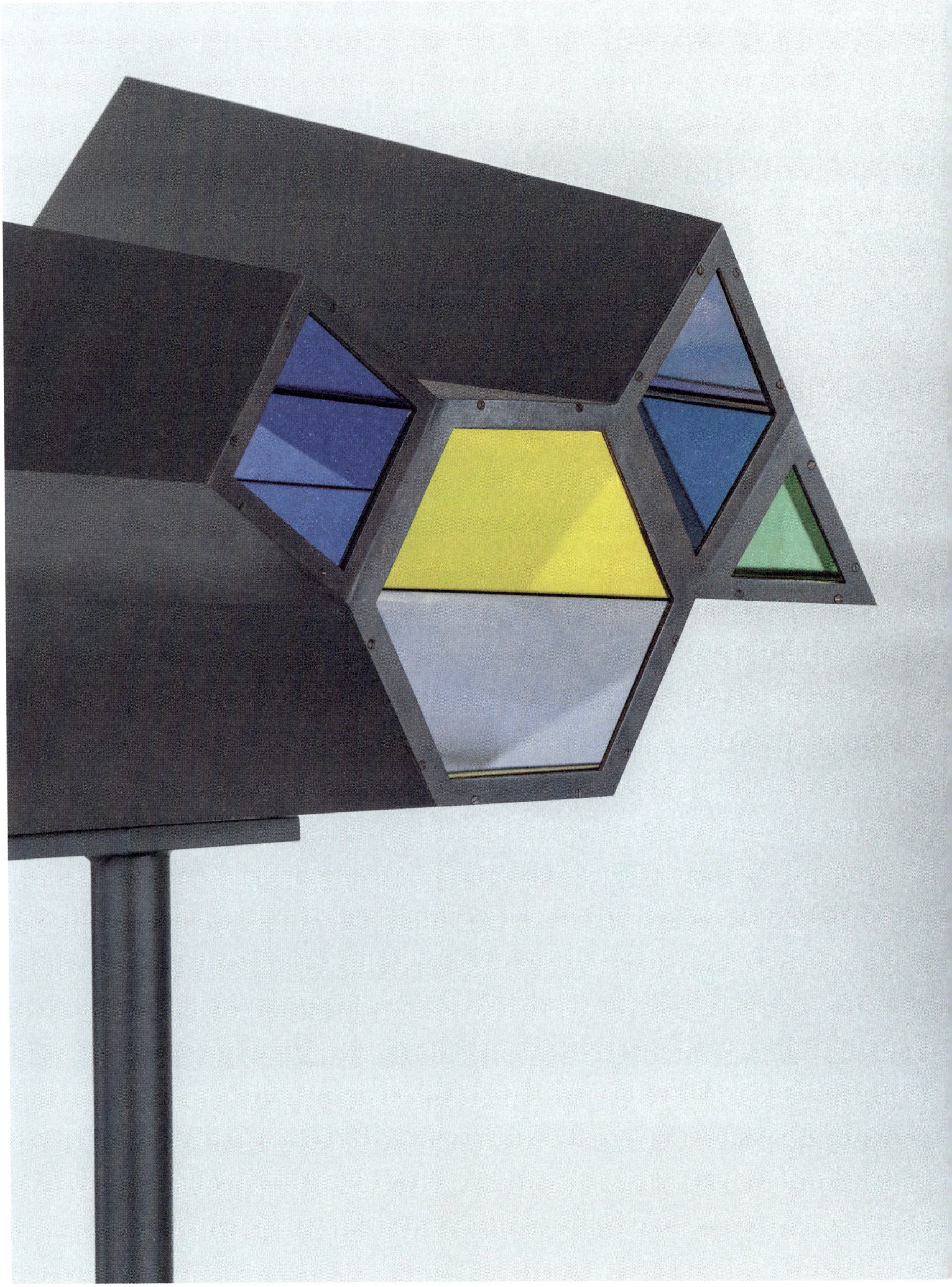

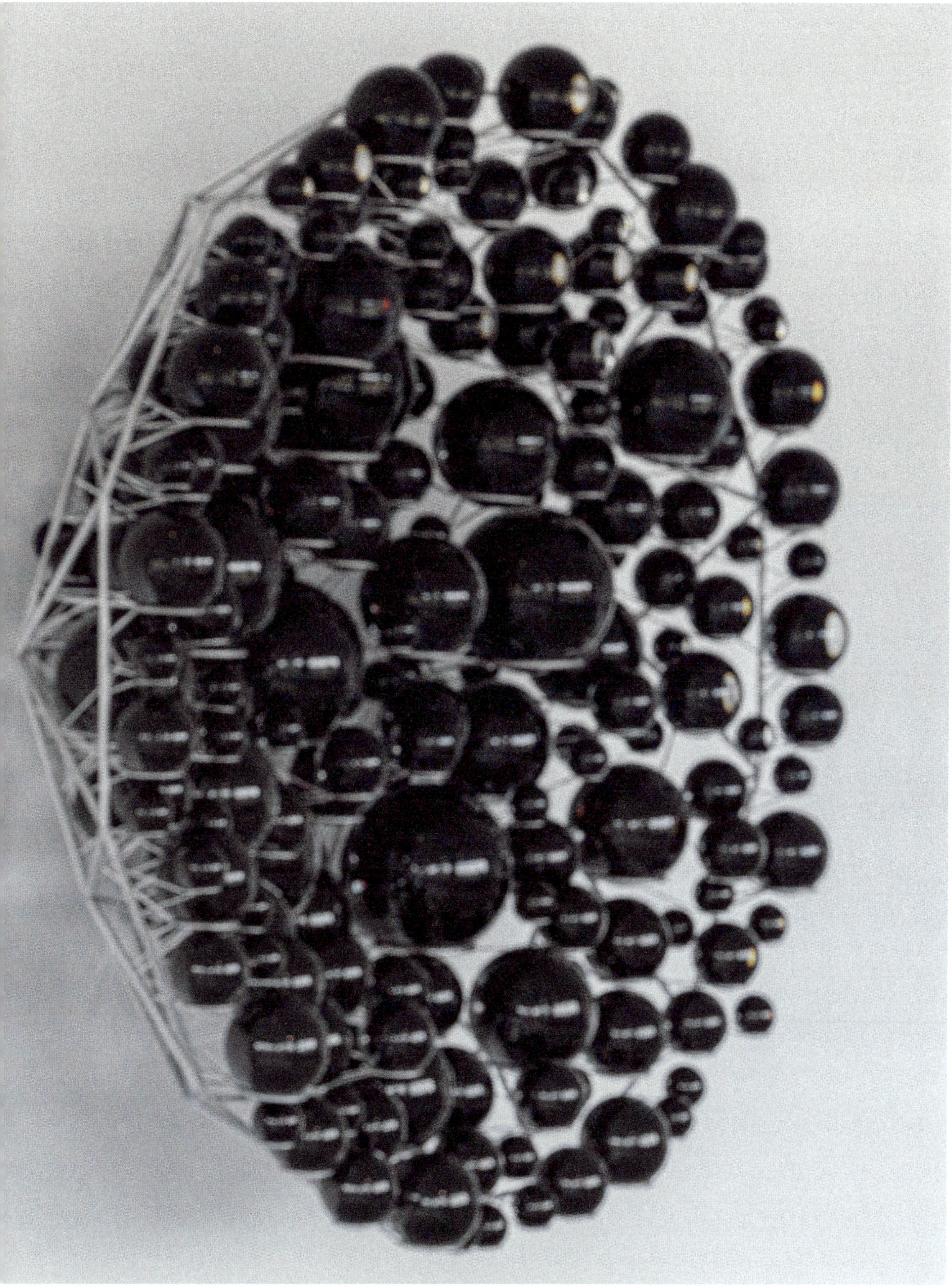

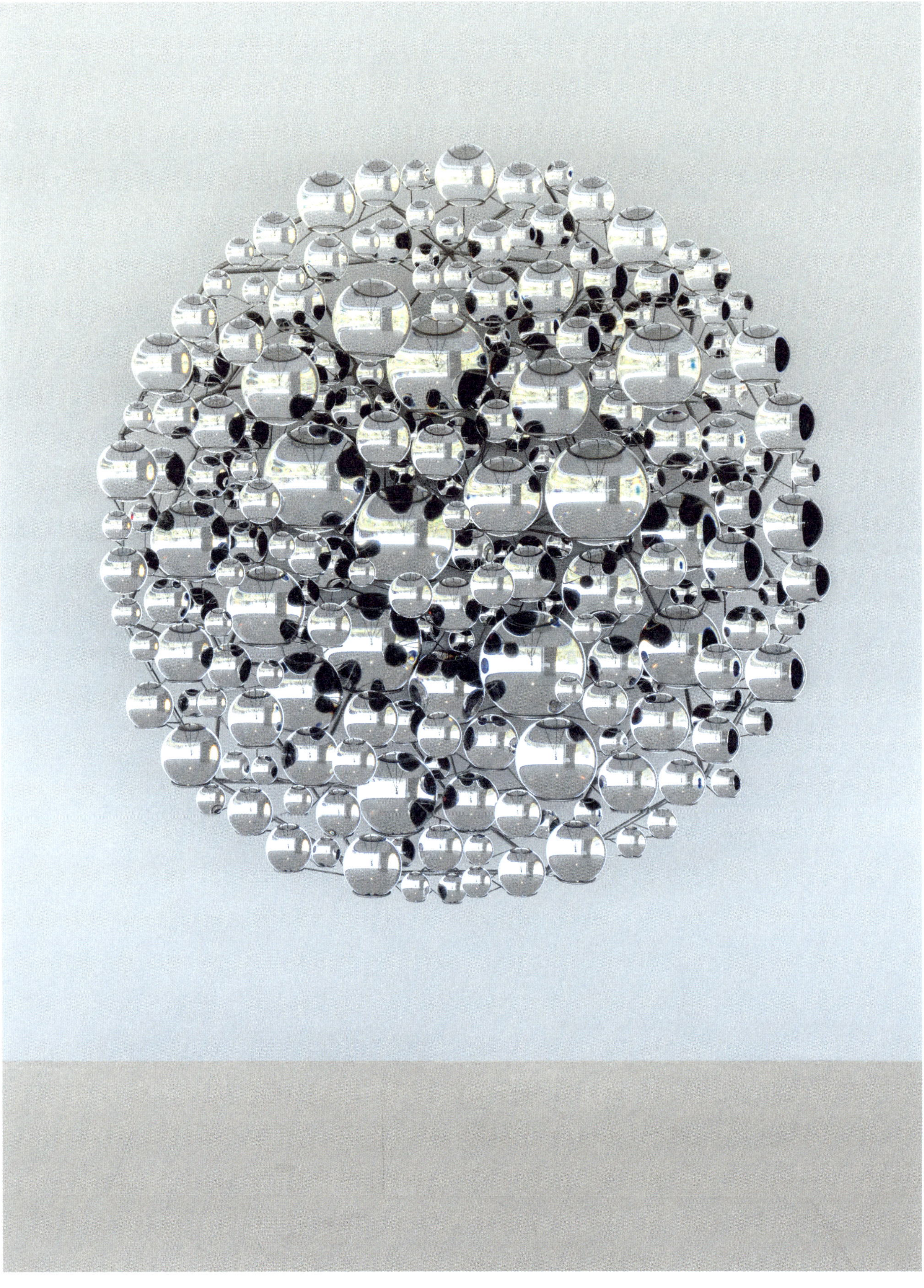

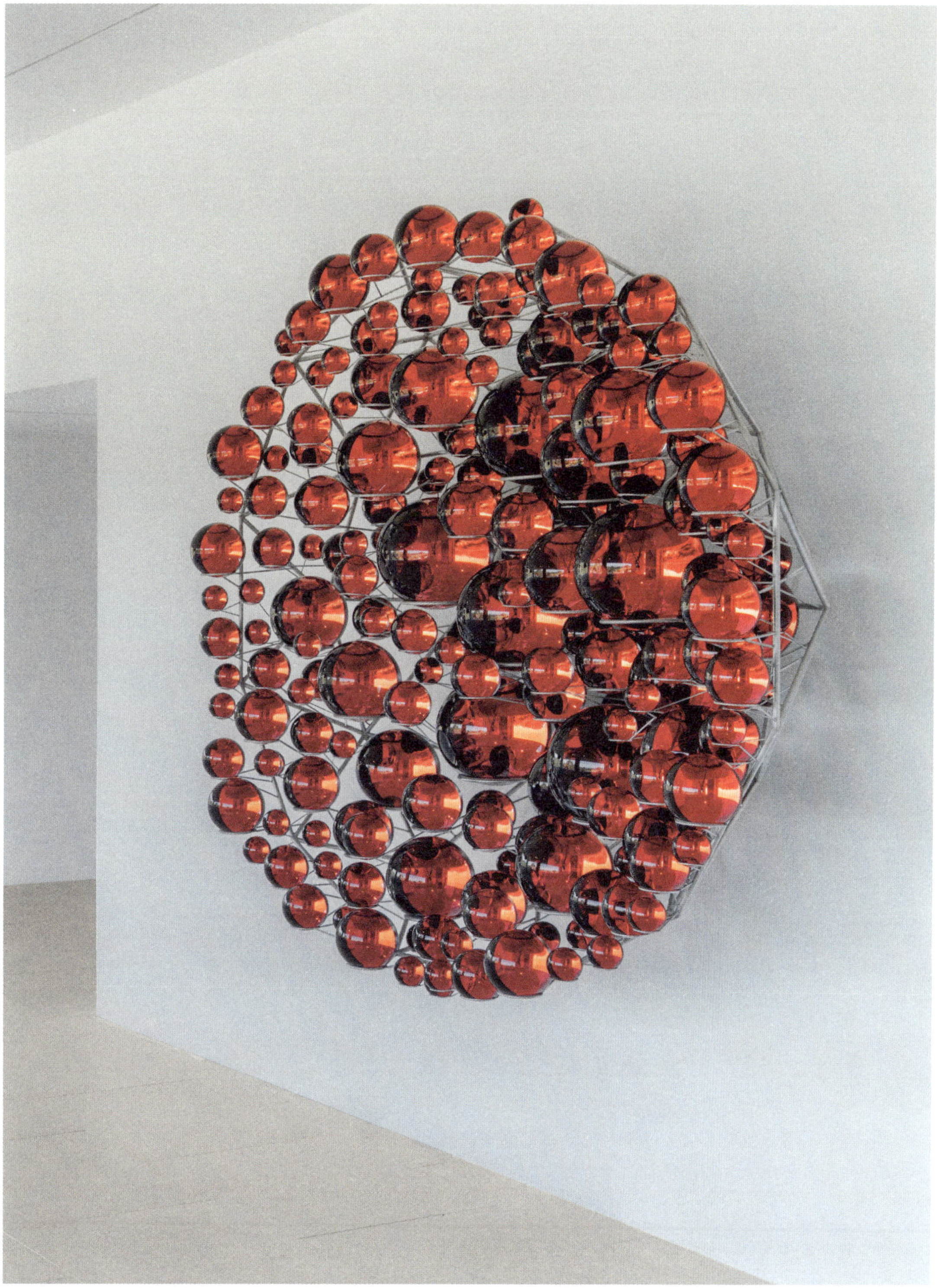

Olafur Eliasson, *The collective consequences of focus on focus*, 2022, partly silver-plated crystal glass spheres, paint (black, red), stainless steel, 171 × 169 × 67.5 cm

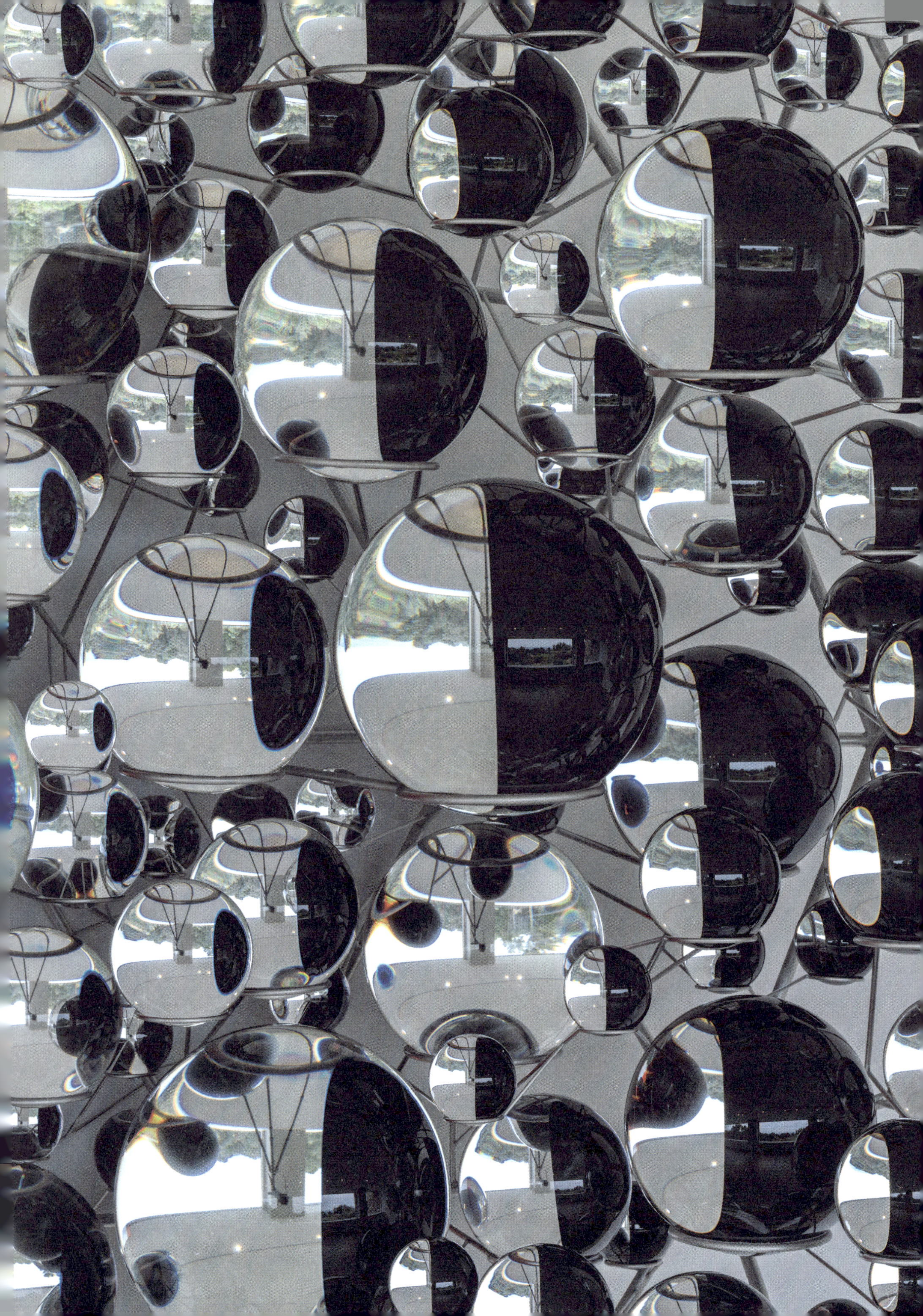

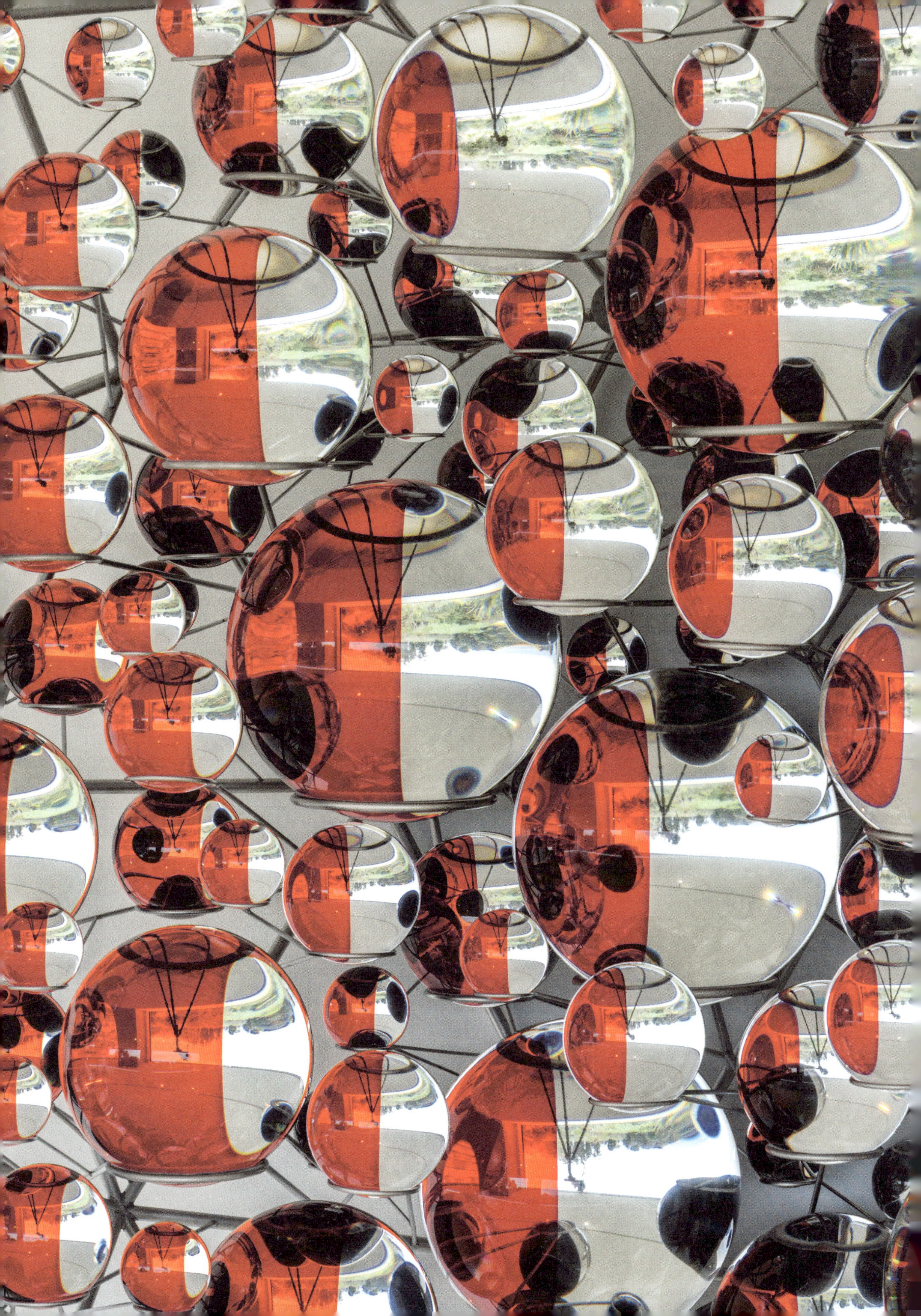

HEINZ MACK

(Germany, 1931)

Ohne Titel, 1950

Graphite on paper
48.5 × 62.9 cm

The *Vertigo* exhibition emerges from a vertiginous contemplation of nature and its phenomena.
A sensitivity to this developed very early on for Heinz Mack, after he experienced an unforgettable moment. Aged nineteen, while on a trip to Bordeaux to visit his father's grave (a German soldier who had died during the war), Mack saw the ocean for the first time. Looking out at the reflection of the sun's rays on the water, as if a kind of mirage was being projected into the air, he was overcome with emotion. This experience was to form the basis for his luminous reliefs (such as those exhibited in the "Atmospheric Turbulence" and "Threshold, Mirage and Abyss" sections) and was a key moment for perceptual art. On the work on paper presented here, two types of horizontal lines – straight and serrated – simultaneously come together and stand apart from each other. This visual interference, as well as the interaction of the lines with the background of the paper, generate an optical vibration that disrupts the viewer's gaze, a disturbance heightened by the gradual erasure of the stroke.

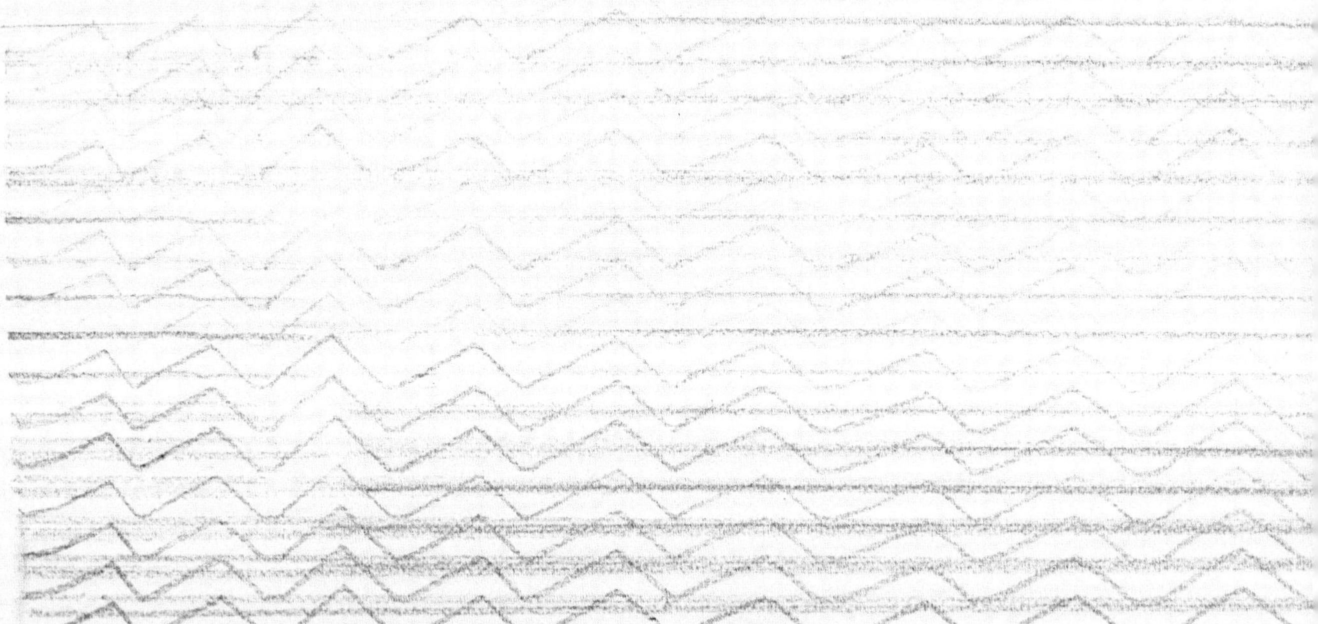

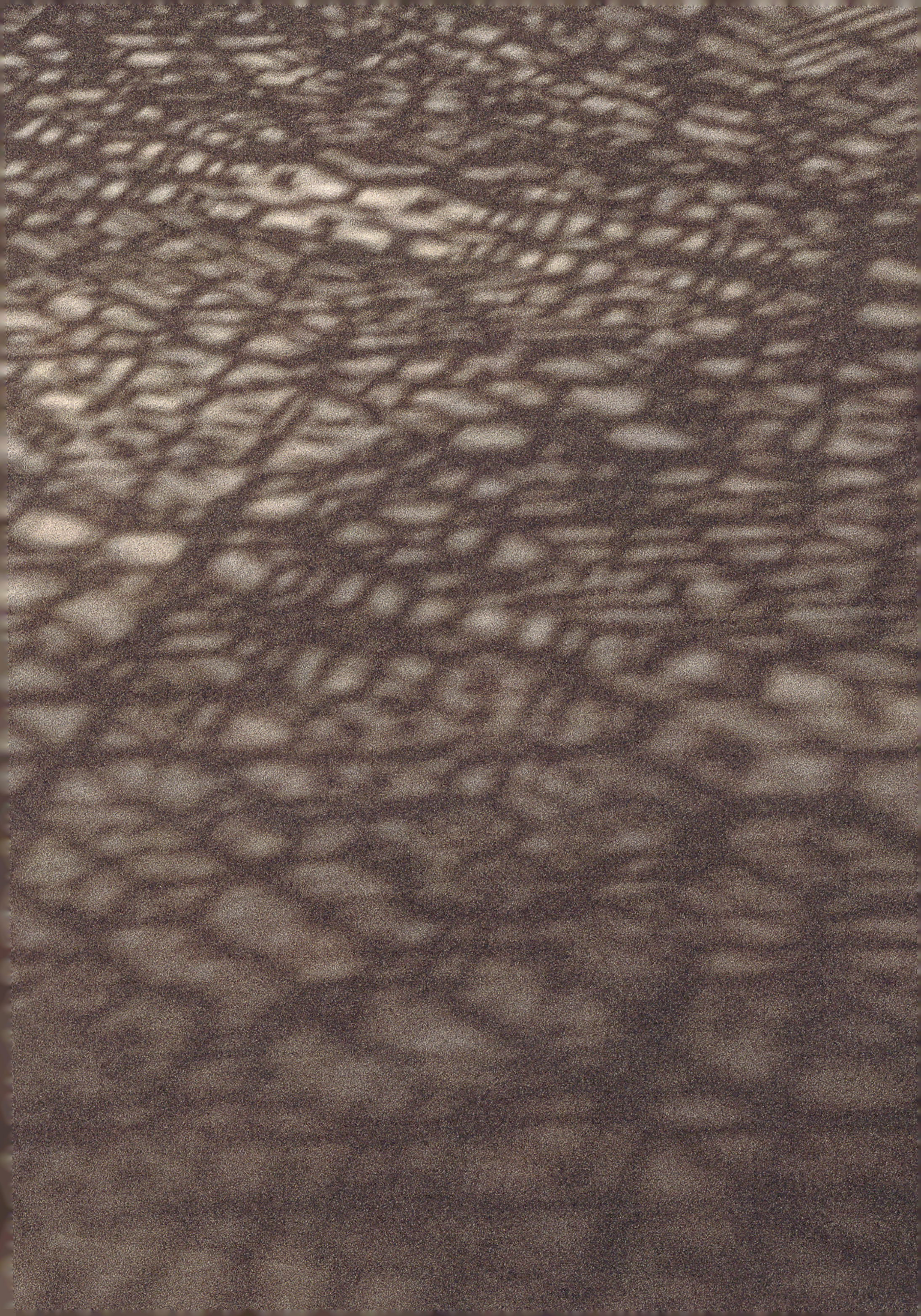

FIELDS OF VISION

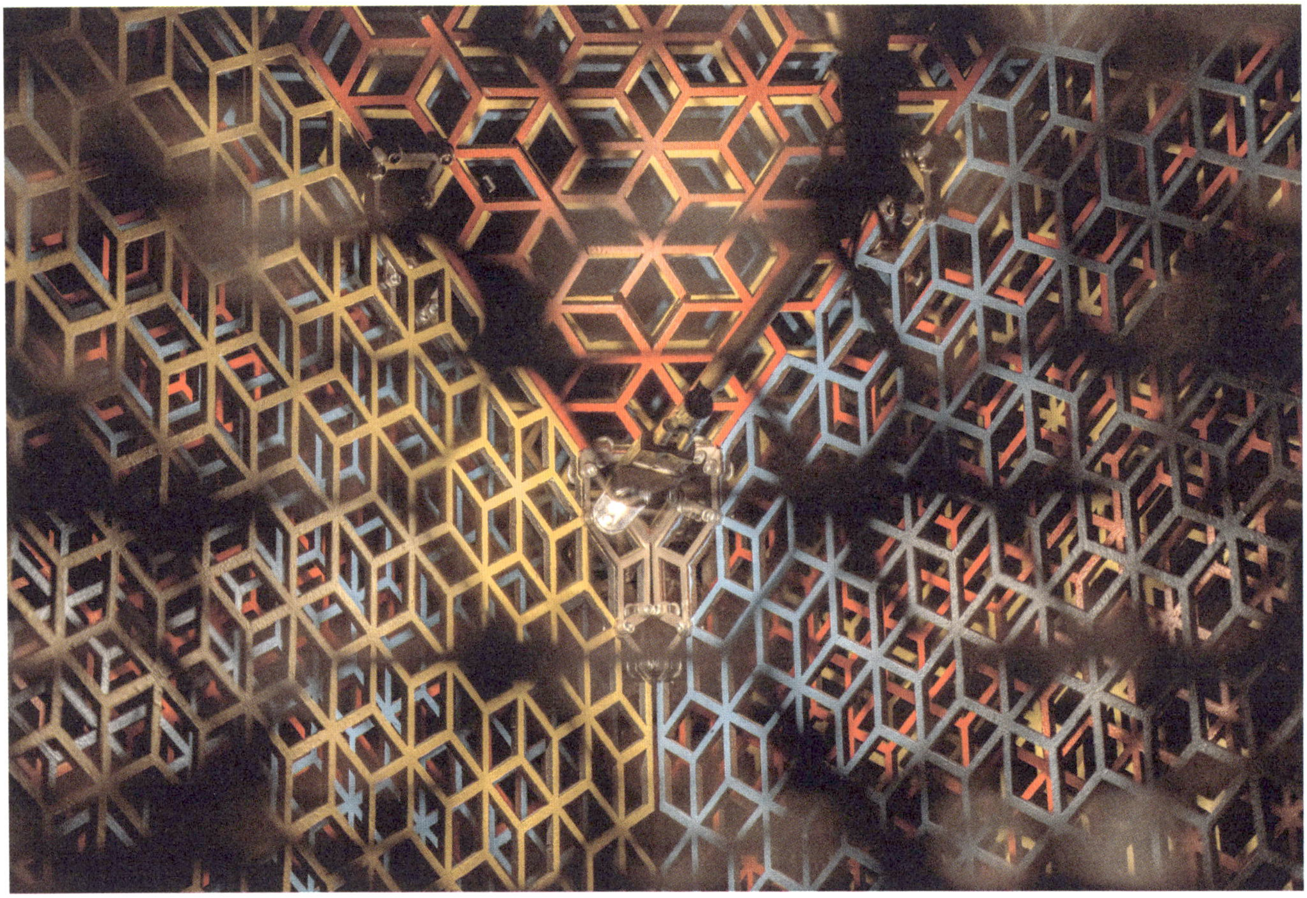

The visit throughout the *Vertigo* exhibition continues and finishes outside the Villa, initially in the Pavillon, which contains an artwork by Conrad Shawcross: the projection of moving shadowy grids that retract and dilate the visual space in a huge, windowless room. These unstable forms come from a mobile source of light situated in an openwork polyhedral cage hanging from the ceiling like a simple lightshade. Once out of this cell, which is at once enveloping, fascinating and gruelling, we are next invited to direct our gaze into the concentric mysteries of Jeppe Hein's permanent artwork, which subverts the principle of the hedge maze to create a visually precarious milieu. Comprising metal stelae among which we are impelled to wander eternally, the artwork weaves together reflections and nature. These kaleidoscopic mechanisms prove to be highly hallucinatory, or even psychedelic: they make us believe there is some kind of chemical malfunction going on in our brain. They take to the sensory extreme the dizzying impressions used to such great effect in *Vertigo*, emphasising a phenomenon-based abstraction, in an all-encompassing perceptual experience that reminds us of our intimate connections with the universal energy of the visible and invisible forces of nature.

Each of the sections reminds us that throughout the visit we have renounced our neutrality or passivity as mere viewers: providing that we give up our usual museum habits, we become fully-fledged subjects, or even actors in this still little-known sensitivity to abstract art. Admittedly, the artworks in *Vertigo* may be photogenic, but to fully understand the essential aesthetic issues involved, and thus their phenomenological significance, these creations must be experienced *in vivo*, that is, in real time and space – and even more so than for most figurative or even abstract paintings, which remain confined to the static domain of the image. Like a simple walk or hike, it is our movement in time and space through the Villa that allows us to give ourselves over to the sensory exploration of light and chromatic secrets, to feel the universal energy of those visible and invisible forces of nature. With their oscillating mobiles, pulsating monochromes and polychromatic clouds, these artists set aside the traditional idea of construction and composition. This renunciation then enables them to place unprecedented importance on the precipitous, ebullient and whirling substance, creating the oxymoron of a dynamic void, constantly in touch with the perceptible natural world. Such creations, as elusive to our senses as they are powerfully present, achieve the status of a *Fata Morgana*, that very particular atmospheric mirage named after Morgan the Fairy, who, in Arthurian legend, not only had the power to raise palaces above the waves but also to influence the wind.

Opposite and following pages: Conrad Shawcross, *Slow Arc Inside a Cube XI* (detail), 2020, painted steel, light, mechanical system, 165 × 72 × 62 cm

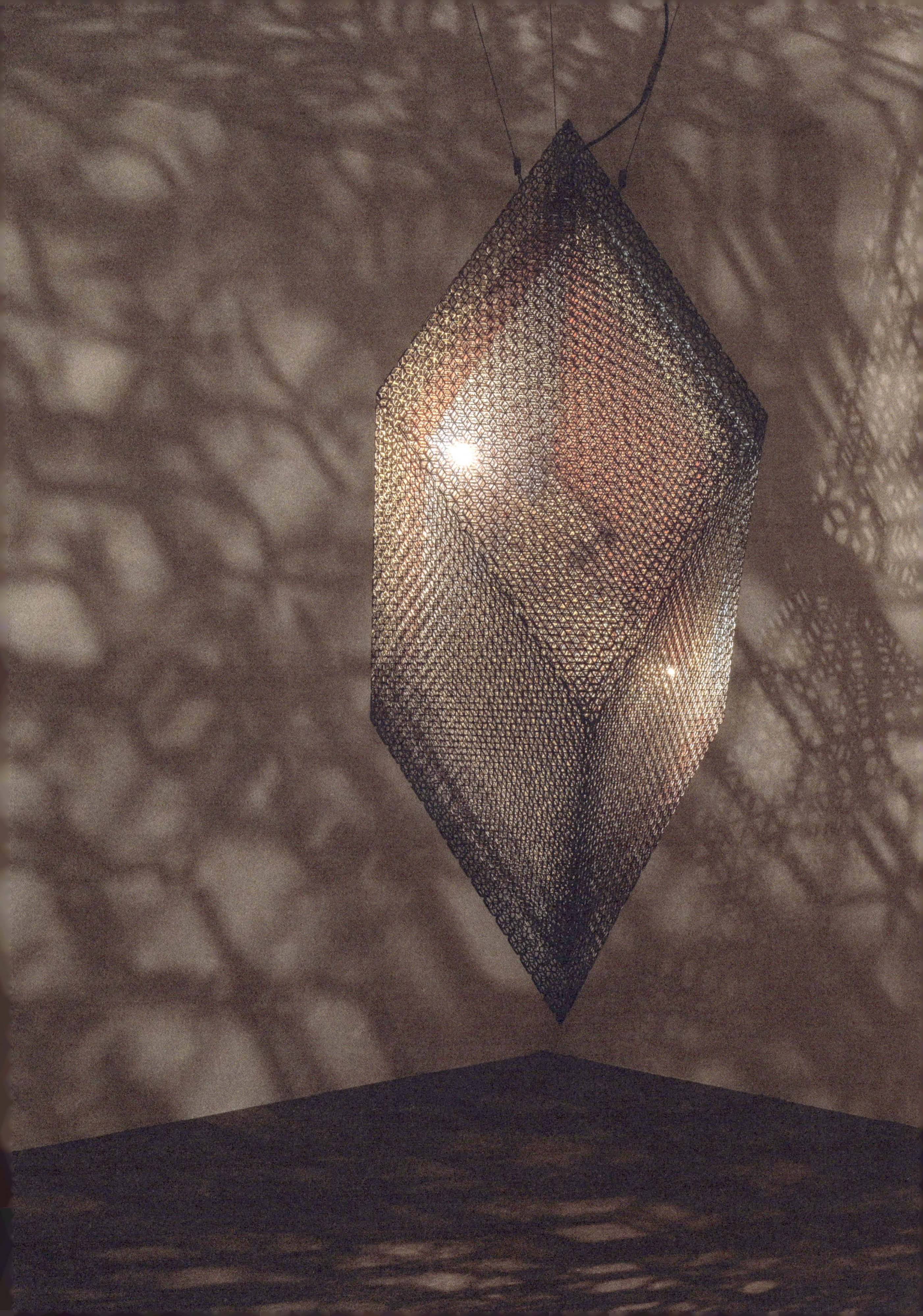

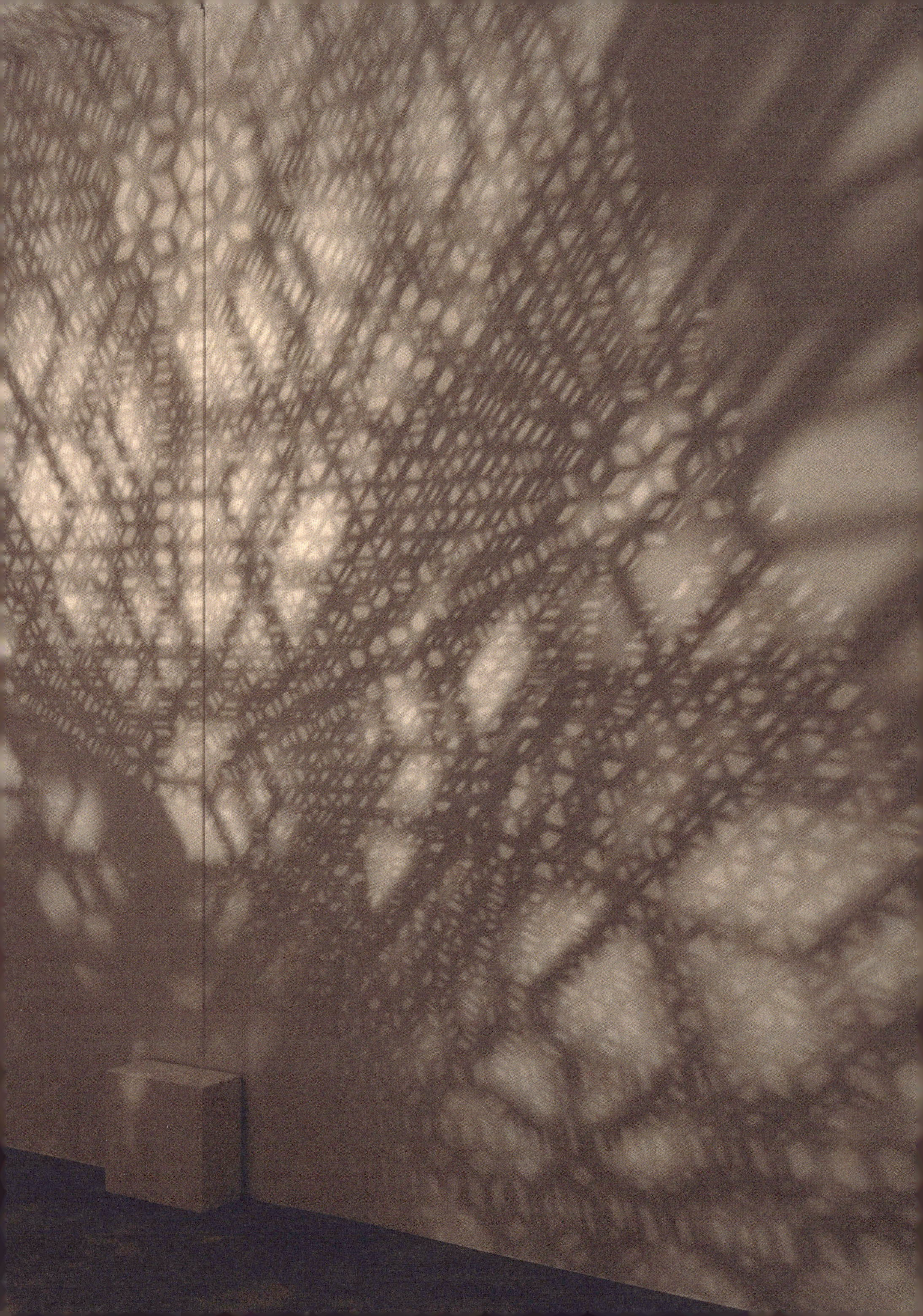

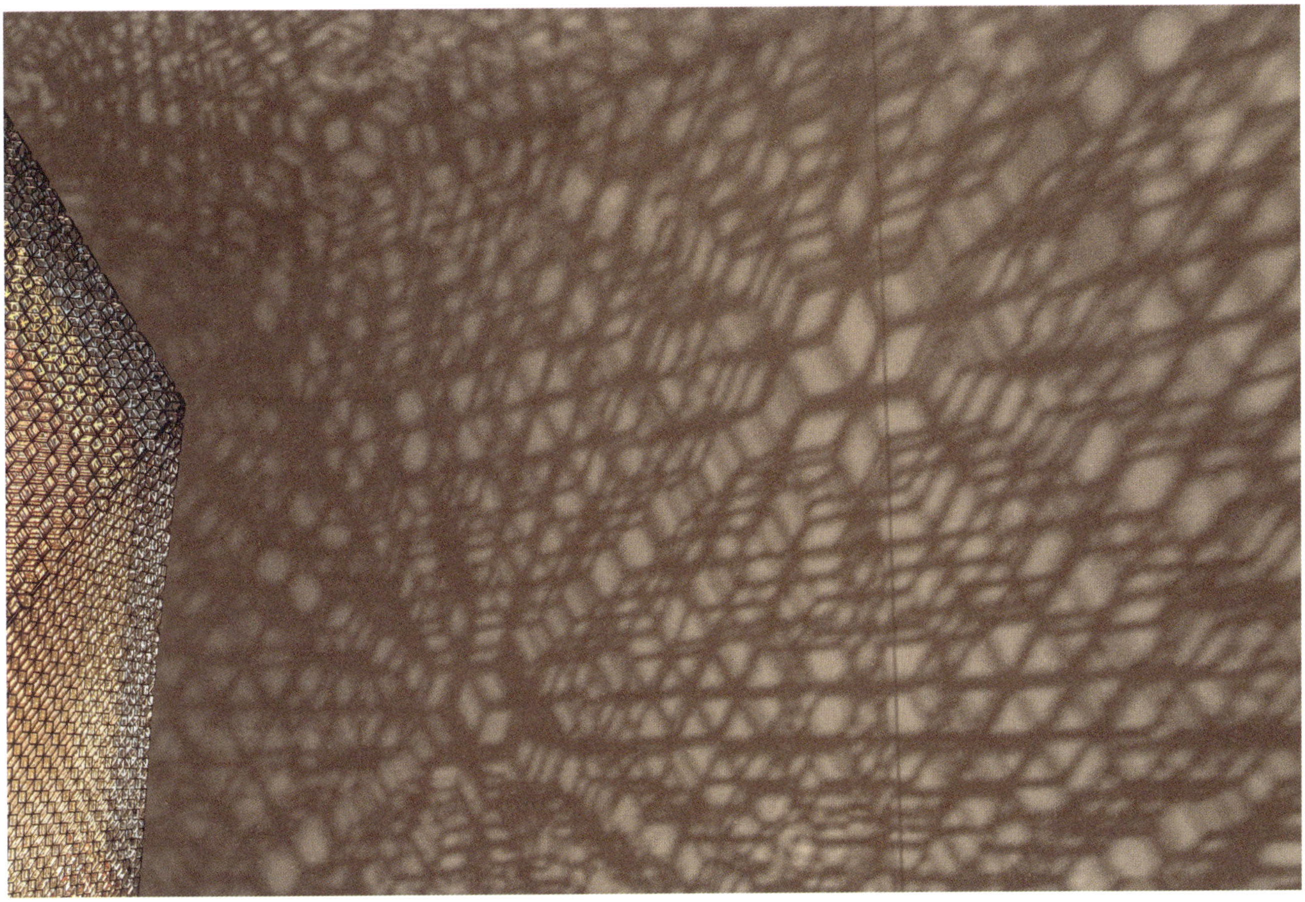

Conrad Shawcross, *Slow Arc Inside a Cube XI* (detail), 2020, painted steel, light, mechanical system, 165 × 72 × 62 cm
Opposite and following pages: Jeppe Hein, *Path of Emotions* (detail), 2018, high polished stainless steel, 280 × 1,216 × 1,493 cm

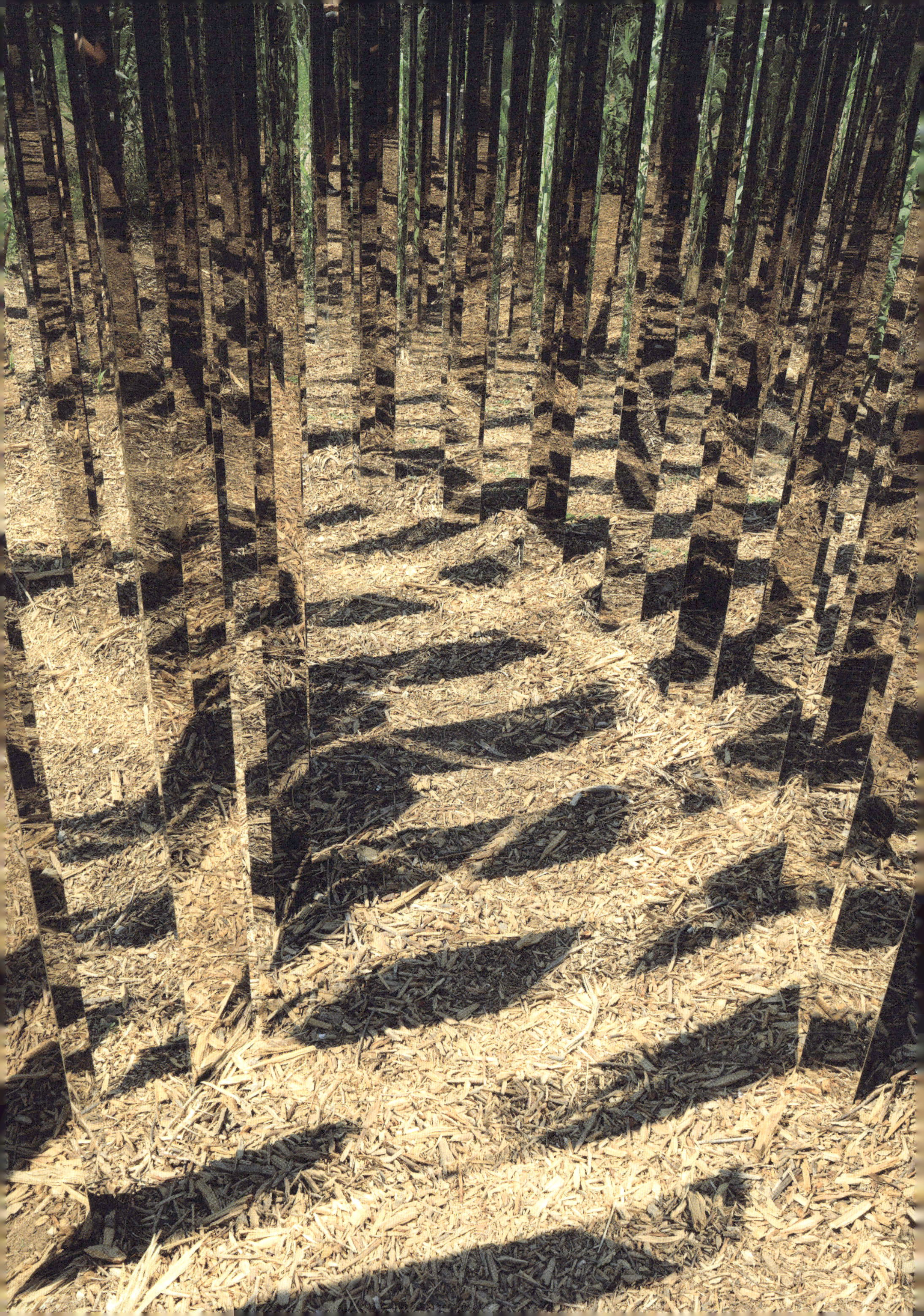

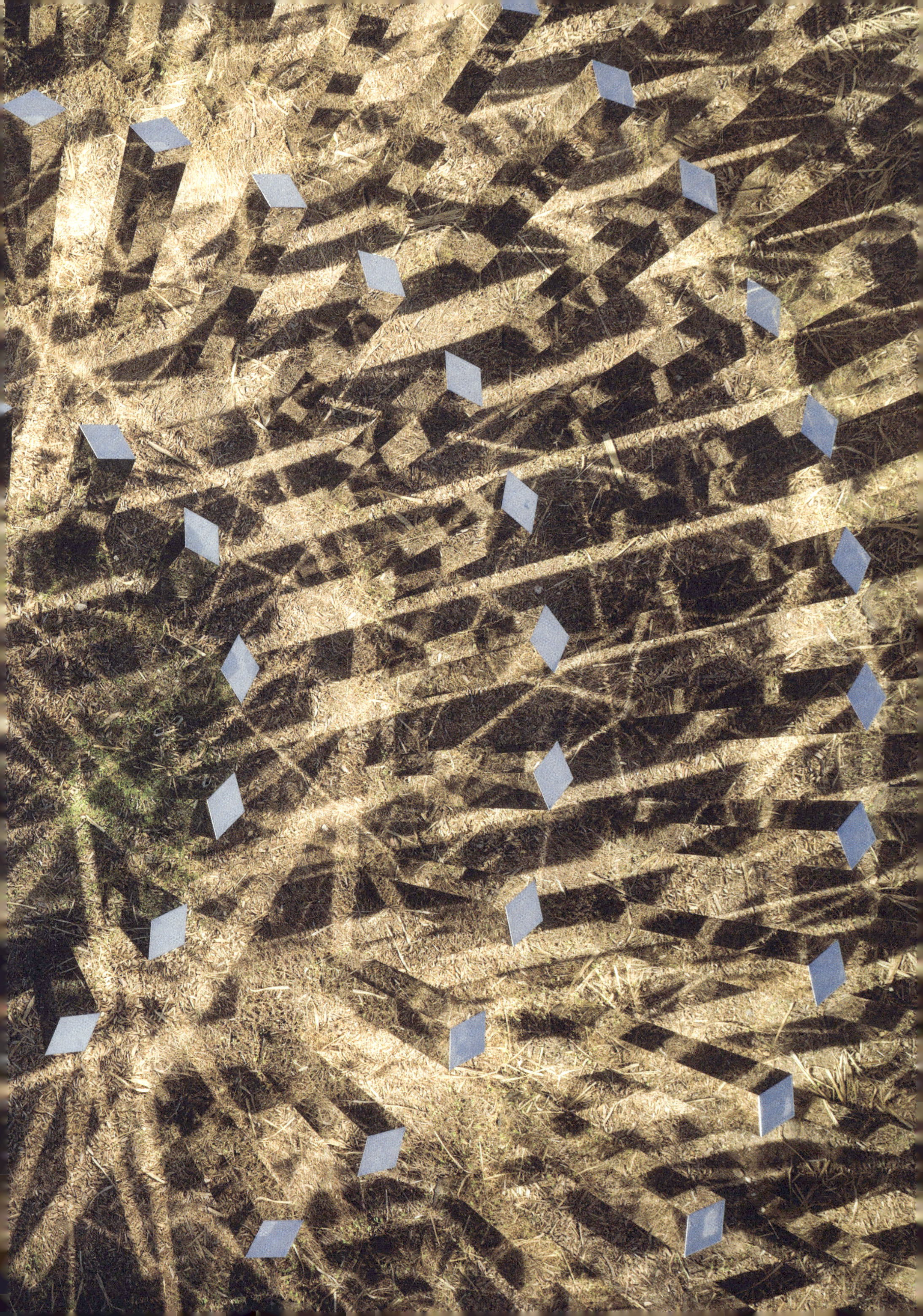

ALMOST A LIGHT

Nina Leger

It's a pity, he said this morning, before I took the train for Hyères.

It's a pity, said the driver who drove me to the Port de la Tour Fondue.

It's a real shame, the woman seated next to me on the boat was saying. All of them were gazing at the utterly grey sky, and so was I, also telling myself, it's a pity.

When you live on the mainland and you're going to an island, you want it to be faithful to the image you have of it: you want it to be blue. Blue sky above, blue sea below and the horizontal island in between.

I arrived in Porquerolles in the morning and, probably because I know of nothing more enclosed than an island, I planned to stride across it following the symbol of infinity. Starting from the port, situated in the middle of the northern side, tracing a loop eastwards, then another westwards, and at the junction of the two lies the Villa. I will place the exhibition at the centre of an infinity carved out of the finite.

Setting off eastwards, I'd wanted to follow the sun – but it doesn't exist. The grey attenuates everything, the grey requires more work. Perceptions must grow accustomed, great intensities relinquished and the static beam outstretched across the sea must be celebrated. I walk on the sandy path that leads down to the first beach. Suddenly, a nightingale sings. It makes the exact sound of the absent light.

I look at my map. The island exists, there, alone in the compact blue of the sea; it has lost its archipelago, abandoned its coastline, it seems distant, almost Pacific. But, when I lift my eyes, I see only land on the horizon, and the sea, viewed from here, looks like a lake caught between the island and its coast.

Not long ago, I discovered that some islands exist inside other islands. On the island of Luzon, in the Philippines, there is Lake Taal, and within this lake is Volcano Island, and within Volcano, there is another lake. For several years, there was even a cone of ash in the middle of this lake on the island on the lake of the island, and this cone contained an additional lake. A page of the encyclopaedia is entirely devoted to these vertiginous formations called "recursive islands". It lists them and classifies them by degrees. The first section indexes the "Lakes inside Islands" and the last "Lakes on Islands in Lakes on Islands in Lakes". There is only one line in this section: Yathkyed Lake, in the province of Nunavut, in Canada. A note specifies that in reality, it is not just a lake on an island in a lake on an island in a lake, but that there is an additional island in the final lake, and that it is the only one of its kind that has been discovered in the whole world: it is the most recursive island in the world – and it has no name.

The sea comes and goes on the thin strip of sand, it undulates beneath the seaweed, glides into their dense darkness, withdraws and starts again. Plage de la Courtade. I look at the map again. The island is a contour on it, that of an arc or a cradle that nothing can budge. But the movement of the waves contradicts the map. There is no fixed line or design and there are no limits. The island continues. For the island, the sea is not an ending or the open air of a beginning. The endings, the beginnings and their demarcations are fictions invented by eyes that look down on the world.

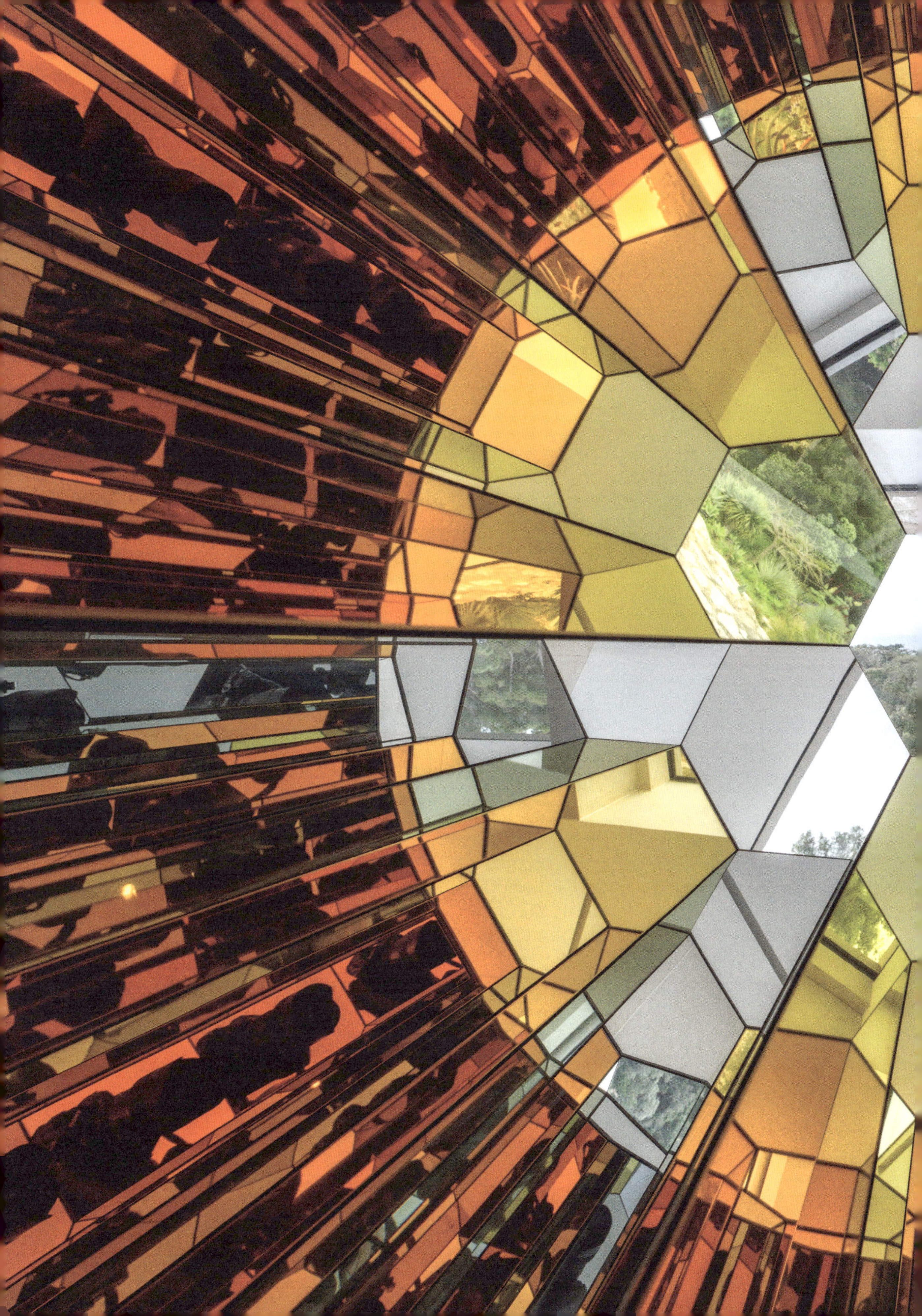

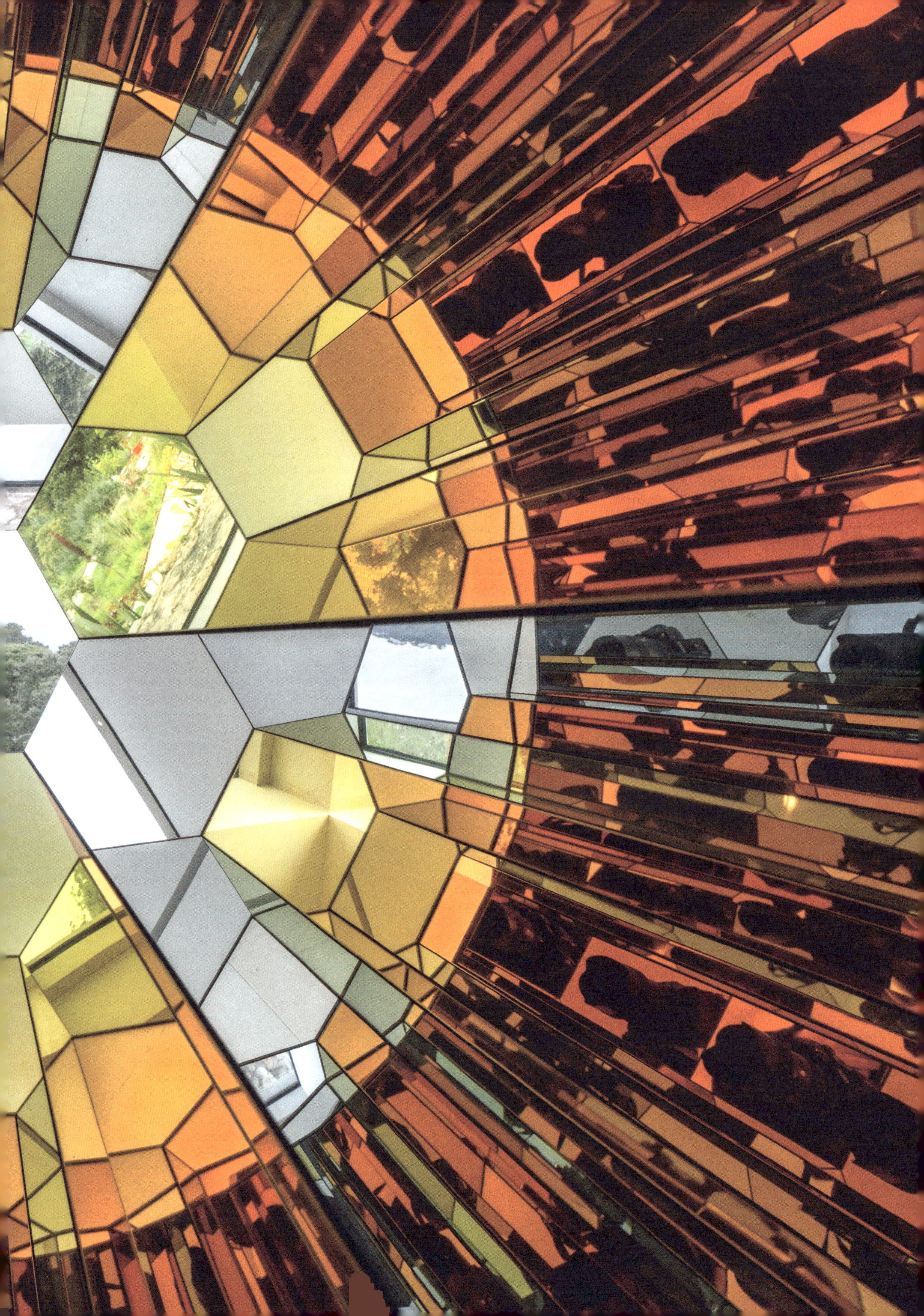

Islands in lakes in islands are also fictions of perspective, creatures of maps and satellites. Once you abandon the high-angle for a cutaway shot, the concentric circles that were strictly defining the lands from waters will change their relationship into one perpetual undulation. Their seperation will turn into a dance; surface into depth.

Seen vertically, all islands are limitless.

The most recursive island in the world is inaccessible. It can only be seen on satellite images. Zoom in, zoom out, the vertigo of a shape that appears against a background in a shape on a background in a shape on a background; zoom in, zoom out, island in a lake on an island, etc., on a screen. The island is recursive only because it is only seen from above. It is only seen from above because Yathkyed Lake is owned by a goldmining company. Those who extract things from the earth know very well that the world must be looked at vertically rather than making do with the illusions at the surface. By producing a cross-section of the vertigo in Yathkyed, a company saw gold. It bought the area, closed it off and since then has been excavating the recursive island. Zoom in, zoom out, completely cut off from reality, the island now only exists on our screens.

Before coming here, I read the encyclopaedia page on Porquerolles, and I noticed the verbs used to describe its history: occupy, settle, found, flight, concede, belong, buy, buy back, sell, give, erect, possess, take, cede, take back. Usually when I write about a place, I'm looking for the traces of those words, usually I take an interest in those who build, as well as those who excavate and those who see the world as a cross-section, but today, I'm looking for feelings rather than stories, so I circumvent them. I have decided to avoid the forts built on the island's capes, headlands and promontories; I refuse to look at the batteries and their cannons pointing in all directions; I block out anything that would convey the island's epic narrative. Five forts and four batteries for an island seven kilometres long and three wide: take, occupy, found, fight, cede, possess. I ignore Fort du Lequin, Fort de l'Alycastre and Fort des Mèdes, mentally piling up those verbs of history within them; I head inland and cross through to the other side of the horizon.

Calanque de la Galère. On the eastern side of the island the coast loosens its grip, leaving only the odd rock. Grand Sarranier, Petit Sarranier. It's not the high seas, but it is no longer a lake. I could look out into the distance, but my eye is caught by what is near: the crenellated rocks of the calanque, hewn from a gentle silver, slightly dirty, serrated like a weapon, foliated like an ancient book.

I pass my hand over it, it crumbles. The island comes away under my fingers, it changes, and, most of all, it leans. The ground is at a 45° angle. The sheets of stone rise obliquely; they extend the matte light of the water into the sky and bring the dull silver of the clouds into the sea. The island lives continuously between open air and underwater air. The island is amphibious.

With whitened fingers and whitened clothes, I leave the calanque, covered in powdery stone. The island and I begin to merge, I lose my own outline, and, at the same time, I stop assigning it one too. I was seeking the island through its forms; I find it in its textures. I was envisaging it through separations – what it is, what it isn't – but I'm discovering it through porosities; I mistook rocks for trunks – their wood polished like pebbles – and stumps for stones – veined like wood. I had imagined a single moment of understanding, but the island comes to me slowly.

I go back down via a small path. I've abandoned the map – since the map lies. I play at losing my way, I don't get lost.

I pause among the trees, go through a gate, take off my shoes, go down some stairs. I am standing at the intersection of my infinity loop.

Interior. Here is colour.

Electric blue, iridescent green, oceanic pink, euphoric yellow, green once again, as tender as spring, fires of dark stars against a background of explosions, the vibration of a pale sun underwater, light waves, echoes, threatens to collapse into a thousand pieces, then absolute or total blue, deep red, a silver filter, absorption, brightness and finally – having ascended the stairs – tremor, propagation, multiplication. Through an eyepiece I see the island becoming several, I see, on a sheet, the sea sparkling above itself – and I leave.

Exterior. Here is light.

The colours have returned to the world as if all that was required was to collect them from where they were resting.

I start walking again. The contrasts walk with me. As it becomes luminous, the island is joined by shadow. Scents rise. Eucalyptus. Pittosporum. I walk on. The island takes the colours of the paintings and deploys them as worlds.

I head due west. Already the sun is slowly setting. I have walked the entire island. I move through the tall bushes on the strip of land separating the two last bays. One with white sand, the other with black. Two parentheses that open onto the sea.

The sun is about to disappear. I reach the island's farthest point. Standing on the rocks, I hold it tightly to me, gathered together with its lights, held into a contour that is no longer a fictional space but an imprint of time.

The sun drops and the wind rises. Furiously. It sweeps away the light, disperses the island I thought I had taken in, refuses all conclusions, all contours, all closure.

The sun has set. The wind blows.
No end in sight.

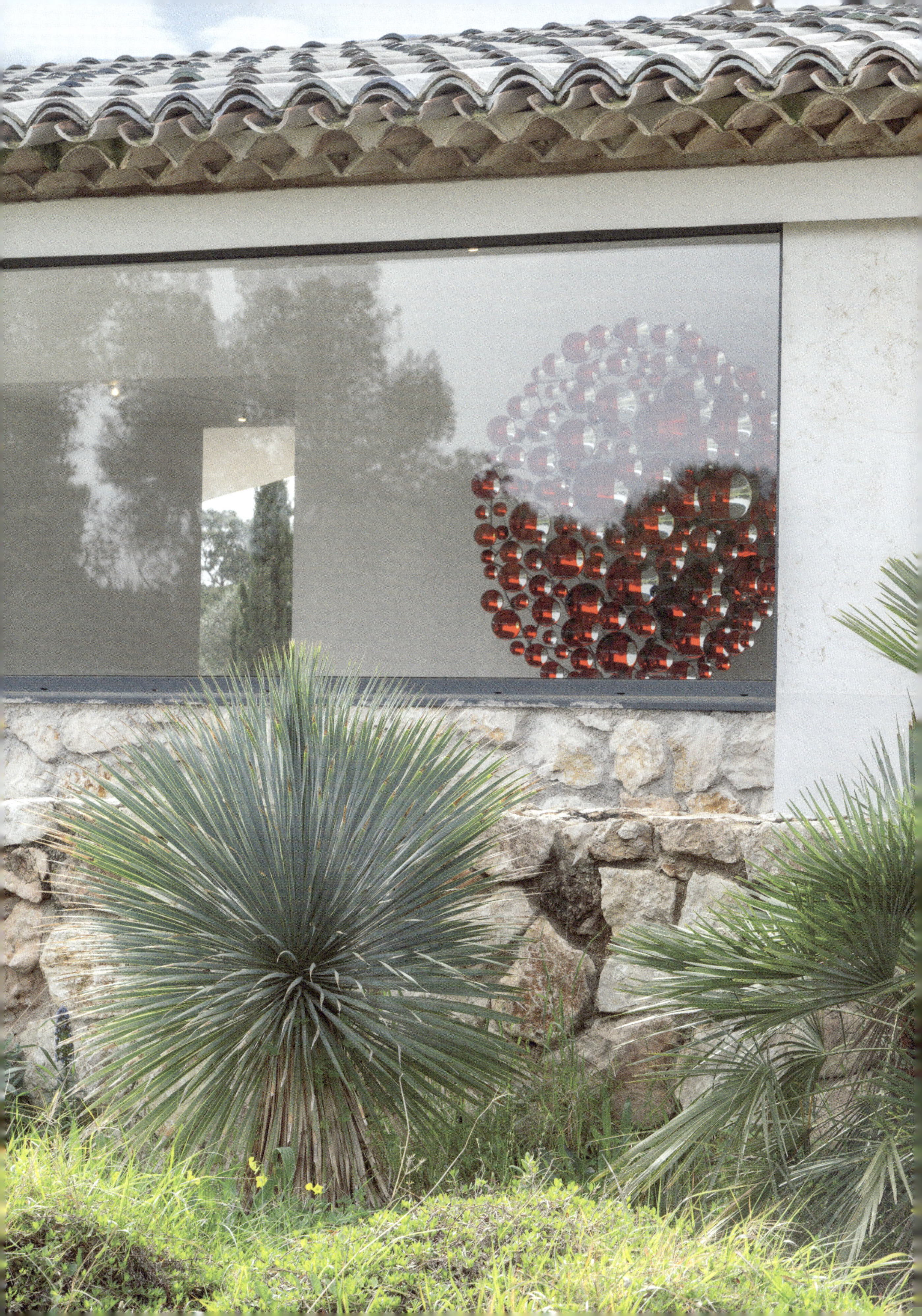

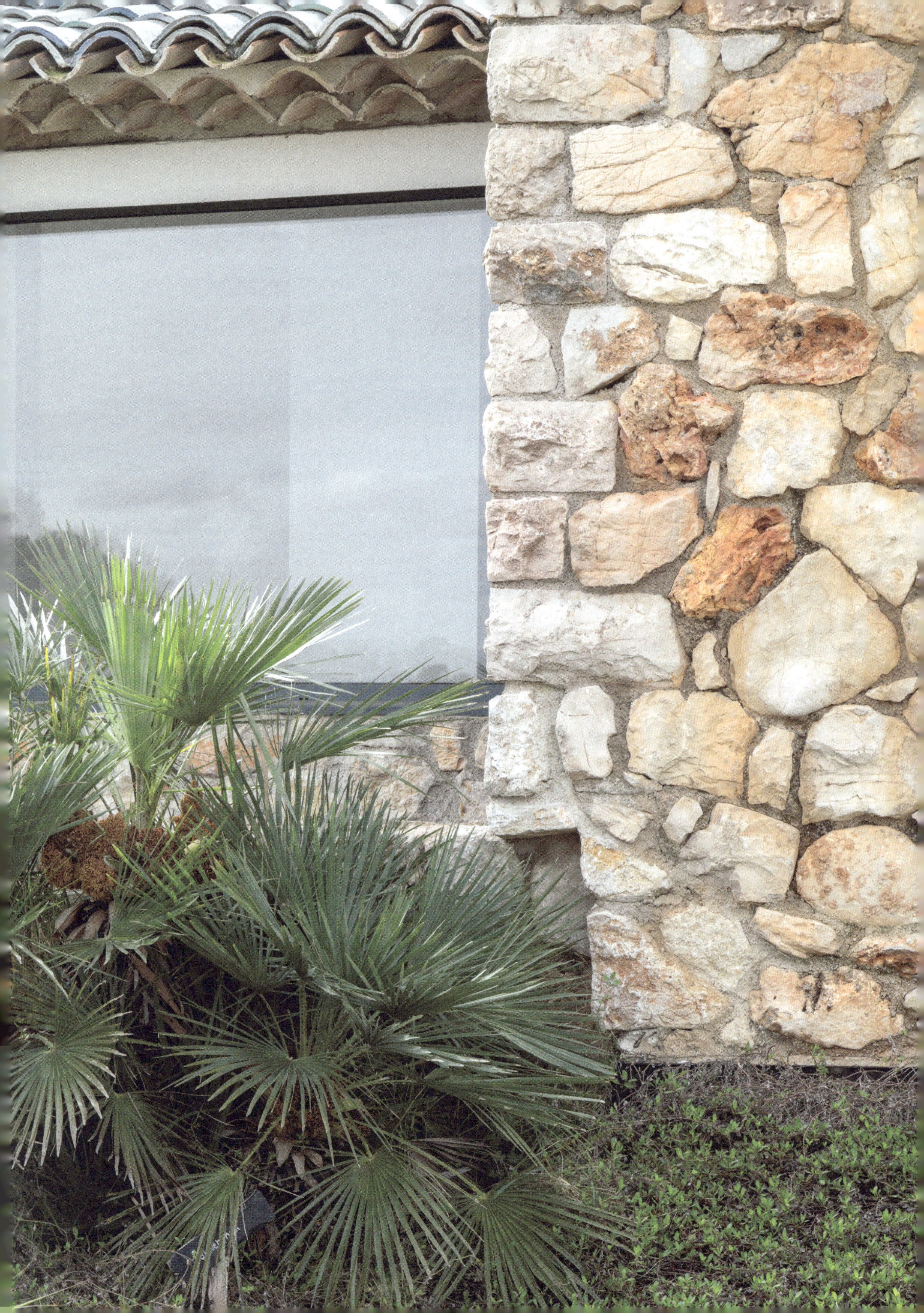

LIST OF EXHIBITED WORKS

Unless otherwise specified, all artworks are © and courtesy of the artist, and the photographs were taken by Nicolas Brasseur.

John Armleder
L.A. Gold, 2014, sequins on wood panel, 200 × 300 cm, courtesy the artist and Galerie Devals, Paris

Oliver Beer
Resonance Painting (Lovesong), 2024, pigments on canvas, 200 × 150 cm

Anna-Eva Bergman
N°15B-1963 Néant d'argent, 1963, vinyl paint and silver leaves on canvas, 146 × 114 cm, Fondation Hartung-Bergman © Anna-Eva Bergman, ADAGP, Paris, 2025

Jean-Baptiste Bernadet
Untitled (Feelings), 2021, oil on canvas, 205 × 390 cm, courtesy the artist and Almine Rech © Jean-Baptiste Bernadet, ADAGP, Paris, 2025

Frank Bowling
Hello Rosa New York, 1973, acrylic on canvas, 286 × 693.5 cm, Collection Carmignac, courtesy the artist and Hauser & Wirth © Frank Bowling. All Rights Reserved, DACS, 2025 / ADAGP, Paris

Alexander Calder
Mobile, 1970, painted metal, 95 × 305 cm, Musée de Grenoble Collection © Alexander Calder, ADAGP, Paris, 2025

Lynn Chadwick
Mobile (Version II White), 1952, steel rods and shapes, 105 × 133 × 133 × 122 cm, courtesy The Estate of Lynn Chadwick and Perrotin © The Estate of Lynn Chadwick

Chu Teh-Chun
Mémoire du regard, 1989, oil on canvas, 180 × 200 cm, Fondation Chu Teh-Chun © Fondation Chu Teh-Chun, ADAGP, Paris, 2025

Caroline Corbasson
Collapse, 2017, serigraphy with chrome ink on aluminium black Dibond, 350 × 260 cm © Caroline Corbasson, ADAGP, Paris, 2025

Isabelle Cornaro
Reproductions I (#4), 2010, acrylic spray paint, 250 × 332.5 cm, Aimery Langlois-Meurinne Collection © Isabelle Cornaro, ADAGP, Paris, 2025

Carlos Cruz-Diez
Physichromie 1857, 2013, chromography on aluminium, strips of plastic, 150 × 100 cm, private collection, Cruz-Diez family © Carlos Cruz-Diez / Bridgeman Images 2025

Philippe Decrauzat
newwave, 2025, acrylic on canvas, iridescent blue, 2 sections: 204 × 250 cm; 204 × 500 cm (overall) © Philippe Decrauzat, ADAGP, Paris, 2025, commissioned by the Fondation Carmignac

Olafur Eliasson
Colour experiment no. 118 (Blue Lagoon), 2023, acrylic on canvas, diam. 160 cm, courtesy the artist; Tanya Bonakdar Gallery, New York / Los Angeles; neugerriemschneider, Berlin
The collective consequences of focus on focus, 2022, partly silver-plated crystal glass spheres, paint (black, red), stainless steel, 171 × 169 × 67.5 cm, courtesy the artist; Tanya Bonakdar Gallery, New York / Los Angeles; neugerriemschneider, Berlin
Your vanishing, 2011, bronze, filtered glass with a coloured effect (blue, pink, cyan, yellow), mirror, stainless steel, paint (black), 181 × 70 × 70 cm, courtesy the artist; Tanya Bonakdar Gallery, New York / Los Angeles; neugerriemschneider, Berlin

Helen Frankenthaler
Petroglyphs, 1990, acrylic on canvas, 116.8 × 299.7 cm, Helen Frankenthaler Foundation, New York © 2025 Helen Frankenthaler Foundation, Inc. / Artists Rights Society (ARS), New York / ADAGP, Paris, 2025

Bernard Frize
RAMI, 1993, acrylic, ink, mother-of-pearl and resin on canvas, 205 × 194 cm, courtesy the artist, Perrotin and Marian Goodman © Bernard Frize, ADAGP, Paris, 2025

Hans Hartung
T1967-H22, 1967, vinyl paint on canvas, 154 × 250 cm, courtesy Perrotin © Hans Hartung, ADAGP, Paris, 2025

Raphael Hefti
Exit, pursued by a bear, 2025, bismuth, 70 × 40 cm each

Jeppe Hein
Path of Emotions, 2018, high polished stainless steel, 280 × 1,216 × 1,493 cm, Collection Carmignac. Photo Camille Moirenc

Leiko Ikemura
Praise of Light II, 2020, tempera and oil on jute canvas, 290 × 190 cm, Collection Carmignac, courtesy the artist and Fergus McCaffrey

Ann Veronica Janssens
Magic Mirrors (Pink & Blue), 2013-2023, dichromic laminated glass made of shattered glass, float glass and gelatin filters, 300 × 150 × 1.8 cm each, courtesy the artist, Esther Schipper, Berlin / Paris / Seoul; Alfonso Artiaco, Naples © Ann Veronica Janssens, ADAGP, Paris, 2025

Véronique Joumard
Paravent, 2018, steel and Fresnel lens, plexiglas, 180 × 60 × 2 cm, Billarant Collection, Paris © Véronique Joumard, ADAGP, Paris, 2025

Yves Klein
Monochrome bleu sans titre (IKB 68), 1961, pure pigment and synthetic resin, gravel, on gauze mounted on wood panel, 194 × 140 cm, private collection © Succession Yves Klein c/o ADAGP, Paris, 2025. Photo © All rights reserved
Peinture de feu sans titre (F 24), 1961, burnt cardboard on wood panel, 139 × 299 cm, private collection © Succession Yves Klein c/o ADAGP, Paris, 2025. Photo © All rights reserved
Pigment pur, original artwork 1957 – posthumous installation 2025, pure pigment, 300 × 500 cm, private collection © Succession Yves Klein c/o ADAGP, Paris, 2025
Pluie bleue (S 36), original artwork 1957 – posthumous edition 2018, pure pigment and synthetic resin on 12 wooden rods, 209 × 1.1 cm, private collection © Succession Yves Klein c/o ADAGP, Paris, 2025

Emily Kraus
Stochastic 1, 2022, oil on canvas, 170 × 300 cm, courtesy the artist, The Sunday Painter, London; Luhring Augustine, New York

Artur Lescher
Apolinário, 2014, brass, 400 × 100 × 100 cm, courtesy the artist and Almine Rech
Cardenal, 2014, nylon, 220 × 60 × 60 cm, courtesy the artist and Almine Rech

Heinz Mack
Das Meer I – Licht-Relief, 1963, aluminium on bronze-and silver-plated wood, 199 × 99 × 4.5 cm © Heinz Mack, ADAGP, Paris, 2025
Ohne Titel, 1950, graphite on paper, 48.5 × 62.9 cm © Heinz Mack, ADAGP, Paris, 2025
Silberrelief, 1965-1967, hand-embossed aluminium on wood, stainless steel, acrylic glass, 206 × 203 × 12.5 cm © Heinz Mack, ADAGP, Paris, 2025

Flora Moscovici
À la poursuite du rayon vert / Romancing the Light, 2025, pigments and gouache binder, variable dimensions © Flora Moscovici, ADAGP, Paris, 2025, commissioned by the Fondation Carmignac

Otto Piene
Lightroom with Mönchengladbach Wall, 1963-2013, carboard, wood, metal, motor, light, variable dimensions, courtesy Sprüth Magers © Otto Piene Estate / VG Bild-Kunst, Bonn / ADAGP, Paris, 2025

Gerhard Richter
Abstract Painting, 2009, oil on canvas, 180 × 180 cm, Collection Carmignac © Gerhard Richter 2025 (23042025)
Wolken (Grau), 1969, oil on canvas, 150.2 × 200 cm, Collection Carmignac © Gerhard Richter 2025 (23042025). Photo Thomas Hennocque

Bridget Riley
For Genji, 1995-1996, oil on linen canvas, 165.1 × 228.6 cm, Centre national des arts plastiques (FNAC 01-010), on loan at Musée de Grenoble © Bridget Riley / Cnap

Rotraut
Éclipse, n.d., mixed techniques on canvas, 130 × 89 cm, private collection © Rotraut, ADAGP, Paris, 2025

Thomas Ruff
d.o.pe.05, 2022, colaris on velvet carpet, 267 × 200 cm, courtesy the artist and David Zwirner © Thomas Ruff / Artists Rights Society (ARS), New York / VG Bild-Kunst, Germany / ADAGP, Paris, 2025

Hugo Schüwer Boss
Eleonor, 2024, acrylic and varnish on plywood mounted on concealed wooden frame, 160 × 120 cm © Hugo Schüwer Boss, ADAGP, Paris, 2025

Conrad Shawcross
Slow Arc Inside a Cube XI, 2020, painted steel, light, mechanical system, 165 × 72 × 62 cm, courtesy the artist and Victoria Miro

Francisco Sobrino
Structure permutationnelle, 1963-2014, polished stainless steel mirror, 150 × 60 × 60 cm, Atelier Sobrino, Paris © Francisco Sobrino, ADAGP, Paris, 2025

Jesús Rafael Soto
Esfera Amarilla, 1984, painted metal and nylon thread, 300 × 300 × 300 cm, private collection, courtesy Galeria Elvira González, Madrid © Jesús Rafael Soto, ADAGP, Paris, 2025

Pier Stockholm
Ygor XLI, 2025, ink, polyester putty for cars, paint and plywood, 190 × 240 cm

Thu-Van Tran
Les Couleurs du gris, 2025, whitewash and pigments on linen canvas, 130 × 195 cm, courtesy the artist and Meessen, Bruxelles © Thu-Van Tran, ADAGP, Paris, 2025

James Turrell
Prado, Red, 1968, projection, variable dimensions, courtesy the artist and Almine Rech

Günther Uecker
Spirale I, 2002, paint, latex, graphite and nails on wood panel, 200 × 200 × 16 cm, Collection Carmignac © Günther Uecker, ADAGP, Paris, 2025

Fabienne Verdier
Ti ricorda il primo amor, 2020, acrylic and mixed techniques on canvas, 212 × 137 cm, courtesy the artist and Waddington Custot © Fabienne Verdier, ADAGP, Paris, 2025. Photo Inès Dieleman

Jef Verheyen
Natte zielen, 1979, matte lacquer on canvas, 120 × 120 cm, Jef Verheyen Archive © SABAM Belgium, 2025, Jan Liégeois on behalf of Axel Vervoordt Gallery / Jef Verheyen, ADAGP, Paris, 2025

VERTIGO

From 26 April to 2 November 2025
Guest curator, **Matthieu Poirier**

Fondation and Villa Carmignac would like to thank the artists, art lenders and institutions who contributed to this exhibition.

Charles Carmignac
Grégoire Robinne
Editors

Kévin Le Squer
Director of the Publication

Sirrine Laalou
Editorial Manager ,
assisted by Chris Marie Tyan

Dune Lunel
Graphic Designer

Ann Veronica Janssens
Nina Leger
Matthieu Poirier
Riccardo Venturi
Authors

Kévin Le Squer
Lilah Remy
Notices

Anna Knight
and Jo Nicoud-Garden
Translation and Proofreading

Charlotte Othman
Editing

Nicolas Brasseur
Photographer

Fotimprim, Paris
Photoengraving

Printed at Syl in Spain, June 2025
Legal deposit: July 2025
ISBN : 978-2-37372-227-7
Price: 39 €

Diffusion-Distribution
France, Belgium, Switzerland
Belles Lettres
Diffusion-Distribution
25, rue du Général-Leclerc
94270 Le Kremlin-Bicêtre
T +33 1 45 15 19 70
bldd.fr

North America (USA and Canada), Latin America, UK, Asia, Australia, Middle East
ARTBOOK D.A.P.
75 Broad St, Suite 630
New York, NY 10004
artbook.com

FONDATION
& VILLA CARMIGNAC

Edouard Carmignac
President

Charles Carmignac
General Director

Emeric Glayse
Deputy Director

Kévin Le Squer
Exhibition Manager

Anne-Louise Amanieu
Production Officer and Registrar

Lilah Remy
Exhibitions and Editorial
Project Assistant

Olivier Ibañez
Director of Communication
and Development

Aurore Gallarino
Deputy Director of Communication
and Development

Angie Linconnu
Communication Officer

Loula Msellati
Communication Intern

Margaux Granjou
Carmignac Award Manager

Frédérique Yourath
Executive Assistant

Jean-Marie Toche
Operations Director

Béatrice Gallyot
Operations Deputy Director,
Public Relations Manager

Lilia Khadri
Public Relations And Cultural
Mediation Officer

Thibault Garnier
Administrative and Financial
Manager

Cécilia Renoux
Administrative and Human
Resources Officer

Olivier Deredec
Intendant/Gardens Manager

Alexandre Da Silva,
Olivier Haberey
Intendant/Gardeners

Florian Bruno
Shop Manager

EXHIBITION

Géraldine Mercier
Project Manager

Alice De Bortoli
for Ortiche Studio
Set Design

Produzioni Milano
Construction

Reflet
Lighting

Dune Lunel Studio
(Graphic Design)
and Œil de Lynx (Signage)

Christine Cameau,
Susan Pickford,
Bernard Wooding
Translation and Proofreading

Fræme; Ismaël Genoun
Sanz, Rosanne Moulin,
Nicolas Rousseau
Mediation

Marianne International
Reception and Shop

Chenue, Crozier, Fræme
Transport and Installation of Artworks

La Réserve
Conservation-Restoration

Morel & Cie
Insurance

ATM
Security

Media Partners:
Le Monde, Beaux Arts,
AD, New York Times, Konbini,
Le Bonbon, Marie-Claire, Infrarouge,
Nice Matin, Ici Provence, MK2, FNAC,
JC Decaux, Gares & Connexions,
Métropole

With the support of:
Profirst, Perrier-Jouët, Malongo,
Zecabas

Oliver Beer, *Resonance Painting (Big Distant Crush)* (detail), 2024, pigment on canvas, 200 × 150 cm, courtesy the artist and Thaddaeus Ropac Gallery. Photo: Juan Cruz Ibañez (cover)